COLLECTIVE LEADERSHIP *COMPASS*

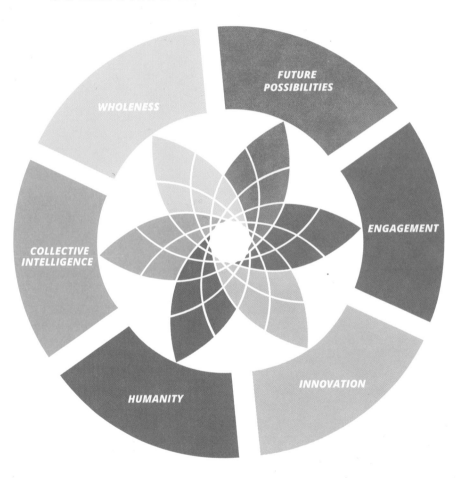

Praise for *The Art of Leading Collectively*

"If we are serious about taking on the pressing challenges of our time, we need fresh ideas about the art of leadership, new approaches to practicing it, and courageous minds willing to make that journey. In *The Art of Leading Collectively*, Petra Kuenkel has given us an inspiring book, that is also a vital roadmap, for any and all who feel called to accelerate the great transition our world so urgently needs."

—ALAN ATKISSON, author of *Believing Cassandra*
and *The Sustainability Transformation*

"Corporations, governments, and NGOs alike will benefit from the shift in collaboration across sectors that will be opened with collective leadership. I highly recommend *The Art of Leading Collectively* to anyone interested in the future of leadership and anyone committed to systems transformation for sustainability and humanity."

—KATHRIN WIELAND, CEO, Save the Children Germany

"Through rich examples of her own experience and that of others, Petra Kuenkel shows that co-creation is at the heart of our lives. Moreover, she gives invaluable material to help us co-create in more conscious, fulfilling, and effective ways. Her method is core to addressing critical challenges-come-opportunities that we face as individuals, in our work lives, and as increasingly interconnected citizens of planet Earth."

—STEVE WADDELL, author of *Global Action Networks*;
principal, NetworkingAction

"*The Art of Leading Collectively* is an amazing journey into taking diverse actors through collaborative change. Beautifully articulated with case studies in its implementation in individual to global change initiatives, this is an inspiring and invigorating read—most relevant to our complex, urgent, and interdependent world."

—PAVAN BAKSHI, CEO, Prime Meridian Consulting, India

"In our complex world, strategies for harnessing collective intelligence and mobilizing collective leadership will be critical to achieving transformative change. Kuenkel eloquently champions an approach to leadership that is surprisingly under-explored in the literature, offering a clear conceptual framework to underpin her argument."

—DANNY BURNS, co-author of
Navigating Complexity in International Development

"The Collective Leadership Compass is a fascinating multi-dimensional framework that has the potential to open up new perspectives on systemic change from a complex systems perspective. This book should be read critically, but it should be read."

—DAVE SNOWDEN, chief scientific officer, Cognitive Edge;
creator, The Cynefin Framework

"Unleashing the potential of multi-stakeholder collaboration is paramount for achieving the 2030 development agenda. *The Art of Leading Collectively* is a powerful guide for change agents, from those in business to those in international organizations who want to make change happen and address global challenges at scale. The beauty of this book lies in its appeal to thinkers and practitioners alike to embrace systems change, organizational development, and individual daring as key ingredients to collectively and decisively acting on creating a better world."

—ARJAN SCHUTHOF, Global Partnership for
Effective Development Cooperation

"The Collective Leadership Compass, the tool elaborated on in *The Art of Leading Collectively*, enables people from very different backgrounds, perspectives, and beliefs to come together, meet as equals, and develop common ground and solutions that go beyond what each could have achieved individually. These solutions are truly carried by all members of the group and hence translated into action. Having had the privilege to experience the method firsthand, I know that its effects are profound and just what is needed to bring forth the kind and level of innovation we urgently need today."

—BETTINA VON STAMM, author of *The Innovation Wave*
and *Managing Innovation, Design and Creativity*;
founder, Innovation Leadership Forum

"The complex challenges of our time call for systems-based, collaborative leadership. Petra Kuenkel shares her breadth of experience about developing this capacity, showing how leaders can use her approach to mobilize organizational, multinational, and multi-sectoral networks for sustainability. She reminds us that becoming a more effective collaborative leader is both an inner and outer journey, and that we can best realize our individual visions by accessing people's collective humanity, power, and creativity."

—DAVID PETER STROH, author of *Systems Thinking for Social Change*

"Implementing the seventeen global sustainable development goals successfully will require us to take collaboration between institutions, stakeholders, and nations to the next level. *The Art of Leading Collectively* prepares us for this journey."

—CORNELIA RICHTER, management board member,
Deutsche Gesellschaft für Internationale Zusammenarbeit (GIZ)

"The level of complexity in development challenges requires new approaches and new forms of leadership. Persuasively and vividly laid out through both storytelling and deep analysis, Kuenkel provides the tools and understanding that are essential to the science and art of leading collectively."

—DARIAN STIBBE, executive director, The Partnering Initiative

The Art of
LEADING
COLLECTIVELY

Co-Creating a Sustainable, Socially Just Future

PETRA KUENKEL

Foreword by Ernst Ulrich von Weizsäcker

Chelsea Green Publishing
White River Junction, Vermont

Project Manager: Angela Boyle
Developmental Editor: Joni Praded
Copy Editor: Laura Jorstad
Proofreader: Helen Walden
Indexer: Peggy Holloway
Designer: Melissa Jacobson

Printed in the United States of America.
First printing January, 2016.
10 9 8 7 6 5 4 3 2 1   16 17 18 19 20

Chelsea Green Publishing is committed to preserving
ancient forests and natural resources. We elected to print
this title on 100-percent postconsumer recycled paper,
processed chlorine-free. As a result, for this printing, we
have saved:

40 Trees (40' tall and 6-8" diameter)
18 Million BTUs of Total Energy
3,421 Pounds of Greenhouse Gases
18,550 Gallons of Wastewater
1,242 Pounds of Solid Waste

Chelsea Green Publishing made this paper choice because
we and our printer, Thomson-Shore, Inc., are members
of the Green Press Initiative, a nonprofit program
dedicated to supporting authors, publishers, and suppliers
in their efforts to reduce their use of fiber obtained
from endangered forests. For more information, visit:
www.greenpressinitiative.org.

Environmental impact estimates were made using the Environmental Defense Paper Calculator.
For more information visit: www.papercalculator.org.

Our Commitment to Green Publishing

Chelsea Green sees publishing as a tool for cultural change and ecological stewardship. We strive to align our book manufacturing practices with our editorial mission and to reduce the impact of our business enterprise in the environment. We print our books and catalogs on chlorine-free recycled paper, using vegetable-based inks whenever possible. This book may cost slightly more because it was printed on paper that contains recycled fiber, and we hope you'll agree that it's worth it. Chelsea Green is a member of the Green Press Initiative (www.greenpressinitiative.org), a nonprofit coalition of publishers, manufacturers, and authors working to protect the world's endangered forests and conserve natural resources. *The Art of Leading Collectively* was printed on paper supplied by Thomson-Shore that contains at least 100% postconsumer recycled fiber.

Library of Congress Cataloging-in-Publication Data
Names: Kuenkel, Petra, 1956– author.
Title: The art of leading collectively : how we can co-create a better future : a guide to collaborative impact
    for sustainability change agents from companies, the public sector, and civil society / by Petra Kuenkel.
Description: White River Junction, Vermont : Chelsea Green Publishing, [2016]
    | Includes bibliographical references.
Identifiers: LCCN 2015034159| ISBN 9781603586269 (hardcover) | ISBN 9781603586276 (ebook)
Subjects: LCSH: Cooperation—Social aspects. | Leadership—Social aspects. | Organizational change.
    | Sustainability.
Classification: LCC HD2961 .K76 2016 | DDC 658.4/092—dc23
LC record available at http://lccn.loc.gov/2015034159

Chelsea Green Publishing
85 North Main Street, Suite 120
White River Junction, VT 05001
(802) 295-6300
www.chelseagreen.com

This book is dedicated
to all leaders, drivers, innovators,
change agents, managers, and visionaries
who join the global learning journey
toward more effective collaboration for
a sustainable, socially just world.

Contents

Foreword

In July 2012, invited by UN Secretary-General Ban Ki-moon, a high-level panel of twenty-seven leaders from around the world began to work on their consultative advice for a global development framework beyond 2015.[1]

The report, published in May 2013, emphasised "the central importance of a new spirit to guide a global partnership for a people-centred and planet-sensitive agenda, based on the principle of our common humanity."[2] The report suggests five big transformative shifts:

The first shift: Ensuring that no person—regardless of ethnicity, gender, geography, disability, race, or other status—is denied universal human rights and basic economic opportunities.

The second shift: Putting sustainable development at the core of all development activities.

The third shift: Transforming economies in the way that they provide jobs and inclusive growth.

The fourth shift: Recognizing peace and good governance as core to human well-being.

The fifth shift is seen as an underlying support to reach the transformation. This shift involves forging a new global partnership in a "spirit of solidarity, cooperation, and mutual accountability" coupled with the common understanding of our shared humanity, underpinned by mutual respect and mutual benefit. The panel knew that the challenges of sustainability—managing scarce water resources, adapting to climate change, securing access to adequate nutrition, creating responsible value chains, or massively improving energy efficiency—would all require new forms of collaborative inventiveness and, above all, people who would be willing to implement change jointly at all levels of our global society.

What would this look like in practice? One of the greatest potentials of human beings is that their individual and collective mindset can change, and—for better or worse—a mindset change is often contagious. When people come up with daring ideas, others get inspired and encouraged to think beyond their own limits. They fuel the mindset shift and develop it further.

Some thirty years ago nobody would have understood the term *ecological footprint*, yet today the term has spurred ideas, research, and new practices. The need to reduce our ecological footprint has been ingrained in the consciousness of individuals but also in the business strategies of the corporate world. While some may see this need as a burden undertaken solely to maintain their company's reputation, others have discovered it as a business development opportunity. When they began to shift their mindset, the opportunities to combine a better ecological footprint with economic prosperity became not only obvious but also exciting. In *Factor Five*[3], my latest book, co-authored with an Australian team from The Natural Edge Project, we present examples showing the availability efficiency improvements at a factor of five for entire sectors of the economy. With numerous examples we show that a concern for our planet as a whole, our innovative capacity to find new technological solutions, and our drive to think in terms of future possibilities can work hand in hand. But there is even more to it.

One way to describe sustainable development is to see it as a combination of a reduced ecological footprint and an increased Human Development Index (HDI)—a measure of human well-being. The current world, however, shows a dangerous imbalance. The carrying capacity of the earth can be assumed to be sufficient to accommodate seven billion people, each with a footprint of a bit less than two hectares. A decent living standard means an HDI rating above 0.8. Sustainable development, in this view, would be defined as a footprint below two hectares and an HDI rating above 0.8. When we apply this to the world's countries, we discover a striking result that might not be surprising but simply forces us to rethink our action. The countries with the lowest level of HDI are those with the lowest ecological footprint, and the countries with the highest ecological footprint have the highest HDI.

I think humankind got something wrong here, and it is time for a courageous shift. The message is clear: in order to achieve sustainable development, we should be aiming at a five-fold shrinking of rich countries' footprints (with no shrinking of their HDI ratings) and a five-fold increase in poorer countries' HDI ratings (without increasing their footprints). That, roughly speaking, would render both types of countries sustainable.

So much for the challenge, but how do we get there? One important route to take is radically stretching our thinking and pushing ourselves out of our comfort zone. Massively reducing our ecological footprint can be done through brilliant technological advances in energy efficiency, and this change can have a positive impact on the HDI because it offers vast economic opportunities. But this time, the new cycle of technological innovation will need to consider different elements than in the past. It will be inspired and guided by a green technology mindset that takes both the planet and its people into account. If we want to increase HDI while reducing our ecological footprint, we cannot conceive of a growth cycle like those we have had in the last 200 years. We need a much bigger shift in thinking and acting if we want to build resilience into our future world.

Such a shift in thinking requires us to enter into conversations of a different kind. No actor can tackle the challenge in isolation. There has to be a broad and continuously renewed consensus among governments, corporations, and civil society actors on the direction to take, on the most appropriate steps to take, and on the roles of each actor. Governments, and even international bodies, need to set a frame for technological innovation that is planet-sensitive. The corporate world needs to shift toward greater responsibility for the future. And civil society should guard and support the interests of the people.

This consensus needs to stretch over borders—real borders and mental ones. This means that the next innovative cycle will not only be a technical one; the breakthrough move will be to contextualize technological innovation in a sense of purpose and meaning for the greater good of humankind's future. Thanks to the last innovative cycle, which brought us the digital revolution, there is an increasing chance that people will realize what Plato suggested: that we are all connected in a "single visible living entity containing all other living entities, which by nature are all related."[4] Hence, not only nature but also the human evolutionary project thrives on connectivity. Our collective human consciousness evolves as a complex, ever-shifting matrix with a growing sense of responsibility for the whole.

Part of this process is the realization that solutions to the challenges of sustainability require us to be agile, willing to venture into the unknown, and committed to continuous learning. What is needed is not so much a disruptive revolution but a more conscious process of sustained transformation. There is an individual and a collective side to this endeavor. We need bold future thinkers who push us beyond the limits of our habitual thought, and we need better skills in collectively negotiating our path into the future.

It is our capacity to inspire each other to drive ecological and social progress and our willingness to collaborate across nations, institutions, and cultures that will help us find answers to complex sustainability challenges.

But how can we move from simply knowing that we need to collaborate to actually mastering the art of collaboration for a sustainable future in a complex world? How does collaboration across sectors, nations, and cultures work in practice? How will we collectively change our path into the future?

With *The Art of Leading Collectively* Petra Kuenkel invites us to think about collaboration in a new way: not as the inconvenient, uncomfortable add-on we need so that we can work towards sustainability, but as a source of inspiration and drive. She reminds us that the human capacity to collaborate is as old as humankind and has not been lost, and that the vitality of human systems—their resilience—is a function of high-quality conversations and mutually trusting collaboration.

Kuenkel shows us that collaboration, done in the right way, inspires a form of technological and social innovation that considers our planet as a whole, leads to building future possibilities from the collective intelligence of people, and unearths our human potential to continuously learn. When people rediscover the art of leading collectively in the context of sustainability, something is touched at the deeper level of human perception: a window opens into the way in which we can more constructively contribute to our evolution.

This rediscovery awakens a latent capacity to engage with each other, with the planet, with the world, and with future possibilities that further our joint planetary project. Collaboration is not about suddenly having all the answers; it is about developing the next questions jointly in a continuous discourse that is fueled by difference and diversity of ideas.

It is time to revive and further develop our skills to collaborate efficiently toward a better future for both our planet and humankind. Improving the HDI while at the same time reducing the ecological footprint is an ambitious goal. It can be reached if we build our pathways on the human competencies for collaboration outlined in the pages ahead. This book encourages you to join the collaboration journey and get inspired by the results.

ERNST ULRICH VON WEIZSÄCKER
Co-President, The Club of Rome
Co-Chair, International Panel on Sustainable Resource Use

Introduction

The meeting room was much too small for the group of almost forty-five people. It was hot; the cheap white plastic chairs were not particularly comfortable, and the tiled floor did not help. Little wind was coming through the open door, and passing cars played havoc with the acoustics. Down the hill we could hear the sea roaring, the vast Atlantic Ocean of Salvador de Bahia in Brazil, though the invitation to swim was ignored. Instead, and despite the almost unbearable heat, the group—comprising men and women from all across the global coffee chain along with me, their facilitator—passionately concentrated on a written document projected onto the wall. Step by step we worked through it. A lot was at stake. Would this very diverse group jointly agree on the rules of participation for a global initiative for sustainable coffee production?

Different versions of the document had been under discussion for months. They had been the cause of conflicts, threats, and waves of mistrust between the coffee industry and international NGOs. These stakeholders had been meeting regularly in various constellations for more than a year, but I could feel the subtle and silent presence of collective leadership that arises in a group when a mutual move into the future is at stake.

They were getting ever closer to jointly developing a sustainable coffee standard and reaching an agreement on how cash-strapped small-scale farmers could green their operational practices without going out of business. And they had grown into a community of people who had joined a movement for sustainable business practices rather than just a diverse collection of coffee growers, roasters, company representatives, leaders from workers' unions and coffee cooperatives, researchers and activists, presidents of coffee federations, government officials, lawyers, and sustainability managers.

Why were they working together? Greening something as complex as the global coffee value chain required the collaboration of diverse actors. These were people who would not necessarily talk to one another under normal business circumstances. Their lives and worldviews differed in the extreme. Still, despite all the vested interests, the lingering mistrust, the phases of disagreement, we did eventually reach an agreement. When my last call for changes to the document was met with silence, I knew we had arrived. Everybody knew. The relief erupted in spontaneous applause as we honored one another. It felt as if we had achieved the impossible, proving that people can tend the commons.

What is it that engenders commitment to such a strenuous international learning process with an ambitious goal and an unclear outcome—across cultures, sectors, institutions, and business entities? When will people risk crafting an emerging possibility collaboratively, despite all the setbacks and doubts?

The coffee initiative showed me that the possibility of co-creating a better future rekindles a latent desire to contribute to making the world a better place. As this happens, the energy changes; people become more present, more open. They are more willing to cooperate while respecting one another's differences. When there is emotional exposure to the possibility of jointly making a difference in the world, we are drawn to it—not without doubts, but with progressive commitment. It is contagious.

That meeting in Salvador de Bahia took place in 2004, and the Common Code for the Coffee Community became a pioneering industry-wide model for improving the lives of many small-scale coffee farmers and for giving consumers environmental and social peace of mind when they enjoy a good conversation over a cup of coffee. Today sustainable sourcing of coffee has been integrated into business strategy and supply-chain management in most large coffee-roasting companies.

But other changes, too, have occurred: Now there is a multitude of such cross-sector collaboration initiatives in sustainable development. The world is not the same anymore. Our challenges of sustainability have grown, and so have our attempts to address them collectively.

Why It Matters How We Co-Create

Stakeholder collaboration is a form of co-creation. Yet co-creation is not, as many may think, a special skill of a group of innovators who are in a collaborative mood. On the contrary, it is something you and I do every day. We co-create all the time. Everything we do, or do not do, contributes to the co-creation of our world. If we leave our home in the morning and quickly grab a Fair Trade coffee at the next corner, we participate in co-creation. If we happily jump into our privately owned SUV to get to work while ignoring its CO_2 emissions, we co-create. If we passionately advocate for a better life for refugees in our country, we co-create. If we take our company on the road to becoming a more responsible business, we co-create. If we push a cross-sector sustainability initiative forward, we co-create.

We do not always co-create in the most sustainable or successful way. At times we enact reality in a constructive, life-enhancing, and responsible way. At other times we are destructive, to ourselves or to others. If we look at the world as a whole, we may conclude that the balance of co-creation is positive so far. The evolution of humankind has taken its toll, but we are still here as a species and we continue to develop. Things get better, despite setbacks. The future is not something to fear. There is evidence that human-kind can learn from the past. But the future does not just happen. We create it together. Every year. Every month. Every day. Every minute. Every second.

Could we do a little better in co-creation? Could we become a little more conscious in creating a world we are all proud living in?

The unfortunate truth is that our co-creation remains fairly unconscious and invisible to us. The idea that there is no thought and no action without impact on human co-creation can be overwhelming. So we continue to act, oblivious to our impact. We don't want to know how co-creation works at the level of the whole of humankind; it seems too large a perspective, too far away from the daily rhythm of work and life.

I agree and offer, as antidote, the world of fractals. One feature of our evolutionary nature is the existence of patterns that are similar in small and large scale. If you zoom into a fern leaf, you will find the same design structures in ever-smaller units. The self-similarity of smaller and larger systems often goes unnoticed in our daily professional environment. We forget that how we act in a small team may have an impact on the entire organization; that how we act as an organization may have an impact on the entire community, the entire world.

Better co-creation starts small. It is not a waste of time to start with yourself, to improve your team, your organization's sustainability contri-bution, and your collaboration initiative. There is a reason why so many people love the quote from Mahatma Gandhi: "You need to be the change you want to see in the world."[1]

Why Is Stakeholder Collaboration So Important?

Sustainability is on the agenda of every nation, every organization, and many citizens today; it is a global movement that cannot be ignored. If we do nothing, unsustainable global trends will impact businesses over the next twenty years, as well as governments and civil society organizations.[2] These trends range from climate change to ecosystem decline, from energy insecurity to water scarcity. They affect resource management, poverty, economic justice, food security, demographic change, population growth, and more. Those who are confronted with sustainability challenges notice another global trend: Solutions cannot be found in isolation. As Margaret Mead famously said, "Never doubt that a small group of thoughtful, committed citizens can change the world. Indeed, it's the only thing that ever has."[3] Collaboration among different actors is not only paramount, it is also the sole route to successfully addressing the challenges we face. In a global survey of more than a thousand CEOs, 84 percent were convinced that the corporate world could have a decisive impact on global sustainability challenges if there was a strong commitment to collaboration across sectors and to collective efforts for transformation.[4] Myriad examples speak for themselves.

Developing a mainstream sustainability standard for worldwide green coffee requires a joint approach among major coffee traders, standard organizations, international NGOs, coffee producers, and governments. Improving the infrastructure in southern Africa—railways, ports, telecommunication, and roads—cannot take place without dialogue and collaboration between public and private actors in many fields. Implementing sustainable water management worldwide requires collective action on the ground—by municipalities, companies, civil society organizations, and communities—and an exchange of best practices across nations, regions, and continents. Moving a nation's energy supply away from nuclear energy or fossil fuels entails consensus and collective action among many stakeholders inside the country; the surrounding countries may need to be engaged in the vision as well. Regaining a community's traditional land rights and ensuring sustainable land use necessitates cooperation between public and private stakeholders. Dealing with the consequences of climate change requires the combined efforts of governments, civil society, and the private sector.

If we envision a planet in ecological balance, social justice around the globe, and an economic system that serves humankind while keeping the earth healthy, we must admit that sustainability demands global collaboration. As Eric Lowitt puts it in *The Collaboration Economy*, "We have just begun our journey. Much work remains . . . to create a new era of prosperity that benefits our lives today while enhancing future generations' ability to meet their needs in perpetuity."[5] No matter our own chosen task—managing scarce water resources, adapting to climate change, securing access to adequate nutrition, or creating responsible value chains—the challenges of sustainability are urgent. They require new forms of collaborative inventiveness and, above all, people who are willing to implement change jointly at all levels of society.

This means that we need to acquire new competencies—or revive existing ones—to create change collectively on a broad scale. When speaking about the need to work with multi-stakeholder groups, Unilever CEO Paul Polman admits, "It is an enormous learning curve as no one has been trained for this."[6] The learning includes developing our human capacity for outcome-oriented dialogue, effective collaboration, and future-oriented collective action across institutional or national boundaries. Isolated action needs to be replaced by collective leadership—a paradigm shift in how individuals find their leadership roles in the spirit of collaborative co-creation and contribution to the common good.

An African proverb that has been cited many times in the last few years says, "If you want to go fast, travel alone; if you want to go far, travel together." The route to sustainable development is long and winding. We can only travel together. It is helpful to have a map to understand the geography, and it is even more helpful to have a compass.

Tools and Fellow Travelers for the Journey

The Art of Leading Collectively will help you navigate the collaborative journey. Its goal is to encourage and empower those who have started this journey and those who would like to join.

Large companies may adopt sustainability strategies as a result of public pressure, but they soon realize that the internal structures enabling them to learn faster in collaboration with their stakeholders also accelerate business opportunities. Governments increasingly realize that they cannot prevent connectivity and transparency and that staying in a structured dialogue with their citizens is a more peaceful and prosperous way to move forward. Civil society organizations see their impact increase through collaboration with other sectors. Turning the challenges of complexity, interdependency, and urgency into opportunities requires more than passion, intuition, or excellent plans. We need to learn faster together, collaborate more efficiently, and enhance collective action for more sustainable human behavior—on an everyday basis at the local, national, and global level.

The Art of Leading Collectively will take you backstage, behind the scenes of what the world will need more of if we want to co-create a better future: successful collaboration. It is founded on years of work that has shown there is no perfect leader, no perfect project manager who can navigate complex settings collaboratively without the occasional sleepless night. Conflicts, misunderstandings, failures, and hidden agendas are part of the journey. Human beings need to negotiate the road map into the future. There is no other choice. Addressing sustainability challenges requires people in all sectors to work together in more fruitful and constructive ways. No single actor has the best solution for sustainability issues, but each may contribute a piece of the puzzle.[7]

This book will help you implement more outcome-oriented and constructive co-creation on a day-to-day basis—for yourself, your team, your organization, and—above all—your cross-sector collaboration initiative. It equips dedicated change makers in public, private, and civil society organizations with a tool for better co-creation. My experience is that the dimensions of collective leadership for sustainability can be made transparent. They can be learned and enhanced—individually and collectively.

Perhaps you are trying to start a complex cooperation project, or are in the midst of one you're trying to improve. Or maybe you're trying to rediscover the world of fruitful human interaction, shift the mind-set of your organization toward collaboration, or find new ways to work out difficult challenges. If so, the tool presented in *The Art of Leading Collectively*—the Collective Leadership Compass—helps you keep your collaboration journey on track and find the necessary course corrections. With it, you can:

- Prepare for your journey into collaboration from the outset.
- Locate where you are, defining what is present and what's missing.

- Map the path, adjust your strategies, and know what to shift, to strengthen, or to focus on.
- Convince your colleagues that leading collectively for sustainability can change the world.

Your collaboration journey starts with the first step—understanding your own contribution to better co-creation. You are the fractal that can make a difference in the world, the member of a group of thoughtful citizens that can change the world. You are a leader when you begin to engage with the future, when you draw people into collaboration, when you commit yourself to a larger goal. You are not alone on the journey; you are part of a community for change. There are fellow travelers from around the world.

You will read many real-life stories and hear from many of those fellow travelers in the pages ahead. But first let's meet six fellow travelers who are unique: They will accompany us throughout the book, and they are fictional in the sense that I have changed their names, their organizations' names, countries, cooperation partners, and challenges. They are nonfictional in the sense that they represent a variety of challenges based on real experiences. None of them is a perfect leader. They are human beings with limitations and potentials, searching for meaning, trying to make the world a better place, and they all need to draw others into better co-creation. Like all of us, they are under much pressure to deliver, haunted by too many emails, and struggling to balance their personal and their professional lives. The challenges they face may resonate with yours. The contexts and challenges are based on my experience of the last twenty years in making collaboration work through enhancing collective leadership.

Mike is the CEO of TrendWear in the UK, a company in the textile industry with outlets all over Europe. He was recently appointed successor to the former CEO, who had been under severe criticism for being too weak and indecisive in handling the impact of a price war TrendWear has experienced. The clothes they sell target young people, and the profit margins aren't very high. That's why doing business in a smart way counts at TrendWear. Because the company buys from suppliers in Bangladesh that do not treat their workers well, it has also been subject to attacks from an NGO advocating for living wages and decent working conditions in Asia. The sustainability department is handling the issue. Mike is in his mid-fifties, and this position is the one he always wanted. He is known as a visionary yet decisive leader. He knows the clothing business well as he has held both finance and purchasing jobs in the industry. Sustainability has not been on his leadership agenda, but he has watched Nike get attacked for child labor issues then gradually move sustainable supply-chain management to the heart of the company strategy.[8] TrendWear is far from this goal, but Mike is determined to get his company there. It is dawning on him that the challenges of workers' conditions in the textile supply chain may be something TrendWear will not be able to handle without the help of competitors.

Celine, who just turned forty, is an engineer and a member of the interministerial coordination committee for the management of drinking water in the Democratic Republic of Congo (DRC). She studied in France and was offered a job a few years ago in Paris but decided to come back to her country to help the transition toward a promising future with bright people, along with incredible wealth in natural and mineral resources. She has worked for some years at the capital's university in Kinshasa, but moved out of academia because, as she put it, she wanted "action." Water is her professional expertise and she is up to date with best practices in water management worldwide. Access to drinking water is a particular challenge in the DRC. Although it is a water-rich country, less than 20 percent of its population has access to healthy drinking water. With the help of development agencies and consultants the government put a water policy into place, but the country lacks coordination among stakeholders. Celine believes the lack of management skill worsens the water problems.

Peter is in his mid-forties and two years ago was appointed the executive director of DiverseAct, an international NGO in

Switzerland. He is the successor to the founder, who led the organization for more than twenty years. The mission of DiverseAct is to put biodiversity and natural resource management high on the public's agenda and to implement environmental projects in Africa, Asia, and Europe. When he started his job he realized that the organization was stuck in an old way of operating—funded mainly by donations and the Swiss government—with no collaboration with the private sector. Peter had worked in the private sector, where his colleagues remember him as a leader who engaged his staff in a vision for change. When he decided to switch careers a few years ago, he was tracked down by a headhunter for the position at DiverseAct. Cooperation with the private sector is the agenda he set when he started, because he believes most of the challenges around natural resource management and biodiversity cannot be tackled by NGOs or governments alone. Not everybody on his staff is excited about the new strategy.

Tina is in her early twenties and in her final year at a university in South Africa. Helping people is her passion, but she did not always have the clarity of focus she has today. When she was sixteen she dropped out of school and nearly ended up on the streets, but a cousin gently guided her back onto her path. Years later, when she asked the cousin why he had invested so much time in getting her back on track, he answered: "I saw the artist and innovator in you. Artists can get lost sometimes; they need people who believe in them." Tina decided that her artistic medium would be people and began to study psychology. Recently, she listened to a panel discussion on unequal educational chances for people from disadvantaged communities. Immediately after that she got some friends together and told them about her idea—creating a movement in which university students mentor socially challenged young people to advance their prospects in life.

Nadeem is in his mid-forties and from India. His family still lives there, but he is currently working for a US-based implementation agency that is contracted by foundations and international organizations to do development work. He is leading a complex cooperation project among NGOs, the public sector, and the private sector. Its goal is to help small-scale African farmers improve production and access to international markets. As he was born into a rural family and later received a degree in agriculture, he knows about the life of small-scale farmers firsthand. Nadeem moved into this position because he is known as a people person. He is an empathetic listener who treats everybody equally, whether it be the top manager of an international foundation or a poor widow farmer. Improving the people's lives is Nadeem's passion. This is the first time that he has led a project with close involvement of the private sector (including Indian, European, and American companies). He is struggling with the lack of understanding among these businesspeople about what it means to work with small-scale farmers.

Andrea is in her early thirties and works as a project manager for sustainability at EnergyTech, a large German company that is one of three leading players providing energy in Germany. The company has set a goal of entering into the renewable energy field, but Andrea thinks this is mostly lip service. EnergyTech still runs coal plants and a few nuclear energy plants. Andrea's friends disapprove of her working at such an old-fashioned firm and do not believe that she will be able to influence anything. This annoys Andrea and makes her doubt her decision to apply for the job. She has recently joined a leadership development program for young professionals, which focuses on learning to lead collaboration projects. She had been fighting to get the approval of her boss, but finally convinced him with the argument that sustainability at EnergyTech is all about internal collaboration. What she has not yet told him is that the program's first module has convinced her that EnergyTech will only change when management opens up to external stakeholder collaboration.

These six fellow travelers are members of a global community for change—people who not only believe in the possibility of better co-creation, but go out and do it. They work across sectors, collaborate along value chains, involve stakeholders in strategy planning, build supportive networks, and reinvent a collaborative economy. They have started the collaboration journey—in various places, at various levels, in business, the public sector, and civil society across all nations. They know that we do not need a revolution; we need to partner with evolution and shift the way we co-create.

We meet them again as they face complex collaborative leadership challenges in very different contexts in part 1, which focuses on how we can turn the challenges of sustainability into opportunities to develop—as leaders, as committed groups of citizens, as cross-sector initiatives. They allow us to see ourselves as nodes in a network of collaborating actors. This will shift our perspective from individual leadership to the power of groups of leaders who become catalysts for change. Part 1 also travels to the backstage of initiatives where we can observe the cost of non-collaboration and better understand the purpose of learning the art of leading collectively.

Part 2 will introduce you to the six dimensions of the key navigating tool—the Collective Leadership Compass. It describes the human competencies inherent in collaborative processes and explores examples of interactions among them.

Part 3 takes us into the practice of collaboration by exploring how to make the Compass work for us. With the help of our fellow travelers, we will identify starting points for better co-creation and dive deeper into navigating the collaboration journey in each of the six dimensions. We'll learn how to use the Compass in complex sustainability challenges—with our team, our organization, our initiative.

Part 4 highlights the major scaling-up strategies for collective leadership that enhance collaboration competencies and can be applied in sustainability initiatives. It shows the potential of stakeholder dialogues and cross-sector partnering, encourages you to empower living networks, and helps you integrate collaboration competencies in leadership development. It strengthens your ability to choose the path with heart and align the outer professional journey to sustainable development with your inner path by following the five principles of collaborative impact.

The Epilogue is an invitation to join the global collaboration journey. It shows that the path ahead for all of us is to build our competencies for collaboration and encourages you to take part in this exciting journey.

Better co-creation is all about us human beings—you and me, and the many others out there, all around the world. The challenges are as manifold as there are opportunities for dedicated people to make a difference.

PART ONE

Turning Challenges into Opportunities

I have had the privilege of working with people from many cultures across the globe, to accompany many difficult collaboration projects with ambitious goals, to touch many urgent sustainability topics—from global to local. In the process I have come to see the world with different eyes. It is not the world conveyed through the daily media, where disaster and atrocities dominate the picture. Instead I see the world through the lens of people who are busy changing it toward sustainability, who want to make a difference for the future of humankind. These are humble pioneers prepared to go the extra mile for a better collective future—in business, in government, and in civil society. Uncounted numbers of people align their professional contribution with the common good.

They are often successful, but I also see that initiatives with the best of intentions fail, collaboration processes fall prey to lingering mistrust, different approaches to doing business cannot be aligned, people talk about ambitious goals but never move to action, the emotional connection to a larger goal gets lost, or people feel alone and give up on changing their companies. The journey toward better co-creation is not a road without potholes. People can get diverted by impeding structures, get trapped into measuring questionable metrics, or become depressed by misunderstandings across sectors, organizations, cultures, races, or genders. They set up complicated collaboration structures that result in all talk and no action. Their passion dries up or they become cynical toward weaker stakeholder groups. People then either attribute failure to themselves or blame others and the world "out there."

What if we stopped blaming others for failed or difficult collaboration efforts, and instead saw the global trend toward partnering and dialogue as a way of training our muscles for the future? We need to become fit for collaboration, whether we're in the corporate sector, the public sector, or civil society.

Helping people collaborate successfully has been the core of my work for two decades. If things got difficult, if crises emerged, I found a way to get all the actors back into a collaborative space. If people refused to talk with one another or work together, I gently guided them into listening to others. If people were drowning in a cumbersome cooperation structure, I revived their passion for the larger goal. What intrigued me was discovering how little we actually knew about when collaboration worked and why. Could we identify which ingredients would lead to better co-creation? Rarely.

So I began to ask a question—across cultures, sectors, initiatives, and thematic areas: *Can you remember a situation when a group of committed actors led collectively toward an issue of common concern?* Most people gave me an immediate, and often a passionate, answer. However small or large, they could remember when collaboration had worked, a time when people inspired one another to make a difference. I concluded that deep inside we know from experience how collective leadership works. I then added another question: *What must come into play for this to happen?* People paused; sometimes they could not respond. Those who answered hinted at chance, a special leadership quality in one person, or special circumstances. Gradually they listed factors that contributed to successful collaboration: trust, listening, patience, mutual respect, a larger goal, urgency, caretaking, and persistence.

That list was good but still did not satisfy me. These factors help, but did they empower people to consciously shift the way they co-created? I continued my inquiry and started to observe more closely. What was present when a cross-sector group agreed on a plan of action in an atmosphere of joint commitment? What kept a diverse group of actors together when each had to overcome hurdles in convincing their institution to collaborate? What emerged when a group of managers from competing industries patiently persisted in creating an industry-wide approach to tackling a sustainability challenge despite all legal impediments? How did people build committed teams both within and across organizational boundaries? How did they manage to integrate different organizational cultures into joint initiatives and foster collaboration among diverse stakeholders?

When I looked behind the scenes of collaboration initiatives that included a wide range of actors, one insight emerged. It was simple and at the same time complex. It reminded me of the writings of the American architect Christopher Alexander. He sometimes started his lectures with a simple exercise, showing two different photographs and asking students the question: *In which photograph do you see more life?* The answers were surprising. About 80 percent of the students agreed on one photograph. But what did this mean? After many trials, Alexander concluded that their perception of a degree of "life" in an external structure—a photograph, a building, a painting—was not arbitrary. Nor was it simply a matter of taste. There was a pattern in the structures that resonated with the human heart and mind. The architect took off on a journey of discovery that led him to formulate a language of patterns, a way of ordering architectural space that enhances the life force in human beings.[1] He discovered that built structures are dynamic in that the different parts have impacts on one another. The feeling of awe and deeper connection that many people have when they stand in Chartres Cathedral is not just subjective, but is caused by an ordered pattern of elements in relation to one another. He described this in the following way: "All systems in the world gain their life, in some fashion, from the cooperation and interaction of the living centers they contain, always in a bootstrap configuration, which allows one center to be propped up by another, so that each one ignites a spark in the one it helps, and that mutual helping creates life in the whole."[2]

We all know this feeling of aliveness—when we are happy, when our heart resonates, when we feel most connected with life, when our humanity expands. We are intrinsically linked to the order of life within us and around us—people, architecture, nature. We are constantly being created by this order as much as we participate in creating this order. So one of my simple conclusions was: Co-creation works best in a collaborative space where there is "life"—a sense of vitality, not superficial harmony. Have you ever been part of a team that achieved something remarkable? It gives you a feeling of igniting one another's vitality. It's fun. It is the feeling of being alive. It is energy boosting. What then would this mean for our collective ability to co-create in a more constructive, more sustainable way?

Christopher Alexander developed an elaborate pattern language, a way to order space for art and architecture, modeled after patterns of nature. Would it help us if we understood a little more about the patterns of inter-action among people that further collaborative co-creation? If we knew a little more about how "living centers" support one another and come together as a pattern of vitality, could we more easily create an atmosphere in which collaboration works and people more easily connect with goals that serve them today and future generations tomorrow?

You may argue that this is too far away from your world of logical frameworks for project plans, impact monitoring, balanced scorecards, quarterly growth reports, risk management procedures, performance evaluations, and deliverables. My experience says otherwise. On the contrary, it may make your life easier because there is no other choice: We need to co-create a better future. And in this, collaboration is key. For example, sustainable supply chains are core to delivering long-term good for both suppliers and consumers. But determining all the sustainability issues along the supply chain is a demanding task given the complexity of supplier networks that have evolved with globalization. We can move forward when we understand how a group of collaborating actors can lead for sustainability, and how we can inspire large groups of people to act in favor of the common good.

Over my years of working in complex collaboration projects and institutional change management, I began to notice which ingredients shifted the actors into a more collaborative space. None of the ingredients was radically new—it was the combination, the presence of a pattern of mutually supportive ingredients, that made a difference. These ingredients were personal competencies. People either brought in these competencies or developed them jointly with their collaborators.

In the stuffy room in Salvador de Bahia, all the ingredients were there. When the participants went home, they promoted the business value of sustainability engagement, explained the marketing advantages of sustainable coffee, expressed their conviction that this would really benefit small coffee farmers, and presented the benefits of an ambitious public–private development project to their governments. But in the meeting room in Brazil there was more to this group than the rational explanation for each stakeholder's participation. Despite all the repeated political fights and contradictory positions, people agreed that there existed a climate of collective leadership for the future with respect for one another at its core. Everyone was aware of the responsibility bestowed on them: They could each make this one step toward sustainability fail or succeed. As one of the participants summarized, "There was an atmosphere of commitment that made it impossible to misbehave; you would not withhold your position, but would always stay in the collaborative field. You knew that this was a global learning process we were all in together."

What was the magic? Complex, yet simple, it was the presence of a pattern of these six human competencies in interaction.

1. **A Sense of Future Possibilities.** Over the years of building the coffee initiative, people had developed a sense of future possibilities. What had seemed impossible at the outset—to shift the global coffee market—had come within reach. This had only been possible because people had grown together beyond their differences of opinion, business rationale, culture, earnings, and worldviews. They had learned to interact as people with different positions yet with compassion.

2. **Engagement.** They had built a process of authentic and reliable engagement, a prerequisite for both trust and commitment to tangible outcomes and collective action. All participants in the initiative were prepared to take a risk, to venture into an unknown territory with uncertain outcomes, despite difficulties justifying their actions to superiors.

3. **Innovation.** They were jointly and across institutions piloting an innovation by building an industry-wide value-chain community. None of the stakeholder groups—industry, NGOs, or coffee producers—would have found solutions to the sustainability challenges in green coffee production alone.

4. **Humanity.** They had accessed their own humanity and were able to see the person behind a viewpoint and the intention behind a position. This became a cornerstone of their ability to overcome almost irreconcilable differences.

5. **Collective Intelligence.** It was the gradually increasing openness to collective intelligence that improved the solutions. The patience to listen even to the most critical stakeholders enabled an approach that would work for small-scale farmers as well as large-scale producers. With the participation in the coffee initiative, the picture of reality widened. Exposure to such entirely different ways of operating and of viewing the same issue—coffee production—contributed to people's ability to see the larger context in which they were embedded.

6. **Wholeness.** This sense of wholeness made it easier for people to stay in a collaborative field. People had empowered one another to jointly make a difference. I believe it is time to scale up this empowerment.

Chapter 1

How Collaboration Helps Us Manage Complexity

Collaborative co-creation of a sustainable future is not a simple task. There is not always an easy answer. At times, the solution to one problem causes the next problem. Attention to one part of the system creates havoc for another part. Change is urgent, yet the world is complex and, above all, interdependent. That is why we are on a global collaborative learning journey.

Let's visit the world of sustainability standards as a lesson in complexity. Sustainability standards are a great idea. If you go shopping in various parts of the world—from the US to Europe to, more recently, China—you will find goods labeled with them: organic, FSC (Forest Stewardship Council), Fair Trade, Rainforest Alliance, UTZ, and so on. We consumers find more labels than we can understand. How do we know which ones really indicate a sustainable product? Still, we assume we can be assured that they have a positive impact—even if they are all international voluntary standards. Many governments, particularly in developing countries and emerging markets, cannot enforce high national environmental or social standards. Either they do not make these a priority or they do not have the resources to police industries and sanction misbehavior. The international voluntary sustainability standards often exceed the national standards. Buyers—large companies or the One World Shop around the corner—can make application of the standard a prerequisite for buying the goods. Although this may sound like a trade barrier, research has shown that the overall impact is positive for producers.[1] The application of high voluntary standards at the producer level has positive social and environmental effects at the farm or factory and improves resource management capacity. Fantastic results? Partly yes, but what if the solution creates new problems?

If you ever have the opportunity to visit a factory in Southeast Asia (where your brand-name jeans are produced) or a rose farm in Kenya (where your Fair Trade–certified Valentine's Day roses originate), you may be in for a shock. Both the factory and the farm are getting audited in their voluntary standard application to ensure that you as a consumer can wear your jeans and love your roses without a bad conscience—no child labor, good occupational health and safety for the workers, fair pay. So what is the problem? By asking a few questions you discover that both the factory and the farm have fifteen to twenty different auditors inspecting. Each buyer (Adidas, Puma, H&M, Marks & Spencer, and so on) and each standard (Fair Trade, Rainforest Alliance, or the like) sends its own auditors. Auditing has become a flourishing business. The proliferation of voluntary standards has had a positive impact, but it is costly for producers to keep our consumer conscience clean. This is what we learn in moving toward sustainability: We find solutions that work, the solutions create new problems, and we have to find new solutions. We want sustainable products without depriving the producers of a livable wage through auditing costs. So should we drop sustainability standards? No, but we need to learn anew. That is why sustainability and innovation are married—we need visionaries who take solutions to the next level through collaboration.

One such passionate innovator is Claudine Musitelli, until 2014 vice president of ethical sourcing and food safety initiatives at the Consumer Goods Forum in Paris. Musitelli was the driver behind the Global Social Compliance Programme (GSCP), aimed at improving social and environmental conditions in global supply chains through business-driven initiatives.[2] The GSCP is taking a new approach: working collaboratively among companies to improve the sustainability of their often shared supply base. An elaborate process of comparing standards allows companies to accept other audits for their own supply. One practical outcome is reduced auditing costs for producers. Harmonizing standards is not an easy task, however. Musitelli knows that stakeholder engagement is key. Overcoming mistrust and pulling competitors into the collective vision is a learning journey. But it works; companies are changing their approach.

Such challenges inevitably involve *complexity*, *interdependence*, and *urgency*—which, if understood, can be turned into opportunities. It helps to remember that the three conditions are not trends "happening" to us; we have co-created them (even if not consciously). This means we can also co-create ways to deal with them and equip ourselves with skills that humankind needs in the future.

Collaboration challenges are as manifold as there are attempts to address sustainability issues collectively. Our six fellow travelers are living examples of the variety of change initiatives that require better forms of co-creation. Mike, Celine, Peter, Nadeem, Tina, and Andrea differ in age, professional background, geographic location, culture, work, and life experience, but they do have a few things in common. They all need to collaborate with different actors, and they cannot achieve the changes they envision alone. All of them need to expand their collaboration skills and the ability to effectively co-create with other leaders. What are their challenges?

> **Andrea,** the sustainability manager at EnergyTech, needs to find a way of influencing her company to make a decisive shift in changing their business model toward renewable energy.
>
> **Nadeem** needs to make the complex design of an ambitious cross-sector cooperation project work in practice and to the benefit of small-scale African farmers.
>
> **Tina,** the emerging social entrepreneur, needs to take her dreamlike innovative idea to help educationally disadvantaged young people into reality and convince many people to join her dream.
>
> **Peter,** the executive director of DiverseAct, will have to take his staff from resistance and skepticism about the private sector to innovative collaboration with the private sector.
>
> **Celine,** the seasoned water engineer, needs to enhance coordinated action for drinking water among a variety of players in the DRC.
>
> **Mike,** the CEO of TrendWear, not only needs to align his top management behind sustainable supply-chain management, but also must lead TrendWear into collaboration with competitors.

All need to create a situation where different actors become self-reliant in driving the envisioned change. They need to empower and enact collective leadership. What also unites our fellow travelers is that they have taken a stance for a more sustainable world. They have decided to redefine their leadership contribution, and in that way they are prepared to align their outer and inner journeys.

In an interview with the *Guardian*, London Business School professor Lynda Gratton remarked that people who take a stance for sustainability issues have one thing in common. "Almost always stories begin with one person saying I absolutely believe in this and I want this to happen. What do we know about those people? [They] . . . have taken an outer journey and an inner journey . . . The inner journey is about how the leaders have found their voice, their courage, their authenticity . . . and often this includes what we call crucial experiences . . . things [that] have happened to them in their lives that have given them the courage to let them say: I am prepared to do that."[3] My experience in working with many people who decided to make a difference is that there is a thread running through our leadership development. It is as if we hold something at our core that calls us, gets pushed into the background, and calls us again—a dream, an obligation to help, a compassion for people, a fascination with a future possibility, an interest to understand the world. These are the seeds that get nourished by an engagement in sustainability issues. I believe there are as many longings to make a difference as there are challenges ahead for humankind. A former CEO from an American telecommunications business who founded an NGO in South Africa put it like this: "Collective leadership is not only possible, it is out there and has always been—it keeps the world in balance, barely, but still. If one pays attention to that aspect of oneself, then suddenly one sees and hears how many others there are who have a similar sense of responsibility and a similar focus. It is probably just a matter of heightening the awareness, that we are already doing it and that we are much better connected than we were in the past."[4]

What it takes to expose the core of our potential is encounters with other people, a conversation, seeing something we admire, a book we read, a moment of humanness between people that reaches our hearts and opens us to remembering something we already knew. For Mike it was seeing Paul Polman's strategic move to decouple Unilever's growth from its environmental and social impact.[5] Nadeem's father introduced him to Buddhist meditation at an early age, and the wisdom of compassion has been guiding him ever since. Tina's cousin was the angel she hoped to reinvent for others. Peter's career change was caused by a golf-course conversation with a sustainability manager from a large Swiss food company who praised the role of NGOs. Celine's decision to turn down a well-paid job in Paris and go back and help her country came after an argument with a colleague who wanted a revolution in the DRC while Celine advocated a step-by-step approach to change. Andrea laid her doubts to rest after she was exposed to a book on leadership that said you can always fail, but you must try.

Even though we may know little about how the process of co-creation happens in our daily lives, it is insight that leads to greater humility and a greater feeling of responsibility. Something resonates with us. We engage with the present in a different way. We reconnect, if only for a moment, with our own deeper intention, the history of our voice and our values—with our heart. Learning to take a stance often is a process of unfolding the courage to be who we really are. Our deeper values, our dreams, and our aspirations are gateways to our vitality in this world, our ability to lead and co-create.

But this is only the beginning. Building our capacity for leading collectively toward a more sustainable future requires us to develop personal and strategic abilities that allow us to leverage collective leadership, because it is contagious; where it prevails, people take up responsibility unasked. In building this capacity we need to travel an inner path and an outer path, and we need to do this in conjunction with fellow leaders who are also prepared to take responsibility for a more sustainable future. The two paths are intertwined: Traveling the inner path prepares us for the outer path, traveling the outer path strengthens the inner path. Underlying both pathways are essentially human capacities: the capacity to love, to create, to collaborate, to reflect, to organize, to build, and to bring forth the world collectively.

Each of our fellow travelers sets out on a journey to address one small part of sustainability. They each focus on one of the three aspects of sustainability—an economic, a social, or an environmental piece. I believe it is helpful to remember that *sustainability* refers to long-lasting development in which reasonable economic prosperity, environmental quality, and social equity can be achieved in a balanced way. In the corporate world this is usually referred to as the *triple bottom line* (economic, environmental, social), a new measurement for business performance.[6] Realization of sustainable development would mean an improvement in living conditions for most people in the world and would also ensure that progress is within the limits and capacities of a functioning global ecosystem. Sustainability is not one single issue; it is a complex of issues including political, technological, environmental, social, economic, and above all human aspects. What does this mean for the challenges ahead?

Relaxing in Complexity

You may have sensed that the challenges of Mike, Nadeem, Peter, Tina, Andrea, and Celine are complex. No wonder. Complexity is the future normality, and we'd better learn to enjoy it rather than fight to reduce it.

Four types of complexity characterize the challenges of our sustainable development as humankind:[7]

1. **Dynamic Complexity.** Cause-and-effect relationships are no longer traceable or plannable in a linear fashion. An action in one part of the world may create unexpected havoc in another part. Dynamic complexity suggests that we complement our linear planning with systemic approaches and collective iterative learning mechanisms.

2. **Generative Complexity.** Solutions that worked in the past and habitual patterns of action are often inappropriate for the future; they may even have the ability to pull us into a downward spiral. For instance, our global financial system, in addition to its focus on the way we calculate GDPs, is preventing us from developing an economy that supports human evolution. Behavioral habits, calcified mind-sets, and systemic structures reinforce one another and call for radical innovation and collective intelligence to shift human behavior and thinking toward a new pattern.

3. **Social and Institutional Complexity.** The worldviews and interests of humankind may have been complex in the past, yet in the modern world people experience differences on a daily basis. The complexity of institutions extends to different cultures, interests, and territorial boundaries across the world. At the same time, institutional complexity offers an opportunity. Most of the sustainable development challenges—ranging from climate change to food and water security— require aligned action. It is the multi-stakeholder approach to global and local solutions that will become the norm in societal change.

4. **Value Complexity.** For many people in the world, personal values, institutional values, and societal values are misaligned and often subject to trade-offs. Nothing shows this more clearly than the world-wide corruption perception index. However, the challenge of complexity goes much deeper. Many employees in multinational companies, for instance, feel that they need to leave their personal values at the doorstep if they are to meet their company's performance demands.[8] Sustainability can be seen as a global project to realign deep human values with human behavior in all aspects of development.

For all four types of complexity, collaboration is the only way to turn the challenges into opportunities. Where complexity is high, the capacity to adapt, to evolve, to coordinate, to innovate, and to change is equally high.[9] This is one of the greatest lessons from biodiversity. The diversity inherent in complexity means that we need to learn to operate and to deliver in multi-actor settings, across institutional boundaries, mind-sets, and worldviews. Peter at DiverseAct knows this.

Biodiversity loss is a problem with so many multilevel causes that we are unsure how to even start slowing the decline of species. Discovering how requires a variety of stakeholders to understand what the issues are. Maintaining the complexity of biodiversity will help us into the future. It makes life on earth more resilient. It is Peter's mission to make more people understand this and enhance awareness and responsibility for it.[10] That is why he is determined to get his organization to cooperate with the private sector. It is dawning on him that his leadership challenge might be related to the mission of his organization. Will it be the principle of diversity—in approaches, stakeholder collaboration, and project composition—that will increase the impact of the organization? Does he have to take DiverseAct to the edge of chaos?

Celebrating the Interdependence of Life

Globalization could already be distinguished as a megatrend in the 1990s, and today the effects of global interdependence are becoming more and more apparent. With increased access to Internet and the dissemination of social media, people are connected in a way thought impossible in earlier times.

This interdependence leads to uncertainty and high risks in markets, examples of which can be perceived in the financial crisis in 2008, when the survival of one bank could determine the fate of a whole economic system. However, new media and digital connectivity also have impacts that further sustainability. One example is the growing need of corporations to address sustainability challenges because new communications technologies and social networks have raised consumer awareness.[11]

But how is this need addressed in the workplace? Mike is aware that TrendWear's reputation is more fragile than ever, and he wants to act before the situation gets worse. He might be able to learn from the water engineer Celine, for whom one thing is already clear—the response to interdependence is interdependence managed consciously. She understands that, in a fragile society like the Democratic Republic of Congo, nothing happens without networks—not even getting clean drinking water. *Connectivity* is key. But Celine is also proud of her global network—she will not have to repeat the water management mistakes of other countries. She is up to date with global best practices, yet needs to find the path that is adjusted to the situation in the DRC. Her insight is crystal clear: What helps her is knowing that she is a member of a global network of actors in water resource management. This is the approach she needs to take into her own country—to create a network dedicated to ensuring water supply countrywide.

We can turn the challenge of interdependence into an opportunity by leveraging networks, using information technology for empowerment and collective action. We can harness the power of mutual support across institutions, territorial boundaries, sectors, and limiting mind-sets. The better our feedback loops with stakeholder and collaborating partners, the faster is the learning on all fronts.

Tapping Our Passions

In today's world it seems that everything should have been done yesterday. And indeed, we are facing deep, structural challenges whose root causes need to be addressed with great urgency.[12] This has partly to do with the magnitude of action required and the delay between action and positive effect. Consider the climate crisis. It is caused by anthropogenic lifestyles that emit too many greenhouse gases. The consequences for the decades to come are clear unless we act immediately to keep global warming under two degrees Celsius by 2050. Or consider the collapse of the Rana Plaza complex in Bangladesh in 2013. That disaster—in which an eight-story commercial building containing clothing factories collapsed, killing more than a thousand and injuring more than twenty-five hundred—had complex root causes ranging from a lack of building safety enforcement to price wars for cheaper and cheaper garments. But it also underscored an urgent need for action to address systemic inequalities in the global trade system.

Mike was lucky that his company did not get their supplies from the affected factories, but he also knows that the next such crisis could hit TrendWear. Urgency drives his personal commitment to change. After the Rana Plaza collapse he sent two of his top managers on an incognito trip to Bangladesh to have a look at their suppliers. They came back shocked and changed, and he knew he had new allies.

In order to turn urgency into an opportunity, we need to connect to the human potential to make a difference. This means tapping into the desire of individuals to contribute positively to society and to create a better future for themselves and their children.

Tina felt the impact of urgency when she gathered a group of students to take action after hearing the panel discussion on educational inequalities. When she told them her own story of being mentored out of a crisis that could have jeopardized her life, she felt how strongly her fellow students connected with wanting to make a difference. My experience is that an intention to make a difference that is driven by urgency creates energy fields. It organizes life. It attracts people and opportunities.

Chapter 2

From the Individual to the Collective: A Paradigm Shift

By now we have seen that the challenges lying ahead of our fellow travelers are different in content and context, yet similar in form. They can move forward when they unearth a composition of competencies that enable them as individuals to lead toward their sustainability issue and yet enhance the cohesion of a group of collaborating actors. They may even need to inspire large groups of people to shift mind-sets and act in favor of the common good. Early on, Andrea often confidentially talked with her critical friends about how she could adopt an underground strategy to influence her company, EnergyTech. Her dream was to get the middle and top management aligned behind a renewable energy strategy so that they could then convince the executive board of a strategic shift. Nadeem knew that in his complex multi-stakeholder cooperation project to help small-scale African farmers he could not monitor all implementing partners; he could only help align a joint understanding of success and trust their individual contribution and performance. And these actions and insights took them to the next challenge. All our fellow travelers needed to expand their own leadership skills and to develop a deeper understanding of how a collective of diverse actors operates successfully.

Leadership paradigms often refer only to individuals and the expansion of one person's skills. The challenges faced by our fellow travelers—and indeed most challenges of sustainability—require us to go beyond the individual and build the capacity of groups and systems to move important issues of common concern forward. This requires collective action, dialogue, and collaboration. It is the aspect of collectivity that has been missing in leadership development thus far. It involves awareness of the underlying complex compositions and dynamics of the systems that require change and the dynamics developing in a group of collaborating actors. We need to shift from a self-centered consciousness to awareness of the larger whole.

In the old paradigm, leadership focuses on the capacity of the individual who has a higher position and who needs to enlist followers in order to deliver results. In many organizations, in both the corporate world and the public sector, dialogue and attention to high-quality collaboration relationships are still side issues, soft skills, add-ons. Most employee performance indicators do not measure the quality of collective human interaction. Yet this is what counts most for results.

Gradually, though, the leader-centric paradigm is shifting. Recent events, such as the Rio+20 summit in 2012, have made it even clearer that global challenges from climate to local sustainability can only be addressed when the joint capacity of leaders to become catalysts for change is realized.

Celine realizes that she can only be successful in ensuring access to drinking water in the DRC when she builds the leadership capacity of others in a collaborative context. Depending on expertise and experience, leadership and followership may be interchangeable. Only the capacity of a leadership collective in outcome-oriented dialogue and with future-oriented collective action will result in access to drinking water for all. The collective responsibility for the joint delivery of shared goals in a network of mutual support is beginning to become her ambitious vision.

Can we develop the leadership competency of a collective of diverse actors? This thought is not entirely new. Peter Senge, the conceptual pioneer of the idea of learning organizations, speaks about team learning as a collective discipline. "The championship sports teams and great jazz ensembles provide metaphors for acting in spontaneous yet coordinated ways. Outstanding teams in organizations develop the same sort of relationship—an 'operational trust'—where each team member remains conscious of other team members and can be counted on to act in ways that complement each others' actions."[1]

Let's take this as a starting point while bearing in mind that the challenges of our fellow travelers go far beyond team cooperation in one organization. Indeed, they need to build committed teams of leaders within *and* across institutions. They need to bring together leaders who act within their own institutional boundaries, yet work toward a similar goal on a collective scale—people who need to think together and to cooperate across departmental or institutional territories. They need to integrate different organizational cultures into joint initiatives and foster collaboration among diverse stakeholders. William Isaacs, a pioneer in dialogue as a core competency for leaders, suggests that a system of actors has reached a level of collective leadership "when people are attuned to each other so well that, even when separate, they naturally act in harmony with each other and the goals of the common enterprise."[2]

Most leaders even within organizations are far from such an ideal collaborative state of mind. As Isaacs states, "They meet as individuals, squeezing time from their more urgent work, debating from their individual perspectives and concentrating on their individual domains of authority. Their actions, and the actions of those who report to them, consequently take place at cross-purposes, and they often seem trapped in cycles of opposition and breakdown."[3] My experience of helping people to collaborate better shows me that reality is far from the ideal state of collective leadership Isaacs describes.

Can we find a path from the typical fragmented way of working to the ideal and to better co-creation? I do not believe in perfection, but am convinced we can improve gradually. Rather than seeing the goal of better co-creation as frustratingly far away, I suggest we rediscover and remember what we already know.

Imagine the following: You are in the mountains, surrounded by beautiful views. There may be some snow on the far mountains; there are green bushes beside you, birds are singing, and you are standing in the midst of it all. You enjoy the moment and feel very close to the world, very much at home in the universe, very much at home within yourself. And suddenly you have a feeling: *Wow! Anything can be done, as long as I am able to drive things forward together with others; we could change the world!* With that thought you not only see but also feel the beauty of the interconnected nature that is surrounding you. For a moment you are in awe. After a few minutes you become much more rational and ask yourself: *What created the feeling that I just had? Was it the view of the far mountains? The birds singing? The green hill behind me? Was it the soil under my feet?* You rationally conclude: It is all of it together. It is the composition of the things surrounding you. And it is you in the middle of this composition, because without you present, you would not be feeling the way you felt just now.

You were responding to nature's composition around you and you became part of it. That's the starting point.

Can this happen in a group of people? It certainly happened in Salvador de Bahia when we worked through the coffee community document and finally achieved a far-reaching agreement. You can say this meeting shifted reality; it co-created the future. How did it all begin? In May 2003, thirty-five stakeholders—coffee producers, European coffee-roasting industry players, and representatives of development organizations and major international NGOs—gathered in London for a meeting. On the agenda was a proposal to develop a baseline standard for mainstream coffee production that would better protect the environment, workers, small-scale farmers, and coffee-growing communities. The extremely ambitious project had evoked the skepticism of many participants. Several smaller meetings had preceded the one in London; people had been arguing, blocking progress, and threatening to jeopardize the initiative. By the time of the London meeting the group harbored high levels of mistrust and serious reservations. But a day and a half of structured dialogue led to a promising outcome: Almost all participants explicitly committed to participating in the initiative. This commitment to collective action for sustainability produced an awareness that was palpable in the room.

What did I learn from it? Leading for sustainability is not an act in isolation. It requires leadership by many individuals toward a similar goal on a collective scale. The biggest investment in the beginning is fostering trust among people and visualizing a common goal—even if it is faint, it's still under construction, and the path toward it is unclear. It is the emotional exposure to collectively making a difference that counts; that is when people join in and start contributing. Do not expect people to drop their skepticism, criticism, and doubt in the beginning. Do not develop false hopes of equality and alleviated power differences, but know that you have entered the field of collective leadership when—despite opinionated differences—people are prepared to join a collective learning journey toward a greater goal. Everybody will contribute to the journey in different ways.

I believe the capacity for initiating, leading, facilitating, and sustaining the construction of meaningful futures is within all of us. If you find collective leadership at work, you probably experience the following situation: A group of people has in front of them a big challenge. They come from different backgrounds, they may have different expertise, and they may have different opinions on how to solve the issue. They get into a conversation about the way forward. The issue is so urgent that they can't waste their time with blocking one another. They are aware that time is important and that they all have the responsibility to find a solution. In that way, they are very focused on an outcome, on driving change, and on working toward a solution, but they are also aware that the best solution actually comes from difference and diversity—from an exchange of different viewpoints, even being opposed to one another on certain issues. They use their time wisely and converse about the issue. They carefully listen to what people are saying because they also want to listen to what is not said. Listening helps them come up with ideas, spot creative solutions, identify the innovative areas. While they are talking it gradually becomes clear to everybody what the solution is, because it emerges out of the conversation, out of the differences, out of the diversity. And finally they all drive toward the solution, within their particular area of responsibility in their institution. And they stay connected and come together at a later stage to see how it went, to learn and to evaluate what worked, what didn't, and how they should take the next step.

If you think that this is an ideal situation and far from your reality, I encourage you to observe closely. It does happen, in many teams and in many institutions. It may be happening on a small scale, not yet big enough to see the changes needed for our global sustainability. But the process is very familiar to human nature. It's a way of interacting responsibly and respectfully toward one another. Try to remember a time when you experienced a team acting that way; then you will have a notion of what collective leadership is about. Now you can imagine what would happen on our planet if that way of acting for sustainability and interacting with one another expands and grows. Our task is to make our inherent capacity for collective leadership more explicit, to bring it to the surface, to understand how it works. It is time to empower many more people to lead collectively toward a sustainable future.

This kind of leadership is an entirely new discipline. Greg Koch, head of global water stewardship for Coca-Cola, puts it like this: "I joined the company as a seasoned engineer but have had to develop skills of partnership development, community engagement, media relations, water policy negotiations, even some philosophy, and certainly have become a much better listener. Almost everyone comes to a discussion about water with visceral experiences, memories, cultural and religious ties, economic links, as well as strong opinions and feeling . . . This makes any solution to a water challenge much more than just technical, economical or regulatory."[4]

Successful multi-actor collaborations for sustainability share the characteristic of an orientation toward future possibilities. It is the creative potential in sustainability that inspires people to join in and commit. Collaborative leaders are visionaries in the sense that they see the unknown not as a threat but as a potential and are, therefore, more likely to spot innovative solutions. We cannot travel the path toward sustainability in silos; instead we need to harness collective intelligence and let it complement individual expertise. Even in the midst of performance demands and project pressure we can access our humanity—the deeper layer in the potential of human encounter that connects us all in the world.

Monika Griefahn, the cofounder of Greenpeace Germany and former minister of environmental affairs in the federal state of Lower Saxony, explains how, when she took over her government post, she succeeded in gradually changing the mind-set and culture of a bureaucracy and turned people into change agents. During her time in office, Lower Saxony became a pioneer in establishing renewable energies with procedures, regulations, and approaches that have since been adopted by other federal states and by other countries. "You have to have an image of the future that goes far beyond the operational goals you would normally set yourself," says Griefahn. "You need to inspire people to think in possibilities rather than limitations. And you need to ask people for their point of view. I never expected that we would have such a long-term impact when I took over the Ministry of Environment—suddenly people started to co-operate across ministries. We created round tables and joint initiatives, and people who had been dormant woke up and contributed. It was the feeling of a movement that pushed us forward."[5] *Collective leadership* for sustainability is the capacity of a group of actors to deliver their contribution to a joint purpose collaboratively, while putting high priority on the common good and a balance among the needs of people, profit, and planet.

Chapter 3

Why We Need a Compass for Better Co-Creation

As leaders and change agents for sustainability we are nodes in a some-times invisible network. When we lead collectively, we more consciously operate as the network. But leading collectively means navigating complex, interdependent multi-actor settings on a regular basis. Collaborating well becomes part of our daily management challenge. That's why it's helpful to have a guide like the Collective Leadership Compass presented in part 2. But before we explore how to use that compass, it's helpful to fully under-stand why it's needed.

The Costs of Non-Collaboration

Let's start by calculating the costs of non-collaboration. Frequently situa-tions arise in which collective human interaction is less successful than we intend it to be. How do we calculate the opportunity costs of interactions that were supposed to lead toward a tangible result—conversations, meet-ings, workshops, conferences, and partnerships—but did not? The costs of non-collaboration or lack of collective leadership are often hidden, but the following examples make clear a severe imbalance between costs and return. (I have changed the names, contexts, countries, and issues.)

First example: A two-day multi-stakeholder meeting on combat-ing malaria was convened in an African country. It was initiated by an international organization active in the field. About 120 people from governments, civil society, and research institutions were invited, of which 80 finally showed up. Ten gave a speech or a presentation on issues that most people already knew about—stating how difficult yet important it is to combat malaria and what has been tried so far. Question-and-answer sessions were allowed after each presentation. The aim of the meeting was to agree on a joint action plan, but the attendees did not design the plan together. Instead the plan was presented by the initiating organization with only limited time for comment. Everybody in the room felt that they would simply continue their own work as before.

Actual costs plus opportunity costs (travel and absence from work): a seven-digit figure. The result: It is good to meet; side conversations and making new connections are great, but the impact of the actual outcome is close to zero. What was lacking? In short: attention to engagement. No process was designed to pre-engage people for a collective action strategy—a plan to jointly get better at combating malaria. People enjoyed meeting, but there was no guided interaction. Future possibilities were hardly mentioned, as most speakers reiterated what everybody already knew. Every speaker was concerned about reputation, avoided mentioning failures or lessons, and conveyed the sense of having a winning strategy. No iterative learning occurred that could have sparked innovation or at least an engaged exchange among participants that might have surfaced collective intelligence.

Second example: Different ministries in a European country worked on the issue of consumer awareness for sustainable consumption. Each was concerned that there was too little guidance for the consumer on what sustainable consumption really means. One believed that there should be more information, so it financed a consumer awareness campaign. Another did not think this approach would solve the problem of increasing confusion over the various sustainability labels, so it launched an initiative to compare those labels and financed a website where consumers could access the comparison. A third ministry thought this was not leading anywhere because a much broader approach to sustainable consumption was most important. It contended that labeled products were only useful to niche markets, and so it wanted to collaborate with industry on sustainable production standards in mainstream markets. Communication among the ministries was aggressive as each disregarded the approaches of the others. Meanwhile, consumers remained confused and continued to fund each ministry with their taxes.

The opportunity costs of such non-collaboration were frighteningly high. What was lacking? In short: a sense of wholeness. Each ministry focused only on its own expertise. Nobody bothered to look at the whole, and certainly not together. Lack of engagement prevented them from making use of their collective intelligence. Relationships among representatives from the different ministries deteriorated. The empathy for one another's structures and constraints and any sense of humanity declined. The future possibility of actual consumer empowerment fell to the wayside.

Third example: Many NGOs, governments, and corporations share the concern that workers in Southeast Asian factories are paid too little. A development agency hosted a meeting to discuss joint action. The meeting took place in Europe. With the exception of one person, no stakeholder from Southeast Asia was present. Out of the six invited companies, three declined participation, giving time constraints as an excuse. The remaining three companies were interested but hesitant. Two of them had already conducted an internal study on how to deal with the low wages that their suppliers paid their workers. The conclusions were ambiguous. The price margin for textile products in Europe and the United States was considered too narrow to allow a price increase for the textile products from the Asian factories. Cutting costs downstream or removing intermediaries would not cover the loss in margin. If any of the three participating companies increased the textiles' sales price at the consumer level, they would lose market share and endanger their business. The unspoken conclusion was that the problem could be solved only if governments in Southeast Asia substantially increased minimum wages. That would hit all companies the same way. None of the participants would have to take the risk of increasing consumer prices alone. The meeting ended with good intentions, but no action plan.

The opportunity costs: enormous. What was lacking? In short: engagement—at the level of participating companies and at the level of stakeholders from the countries concerned. A proper process was missing, carefully looking at who needed to be brought on board for a future possibility that the individual companies could not see separately. Wholeness was missing as each actor looked only at one part of a complex picture with a down-spiraling dynamic that none of them could stop alone. This prevented a breakthrough toward an innovative solution that might have involved a joint action with all regional governments. Nobody dared to look at solutions beyond the current constraints, and nobody wanted to take a risk. People reiterated problems without sensing future possibilities and ensuring collective action.

There are many more examples, and some, I believe, may be part of your own reality. Patterns of incompetency in interactions are natural, but if we leave them unaddressed, they have an enormous impact. The most frightful example for this was the Copenhagen climate summit in December 2009. A lot has been written about why the Copenhagen summit failed, what went wrong in preparation and implementation. Still, it remains a mystery why a group of highly skilled and experienced politicians in powerful positions with farsighted views of the world's course could have been interacting in such an unprofessional way—with incredible direct and indirect negative impacts on millions of people.

What happened? A German news agency revealed the taped conversation among the heads of states on a possible global commitment regarding the reduction of carbon emissions.[1] People failed as people, not only as heads of state. How was this possible? The "Copenhagen Minutes" show how the high-level conversations ended up in a diplomatic disaster with the Europeans feeling powerless and China overplaying its new self-confidence. Twenty-five heads of state met in a separate room while one hundred others plus a few thousand visitors eagerly awaited the agreement on a plan of action. The twenty-five could not agree on tangible emission targets. They became concerned with their own interests more than a larger joint goal, even as heads of state.

What prevents us from knowing what we already know? How can we more competently interact as human beings in order to serve the future of this planet? What are the steps that get us back on track? A compass can help us unearth the human competencies for better co-creation. Let's take a quick view behind the curtains of co-creation—it may remind us of how the world works.

Naming the Dragon: Making the Invisible Visible

In his elaborations on personal mastery, Peter Senge has written an important passage: "Structures of which we are unaware hold us prisoner. Once we see them and we name them, they no longer have the same hold on us."[2] For example, if we have an ambitious goal that we are determined to achieve, we might unconsciously hold a belief that success will separate us from the people we love—so we work toward the goal with a little dragon bothering us and jeopardize our chances of success. Unless we name the dragon—in this case, fear—it will have power over us. That is why so many personal trainers and life coaches tell us to admit and name our fears and walk toward them.[3] What applies to us as individuals also applies to groups of people, teams, organizations, actors who want to collaborate.

The dragon in the room during the meeting on living wages in Southeast Asia was competition. Everybody knew it and nobody would say it: Competition among producer countries in Southeast Asia and competition among the buying and trading companies was the known yet invisible structure that maintained the race to the bottom for textile prices. All actors felt paralyzed and could not openly name the dragon to start a dialogue on how to go beyond a structure that held the unjust and exploitative system in place. In my work helping people to collaborate, I have come across many dragons—structures in place that could not be questioned or even named.

Celine's biggest dragon in the DRC is corruption. Hardly any of her government colleagues could claim they'd never used an opportunity to make some extra money. She knows that these are not necessarily bad people—they need to survive on salaries that are far too low in a city that is more expensive than some European capitals. Celine is convinced that through engagement she will access people's humanity, their desire to make a difference, if she enables them to sense the future possibility of a country no longer wasting its human talents and resources. Then she will name the dragon.

Sometimes the dragon is like the invisible part of an iceberg. In 1976 Edward T. Hall developed what's known as the iceberg model to explain culture. With an iceberg, what we see—the upper part—is determined by what we do not see—the part under the water. Yet both parts are the iceberg. The analogy reminds us that the unspoken or invisible may determine our behavior in organizations more than the spoken and visible.[4] It has often helped me make people understand that there is more to reality than the obvious. We become better co-creators if we attend to both aspects of the iceberg. A compass can help us name the dragons, make the invisible visible, and above all attend to the invisible as much as to the visible in planning our change strategies. We will return to this later.

Reconciling Flatland and Wonderland

A sustainability manager from a global consulting firm recently confided that whenever he integrated soft aspects (such as collective reflection, dialogue, or relationship building) into his projects with large multinational companies, it was exactly this part of the proposal that got cut first by his clients.

What counts in the sustainability effort, as much as in all other less-questioned business settings, is *flatland*—a term coined by author Ken Wilber, who uses it to describe the world "out there" that most of us call reality (as if all other parts of life were not real).[5] It is the world of key performance indicators, quarterly reports, monitoring systems, and incentive schemes. It is the dominant culture that runs not only the corporate world, but also government and civil society organizations. There is nothing fundamentally bad about flatland; we need to measure our progress, establish structures to hold complexity at bay, and develop technologies to push us into the future. We need rules that govern our societies. We need to give evidence that sustainability is possible and that it works for people and for business. But will flatland get us to sustainability?

I often meet sustainability leaders who are overworked, rushed, with dwindling personal relationships, haunted by overexposure to new technology, and usually exhausted. In this respect, they are no different from those in any international business setting. Who would dare to admit working less than twelve hours a day? How do you even spell *weekend* or *vacation*? But everyone I meet also has another, rather separate world, which Wilber terms *wonderland*. This is a world where different things count: our personal development, our spiritual growth, our zest for life, our heart's passion, our ability to be with others in mutually supportive communion, our appreciation of others as fellow human beings. In wonderland, we can be in dialogue with nature, with ourselves, and with our colleagues. There we can develop our capacity to learn collectively, our competency to co-create a more sustainable future, our feeling of being connected to something larger than ourselves, our sense of meaning.

We act as if both worlds—wonderland and flatland—need to be mutually exclusive; one can only exist at the expense of the other. As rational human beings, we know that we need more balance. But is balance the only issue here? Or do we need a shift in mind-set? Can we attempt to rethink the unchallenged assumption that these two worlds need to be separated—and that, in our working worlds, flatland needs to always dominate?

In an article published by the Ashridge Business School, Dave Bond and Emma Dolman argue that the practice of meditation—which could be seen as a wonderland activity—has slowly become a more prominent feature of leadership development programs.[6] A research project I carried out with fourteen leaders from eight different countries helps explain why.[7] Over the course of the study, it became evident that incorporating aspects of wonderland into the work world can be a potent driver for mapping a path toward leadership for sustainability. Reflection, dialogue, and encounter all helped the study's participants reawaken the quest that had brought them to this work, reshape their contribution to sustainability, and achieve a deeper fulfillment.

If we consider the challenges of our fellow travelers it becomes clear that they do not have a choice; they need to be creative in integrating the two worlds or they will fail. Mike has probably the hardest nut to crack. His success will only be measured in flatland values, the financial success he brings to TrendWear. And yet he will not achieve it without engaging people in a future vision of doing business in the textile industry. Andrea has to find the silent dreams of her middle managers at EnergyTech—wanting to be the fathers and mothers kids will be proud of. If Tina wants to grow a movement helping disadvantaged kids access their educational potential, she will only gain momentum if she finds the soft spot in students—the desire to give back the gifts of education through mentoring. If we are serious about co-creating a more sustainable world, we need to reintegrate the worlds we have separated, and defragment what are actually parts of a whole.

In his recent book, Joseph Jaworski shows that integrating wonderland into flatland can be more than just productive.[8] He argues that the capacity for dialogue and acute listening skills can increase mutual understanding and respect for difference in teams, and that meditation practices often lead to financially measurable outcomes. If we want to build our capacity for co-creating a more sustainable future, we need both flatland and wonderland; we need to refuse the divorce and get marriage counseling. Both individually and collectively, outer action and inner development need each other and have a reciprocal effect. If one is missing, the other is lost or falls short of its potential.

That's where the Compass becomes a tool for reconciling flatland and wonderland—its dimensions strengthen the competencies that belong to both flatland and wonderland, to the inner path and the outer path. Hence, the Compass helps integration.

Integrating the Female Perspective

The debate is still on about whether the course of the world would change if more women held powerful positions. A CEO survey done by Accenture included photographs of seventy-five of the interviewees.[9] I could identify two women among those seventy-five CEOs. In the S&P 500 and American stock market index, the percentage of women holding CEO positions is 4.6.[10] If that is a statistical sample of the world's most important CEOs, it is frightening and calls for more affirmative action to empower women at the level of top executives. Sheryl Sandberg, the COO of Facebook, shows in her thought-provoking book *Lean In* how mental and societal structures keep gender imbalances in leadership positions in place unless we consciously make an effort to address the situation.[11] That is now happening in Norway, where corporate boards must be at least 40 percent women.

We have come to this point in our human development with a rather unbalanced relationship between men and women in positions of power. Sustainability cannot be achieved operating as we have in the past. The world needs a more balanced relationship between the ways women and men build the future. More than the scientific discussion of how the imbalance developed, more than the heated debate about how to shift underlying power structures in the world to allow women to take their part in determining the world's course, we need to remember that millions of professional women are here now. They are often less interested in issues of power and less interested in being hailed by media. They are doing their jobs—but it is important to get more of them into stronger positions to drive toward sustainability. Women usually consider more aspects and approach strategic issues more holistically. They often take care of elements that are underutilized: relationships, communication, and collaboration—three cornerstones of sustainability. Because many women need to juggle kids, older parents, and workloads, they often make better use of their time. This is what we need more of in sustainability leadership.

In a discussion of female leaders in business, held in the *Guardian* sustainable leadership hub in 2012, one of the participants suggested that more women could drive a new way of doing business that would be more collaborative, more community-centered, and more partnership-focused.[12] Another participant assumed that by adding more women to leadership teams the overall effectiveness would increase. For him the reason is that men are good at technical and strategic levels, while women have a much better understanding of the need for communication and relationship building.

I strongly support the expansion of female leaders in top positions, as I believe that this is an essential component in shifting the way we co-create. The world needs to be moved forward by both men and women working together. But I do see a need to go beyond the socially constructed gender identities and look at driving forces for co-creation at a deeper level. The Chinese philosophical description of yin as the female principle in nature and yang as the male principle invites us to see the necessary complementarity of co-creation that we should make much more conscious.[13] My work experience in many collaboration initiatives shows that an integration of such complementary approaches must take place in order to shift systems toward sustainability. Whether these principles are brought in by men or women, I do think the differences need to be acknowledged and leveraged. There is a strong female principle at work around the competency of relating to a larger context—of seeing one's contribution as part of a larger story. There is also a strong component of caring and nurturing relationships in collaboration that is crucial to high-quality engagement of different actors, and there is a female principle palpable when people really meet as people.

It is not just women who bring what's traditionally been considered female energy to the table, nor men who bring traditional male energy. And we need both sets of principles. Good collective leadership also requires what are often considered male principles (which can equally be displayed by women): the warrior energy of decisiveness to lead future possibilities, the brilliance of inventiveness and courage to venture into the unknown, and that edge of intelligence that sometime shifts the discourse in heated conversations. So it is not only about adding women to leadership seats; it is also about the ability of all of us to expand our way of co-creating and integrate seemingly different but actually complementary approaches. The Compass can help us notice differences in energies and more consciously integrate them so that what moves forward has both female and male contributions.

Finding the Pattern That Works

You may have noticed in that the Compass can guide us to more balance. Balance does not require an equal percentage of all dimensions. It depends instead the overall presence of different yet consciously composed dimensions, so that each dimension can have an impact on the entire constellation and on each of the other dimensions. Much as Christopher Alexander described when writing about the composition of spaces, each dimension of human interaction supports the others. And not unlike architecture, if we remove one dimension or ignore it, the entire constellation loses its impact. So it is all about impact.

Now let me introduce you to an unusual way of seeing our reality. Assume that there are three important layers in which we can perceive reality.[14] There is a layer of actual behavior that I call *action*—what people do and what we can see them doing, what we hear, the world of facts and figures. But different people perceive even this more superficial layer of reality very differently. Take a view of a beautiful mountain range as an example. One person might look at it in awe as the beauty goes straight to his heart; he adores the variation of shades and forms. For this person, a mountain may be a symbol of happiness. Another person could get an immediate fright by looking at a mountain range: Perhaps she had hid in a mountain range while involved in guerrilla warfare, only to be discovered by the enemy. For her a mountain range is the symbol of defeat. These two people are looking at the same view with totally different perceptions. It is still a mountain range; that is a fact.

The difference in perception of "facts" is not the only challenge for people who work in cross-institutional, cross-sector collaboration projects. How we see the "real" world is not only a function of what some people would call facts, but also a function of structures, of which some are explicit, physical, or visible, and others implicit or invisible. That is the second layer. The layer of *structure* includes the layer of action.

Structures can be physical, like nature, architecture, our body, or other visible order, or they can be mental—embedded through experience in our memory. Structure, both physical and mental, informs thinking. Ask experienced facilitators if they would rather facilitate with a U-shaped table at which each participant has a microphone or with a round of chairs without microphones, and they will explain to you that the ability of people to think together will be entirely different, as will the results. U-shaped table arrangements create a structure that encourages positional statements rather than a conversation. People tend to prefabricate their arguments rather than building on one another's thoughts. A round of chairs is a structure that invites a degree of intimacy—people subsequently feel a stronger interrelatedness, which in turn helps them to listen and refer to one another. While we may be able to overcome the influence of physical structure by conscious decisions, mental structure informs our thinking in a more subtle way through memory.

Structure, visible or invisible, mental or physical, informs our thinking and determines the way we see reality. How we interpret facts. How we understand certain behavior. How we react emotionally to something happening. Robin Sharma provocatively writes, "We do not see the world as it is, but how we are."[15] Peter Senge calls this "mental models"—embedded structure in our mind that makes us see and interpret reality in a certain way and that influences our actions, sometimes without us being conscious of it.[16] These could be beliefs, assumptions, convictions, and so on. Becoming increasingly aware of them is a prerequisite for us becoming more conscious leaders for sustainability.

Collaboration among stakeholders is often an exchange among mental models—and ideally these shift and change through conversations. Noticing mental structures is a prerequisite for us learning to better co-create. Awareness precedes insights and insights precede action. The dragons in the costly non-collaboration examples were the implicit structures that were in place ("we don't talk about price and competition"). They could not be named, but they had an enormous impact on the results—or the lack thereof.

There is a third layer of perceiving reality. When I asked you to imagine sitting in a beautiful mountain area, you might have been able to sense the feeling of being whole, the closeness to the universe that people feel when they see a night sky of bright stars. The presence of the stars actually has an impact on us—it creates an atmosphere, a nurturing climate, that makes us feel at ease, at home in the universe. We can re-create this feeling in other places. For some it might be a seaside beach, a place in the desert, a clearing in a forest, or a riverside—or it might be the feeling you have sitting in a coffee shop in New York, that sense of being part of humankind as people pass by. That is what I call *space*. It encompasses the two other layers—action and structure. Space is an entry point to a broader level of consciousness, to the underlying wealth of possibilities.

Often, when we talk about space, we talk about energy. We would, for example, say that there is low energy in the room. Space has an effect on us. Because human beings are different, we choose different spaces in which to feel happy, to pause for a moment, to reconnect with a deeper truth or ourselves. But what we have in common is that we all know there are certain aspects that constitute an atmosphere of a space.

If you have ever facilitated a group, you may have come across the expression, *You need to hold the space*. What does it mean? It refers to a facilitator's capacity to attend to the space, the atmosphere among people, by giving full attention to each human being present and being present personally as well. It is the ability to sense the collective presence of people and be of service to making this presence a fruitful interaction. It is the climate in the room that helps the cohesion of the group. Attend to it, and people can more easily explore differences without getting defensive. Inherently, we all know how to perceive space and attend to it. Facilitators also know that if the space is positive, the meeting will be effective, results achieved. If the space is fragmented, the outcomes are less collectively intelligent.

We need to become more able to see how action, structure, and space are related, how they influence one another. There is a constant interaction among the three layers. Certain behavior creates or consolidates a certain structure—a mental or a group structure. That structure creates a certain atmosphere, which in turn informs the thinking of people and subsequent action. So it goes around in circles. There is a constant making of reality in which we participate. If we become a little more aware of how this making of reality happens, what we do or don't do, how we could influence the space among people toward more healthy structure and more constructive behavior, then we would make progress much easier. This is not an esoteric route. It is simply how the creation of reality works. Deepening our understanding of reality helps us better deal with complexity, interdependence, and urgency.

Peter's challenge is that, as a newcomer from the private sector to an NGO like DiverseAct, he certainly meets skepticism. In addition to lingering mistrust there is a way of doing things (action) at DiverseAct with mental models and procedures (structure) that keep things as they were in the past, yet that's exactly what he would like to change. He can force people to change procedures, but can he change their mental models? His best chance to shift is by attending to space, the atmosphere, the emotional connection to a future vision of DiverseAct. Then both structures and action will change.

Why is this important? If we want to learn to better co-create, we can't skip the attention to action, structure, and space. It expands our ability to adapt and to act in an efficient and effective way. It helps us get unstuck if we are victims of structures that hold us back. There is one element of space that we all know; it is trust. We can track it back to action and to structure, but still, for most of us it belongs to the realms of space. We simply feel it. In an atmosphere of trust people produce different results. Matthias Horx, a future researcher, suggests that "trust reduces the transaction costs of a society."[17] And it is true. This notion is at the heart of high-quality democracies; it is at the heart of companies getting into authentic dialogue with their stakeholders; it is the cornerstone of authentic engagement processes. With trust being present the impossible becomes possible. People act differently.

In collaboration projects I often ask: What are the success factors for good stakeholder collaboration? People mention trust as a key. My response is, great! And do you know how to get to trust? People often consider trust as something others should have, as if they were entitled to receive trust from the stakeholders they involve. Other people say that trust is something you earn. I agree with the latter. Trust is created; more specifically, trust is co-created. And it is at the cornerstone for collective leadership because it contributes to the vitality of a system of actors and it contributes to the vitality of each individual as part of that system.

The trust built enabled us in the coffee initiative to come to an agreement in Salvador de Bahia. Building trust is the challenge ahead for Mike at TrendWear, Peter at DiverseAct, Nadeem in his multi-stakeholder project, and Celine in the DRC. That's where the Compass comes in as supportive tool. It makes the trust building more conscious. It helps people pay attention to action, structure, and space. It helps build a pattern that works—a pattern of mutually supportive dimensions for better co-creation. It supports building a pattern of human competencies that fuel good collaboration. It reminds us that together we need to reach a delicate balance between life-enhancing collective action and iterative collective learning as a cornerstone of innovation. Individually we need to combine our growth of personal maturity with our capacity to lead structural change. So let's have a look at what the Compass is all about and how we can make use of it.

PART TWO

The Collective Leadership Compass

The Collective Leadership Compass is a practice-oriented approach to leading complex change in multi-actor settings. It empowers leaders to navigate successful collaboration settings for sustainable development in an integrative, inclusive way by attending to a pattern of human competencies in interaction. It strengthens the competency to navigate the *how*, *what*, *why*, *where to*, *when*, *with whom*, and *what for* of our initiatives for sustainability. It can be used to strengthen our individual leadership skills, to enhance the leadership capacity of a group of actors, and to shift systems of collaborating actors toward better co-creation.

What do I mean by "a pattern of human competencies in interaction"? The key to better co-creation is paying attention to the recursive pattern of human competencies in the six dimensions of Collective Leadership: FUTURE POSSIBILITIES, ENGAGEMENT, INNOVATION, HUMANITY, COLLECTIVE INTELLIGENCE, and WHOLENESS. Each dimension has its own dynamic and can be fostered and developed in many ways. With sufficient attention to each dimension and ultimately to their togetherness they mutually reinforce one another's strengths. Leading collectively becomes the natural way to bring forth a desirable future when we enhance our competency to make these six dimensions present—as individuals, as a team of leaders, and as a collective. The dimensions are not new; they are as old as humankind. What is new is paying more conscious attention to their *joint* presence. It helps us navigate through human difficulties and enhances the vitality of individuals and collectives.

Using the *Compass* is like learning to design and implement a pattern by keeping the six dimensions in an appropriately balanced composition and ensuring that none gets lost. When we do this on an individual level, we become more efficient, more effective, better at learning quickly, more adaptive, and above all oriented toward a future that our kids also want to live in. As a collective, we become more resilient—a capacity we need in a complex, interdependent, and quickly changing world. Resilience is not the same as robustness. Denise de Luca, an engineer and leadership expert who promotes learning from nature for organizational change and leadership, explains it this way: "From an engineering point of view, robustness means that a system can function under all kinds of circumstances; resilience means that it can recover from disturbances."[1] This is a brilliant way of describing what we need. With climate change, resource scarcity, social imbalances, and the crisis of financial systems we are realizing that our future depends on action based on the human capacity to become more resilient, adapt, learn, re-create, invent, innovate, and—yes—co-create better.

My experience is that the Collective Leadership Compass resonates with people; it strengthens their confidence that the long path into a more sustainable future can be traveled together. We need to remember that people are only prepared to change their behavior when they resonate with a future possibility that is touching their hearts. Then they happily welcome catalysts for change. Humankind is part of life's inherent tendency for creative unfolding into forms of increasing diversity and complexity. The more we realize this, the more we become the partner of evolution—and can learn the art of resilience.

The Collective Leadership Compass can help us stay on track when we have to weather storms and uncertainties. Before we dive into the Compass, I would like to preempt four possible misunderstandings.

1. The Compass is not a recipe for all challenges that humankind faces. It is a tool that, used wisely, can help us better co-create, collaborate, and lead change for sustainability.
2. The Compass does not reduce the complexity of today's world. Instead it helps us structure our approach to dealing with complexity.
3. Some define collective leadership as a direction set by the top that has to be followed by everybody; that is not what is meant here. A collaboratively delivered contribution to a joint purpose, as I have defined it, will inevitably include differences, conflicts, and the search for the right path.

4. In some people's understanding collective leadership excludes hierarchy and power differences; they assume that we are all equal. I would deny this. We are not, but we can acknowledge one another's humanness and each person's right to lead to the future. When we accept that the future is constantly emerging as a result of encounters among people, we become more aware of the pattern of human competencies in interaction that can take us into a better future.

Chapter 4

A Glimpse into the Conceptual Background

The Collective Leadership Compass was born after years of evaluating collaboration initiatives and discerning what made the difference between success and failure. It was also inspired by vast streams of knowledge built by those who pioneered new ways of thinking about leadership and organizational behavior as well as those who developed key theories on the way humans evolved, natural systems work, complexity and chaos shape our world, patterns form, people and systems interact, and so much more. That thinking distilled, for me, into the six dimensions of the compass.

The following selected conceptual thought had the most significant influence on developing the Collective Leadership Compass.[1]

Shaping the Future

Multi-stakeholder collaboration is a way of forming temporary, goal-oriented systems of human interaction. Because of their temporary nature and—in contrast with institutions—their loose structure, they could become catalysts for changing the behavior of participating institutions and individuals.

It was Peter Senge who drew attention to the fact that when we focus on prescriptions for leadership behavior, or on the interaction between leaders and followers, we often forget the essence of leadership. According to Senge, "Leadership exists when people are no longer victims of circumstances, but participate in creating new circumstances."[2] For a long time leadership has been regarded as the capacity of individuals, but it's time to shift this paradigm and explore leadership as the capacity of a collective—be it a team, the core group of a multi-stakeholder collaboration initiative, or the senior leadership group of a corporation.[3] Senge hinted at this long ago when he said that leadership "is the capacity of a human community to shape its future and specifically to sustain the significant processes of change required to do so."[4]

Extending these insights and reading widely in a vast array of additional literature on leadership, as well as my personal experience that people are drawn to the potential of making a difference, enabled me to define the dimension of FUTURE POSSIBILITIES—with aspects such as *future orientation*, *empowerment*, and *decisiveness* as important lenses through which a collaboration system could be enhanced or improved.

Shared Value Creation

Events such as the Rio+20 summit and the recommendations for a post-2015 climate agenda have made it even clearer that in order to address global challenges, the joint capacity of leaders to become catalysts for change is a must. This is the cornerstone of our response to the global sustainability challenges, whether we are creating responsible supply chains, developing innovative technology for climate adaptation, or engaging stakeholders for better water resource management. In their writing about the possibilities of shared value, economist Michael E. Porter and social-change expert Mark R. Kramer point out that in advanced economies the need for products that better meet societal needs is growing fast—be they energy-saving devices, clean cars, or avenues to better nutrition.[5] The same applies to less developed economies. However, the potential of integrating disadvantaged communities in these countries is even more important, whether that's through mobile phone banking or agricultural information for small-scale farmers.

Combining these insights from social change and development cooperation with my personal experience of the importance of high-quality step-by step engagement in change management gave rise to defining the dimension of ENGAGEMENT with aspects such as *process quality*, *connectivity*, and *collective action* as important lenses through which a collaboration system could be enhanced or improved.

The Creation of Novelty

Joe Jaworski suggests that "the deeper territory of leadership [is] collectively 'listening' to what is wanting to emerge in the world, and then having the courage to do what is required."[6] Otto Scharmer developed this underlying idea into his approach of the Theory U, which is a profound guided change process built on the capacity of a group of people to change their structure of attention and subsequently their collective pattern of thought and action.[7] As individuals and teams carry more and more responsibility in complex multi-actor change initiatives, this capacity to jointly become inventive grows in importance. A whole body of research and practice has emerged around our capacity to innovate for sustainability by drawing on diverse perspectives integrating human, business, and technological factors as well as multiple levels of expertise into an interactive process of idea creation, prototyping, and iterative improvement.[8]

Together with my personal experience that navigating results-oriented stakeholder collaboration needs both content expertise and entirely new perspectives, this gave rise to defining the dimension of INNOVATION with aspects such as *creativity*, *excellence*, and *agility* as important lenses through which a collaboration system could be enhanced or improved.

Ethical Know-How

A little booklet with the title *The Future of Humanity* was published in the year 1986. It documents a dialogue between the Western physicist David Bohm and the Eastern metaphysician J. Krishnamurti.[9] Their conversation was centered on the basic assumption that human thought creates divisions—between "me" and "you" and between "me" and "the world." It then acts on these divisions as if they were facts. To nobody's surprise, the human mental activity shows up as polarization in the world: difference, disparity, and conflict. Each person struggles alone, trying to achieve peace, happiness, and security. And yet the very attempt to separate one's own happiness from the suffering of others is a reinforcing activity maintaining separation and creating more suffering, more disparity, and more conflict.

How do we break this cycle? In his lectures on Ethical Know-How, held in Italy, Francisco Varela noted that human perception is not the representation of a pre-given external world, but in itself a co-creator of reality; we create reality as we perceive it.[10] Hence ethical expertise, for him, is not a skill that we acquire, but one we unearth when we remove the layers of obscured consciousness and begin to see this very nature of reality. We become empathetic with humankind and the world if we enact or free this inner disposition.

Together with my personal experience that mutual respect despite difference in opinion is a cornerstone of successful collaboration, this gave rise to defining the dimension of HUMANITY with aspects such as *mindfulness, balance,* and *empathy* as important lenses through which a collaboration system could be enhanced or improved.

Meaning-Making Interaction

All systems, including multi-stakeholder collaboration systems, need to balance their autonomy with the rules and relational patterns of the larger system they belong to.[11] This balance applies to the actors in a multi-stakeholder collaboration as well as to one collaboration initiative in relation to other initiatives or a larger system of actors. A key to negotiated balance is diversity, in nature a crucial requirement for the resilience of a system. The greater the diversity, the more sustainable a system becomes over time.

Similarly, multi-stakeholder collaboration initiatives are built on internal relationship patterns as well as a shared context of meaning, sustained by continuous conversations.[12] Many forward-looking authors have argued that in order for the collectively meaningful to emerge, diversity must be seen as an asset and endeavors must belong to the collective.[13] The importance of dialogue as a contributor to quality communication has long since also been adopted in the corporate world.[14]

Together with my personal experience that navigating complex change, in multi-actor settings, requires space for structured dialogue, this gave rise to defining COLLECTIVE INTELLIGENCE with aspects such as *dialogic quality, diversity,* and *iterative learning* as important lenses through which a collaboration system could be enhanced or improved.

Networked Patterns

An important feature of natural (including human) systems is the ability to connect with one another in relational patterns, ordered in the form of networks, with constant internal communication. Multi-stakeholder collaboration can be best understood as networked action that recognizes power differences between actors rather than falling into hierarchical relationships.[15] Consequently the structure supporting co-creation should consist of a networked composition of actors, with differences in power, expertise, and influence, rather than the layered organogram typically found in organizations.

In my experience, collaboration systems seem to emerge when a sufficient degree of a common identity, even if temporary, develops linked to a pattern of mutual support. As a result, I realized that a navigation tool needs to mirror patterns of referential relationships. The most relevant conceptual approach, depicting structured patterns that create aliveness, can be found in the work of Christopher Alexander.[16] He suggests that the vitality (or life) of a given space is the result of the composition of what he calls *centers*—elements of structure in a given space that influence one another through interaction. My personal observation is that areas of attention in a collaborative space similarly function as a pattern—and subsequently foster or prevent collaborative effectiveness.

This assumption has given rise to developing the six dimensions as centers of attention as a whole as well as defining WHOLENESS, with aspects such as awareness of the larger *context, mutual support*, and *contribution* as lenses through which a collaboration system could be enhanced or improved.

While drawing on its conceptual depth, the Collective Leadership Compass functions as a road map to a new structure of attention—on the individual level, the level of a team and organization, or the larger collaborative system most multi-stakeholder partnerships operate in. It creates a conscious connection between leadership as an individual task and a collective task—the conscious co-creation of new realities. In that way it helps to humanize our global change efforts, while it also ensures that we keep driving progress.

Chapter 5

Rediscovering Human Competencies

Let's journey into the six dimensions to see how we can develop our competencies. Everybody's contribution to a better future counts. In that way, collective leadership is about equity rather than equality. Collective leadership breaks with the dichotomy of leaders and followers by embracing the human ability to collaborate across cultural, political, technical, and disciplinary boundaries. It does not undervalue the wealth and power of individual capabilities, ideas, and vision, or the commitment and sustenance required to bring these to life. However, it adds a significant insight to the individual leadership endeavor: Leaders know that their vision is important, but that it's never entirely manifested and held by one person or one stakeholder group alone. By the time it's expressed, it has undergone a process of its own emergence predicated on encounters and dialogues with many people. Collaboratively delivered contributions to a joint purpose in multi-stakeholder initiatives will inevitably include differences, conflicts, and the search for the right path.

The purpose of the Collective Leadership Compass is therefore not theoretical, but practical: to guide thought and action toward patterns of successful human interaction. The compass diagram shown in figure 1, along with the explanatory table 1, briefly explores the six different dimensions of the Compass in relation to sustainability initiatives.

Let's explore the different dimensions more in depth.

Future Possibilities

Every change endeavor starts with people seeing future possibilities—sometimes an individual grasping the potential of an idea, sometimes a group of

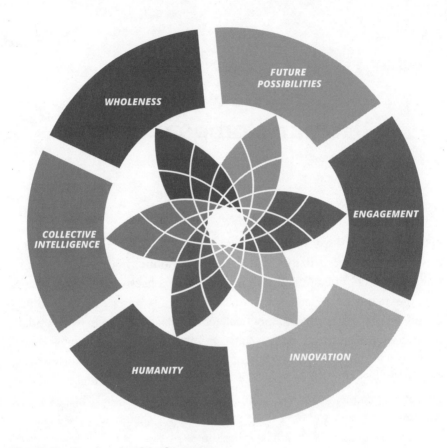

The Collective Leadership Compass

The Collective Leadership Compass, a meta-level guiding structure for developing the pattern of competencies that successful collaboration requires.

Table 1. A Guide to the Six Competencies

Dimension	Competency
FUTURE POSSIBILITIES	Take responsibility and consciously shape reality toward a sustainable future
ENGAGEMENT	Create step-by-step engagement toward building effective collaboration systems
INNOVATION	Create novelty and find intelligent solutions
HUMANITY	Reach into one another's humanness
COLLECTIVE INTELLIGENCE	Harvest difference for progress
WHOLENESS	See a larger picture and stay connected to the common good

people who develop a vision for a future state. This then grows into a more structured change initiative or even a movement. Change starts small, but we all have the capacity to sense future possibilities—small or large. Challenging the "impossible" and seeing new possibilities is a faculty that we can cultivate. It can become a habit to see the glass half full rather than half empty. Inspiring others to access their own creative potential follows naturally.

How can we enhance the dimension of FUTURE POSSIBILITIES? We can develop our competency to inspire and empower (ourselves and) others, stay open-minded, observe trends or developments, acquire new knowledge. We can also stop complaining, overcome the feeling of being a victim, and shift into taking responsibility. When we go beyond problem diagnosis to focus on what improvement a situation might need, we create a pathway into a future that many can own. Setting goals and targets helps in strengthening our competency in this dimension. Our ability grows when we find a cause that is larger than ourselves and when we take a stance for sustainability. It expands as we connect with different minds, and combine complementary expertise and experience. We grow into our own potential of self-efficacy and increase the empowerment of others. It helps if we expose ourselves to the thinking of different people, opening up new pathways for shifting our own habitual mind-sets. The ability of each of us to find our own way to lead future possibilities is important for a sustainable future. This requires us to unearth our own potential to lead, no matter how small or big the task that lies ahead of us.

There are many leaders in the world who encourage our competency in this dimension.[1] Numerous organizations around the world have undergone vision processes to unearth the spirit and commitment of their members to lead future possibilities. In many cases the end result, the vision statement, became more important than the actual process of letting the vision emerge collectively. That is why future orientation cannot be separated from collective intelligence and engagement. As management consultant Harrison Owen puts it, "Vision is never an answer but always a question that initiates a quest toward the fulfillment of the participants."[2]

Engagement

So far, so good. A lot can be achieved by getting our mind-set in place for a future that is in our hands. But even the greatest visions and the best of solutions are futile if not enough people take them up. We need many others to join our collaborative journey to sustainability; we need to engage. Change at a large scale comes about fastest in a web of relationships. How can we enhance the dimension of ENGAGEMENT? When we develop our competency to build meaningful stakeholder engagement processes that create trust and cohesion, invigorate network connections, and foster collective action that leads to tangible outcomes, then we have impact.

There is an art to engaging stakeholders that can be learned.[3] In 2003 I co-facilitated a workshop for BP on a contentious issue—a gas field exploration project in Indonesia. The risk was extremely high, and a lot was at stake. The island chosen for the exploration had a separatist movement. The indigenous people there valued their long-unchanged, nature-dependent lifestyle. Unemployment was high. Lord John Browne, then CEO of BP, had set a clear standard: There would no village resettlement. However, the outcome of the workshop was also clear: Without resettlement the operations would not make economic sense. For the BP managers, all seasoned engineers, an enormous learning curve began. They needed to find a way of aligning business operations with benefits for the people on the island. It was not an easy journey. Many years and many stakeholder collaboration experiences later, Browne had integrated the learning into his core messages when he stated: "External engagement cannot be separated from everyday business; it must be part and parcel of everyday business."[4]

Discovering the needs and benefits of collaboration with stakeholders can be a painful experience. There is an element to authentic engagement that cuts to the core of the challenge. By engaging stakeholders, we might have to adjust our own vision, our strategy, and our plan of implementation. We need openness to a change of path; we need to be able to hold a vision, yet not hold it so firmly that other people cannot shape it. That is why engagement is more than enlisting followers or aligning people behind a goal. The goal itself may be refined so that we create a future that many own.

Innovation

Leading with future possibilities and engaging relevant stakeholders are essential to starting a change process. But we might get stuck, because the danger is high that we re-create the action and behavior that took us exactly to the place we want to leave. Alan Briskin has coined the term *collective stupidity*.[5] We need to learn from the past, but we may limit ourselves to variations on existing solutions. Instead, we need to move beyond the known, most certainly beyond our comfort zone, and the comfortable sphere of the involved stakeholder.

Sustainability requires innovation on a large scale—we cannot walk into the future with our minds focused on present problems. The challenges ahead cannot be addressed by singular solutions, territorial claims, and individual intelligence alone. We need to act and drive innovation in a context of understanding the world as an interconnected system and understanding humankind as a web of relationships. With societal needs in mind, uncounted avenues for innovation are opening for companies, public sector, and civil society groups that think several steps ahead.

How can we enhance the dimension of INNOVATION? We can develop our competency to spot innovative solution. This is easier said than done. Sustainability implies innovation, yes, but not all innovations contribute to sustainability goals. Our inventiveness needs to link to wholeness (we will come to this later) and future possibilities—otherwise brilliant prototypes become isolated solutions. But often, new pathways do not open up when we are busy doing more of the same: staring at our definition of a problem, fighting boundaries, or searching for quick solutions.

Some people I know get their best ideas when they stand under the shower, others when they work out at the gym, and still others when they meditate. Some of the most wide-reaching ideas that arise between people are the results of golf-course conversations, a chat over a coffee, dinner meetings, or long walks with a colleague. The innovation arises when we are not trying to spot a solution to a problem. Ideas pop up; they emerge. This is scary! Do we need to learn the art of not-doing to remove the barriers that we have built between our individual minds and the world's consciousness? Will this help us imagine innovative solutions? Yes and no. *Yes*, because we need to foster our individual and collective creativity and be prepared to venture into the unknown. *No*, because there are many ways to build our competency in the dimension of innovation, because it is also about mastery and excellence, about acknowledging diverse expertise and our ability to adapt to new situations.

We tend to think that innovation is a faculty of individuals, yet it can become a culture of interaction in a team of people. It is helpful to remember that innovation is a manifestation of future-oriented collective consciousness and not simply the product of an individual brain—that's why many ideas pop up at different places in the world at the same time. We can enhance our competency for innovation when we reach deeply into our own consciousness and open ourselves to collaboration with other minds.

People who run leadership retreats know this phenomenon. Otto Scharmer's Theory U process, as mentioned before, can take a group of people to the bottom of the U—a place where mind and heart open and where new ideas can emerge collectively.[6] In recent years many different people have adopted a design thinking approach.[7] This focuses on diverse perspectives by integrating human, business, and technological factors as well as multiple centers of expertise into an interactive process of idea creation, prototyping, and iterative improvement. When we want to establish a culture for innovation, within us, in our teams, in our organizations, and across institutions, we more easily spot innovative solutions if we allow ourselves to meet people as people and let stories emerge that we did not expect to hear.

Bettina von Stamm, an expert engaged in helping companies develop their innovation potential, once remarked: "Because we look at things from very different perspectives, miscommunication and misunderstanding happen. But exactly this is the key to progress. If we see the humanness of another person, if we acknowledge without agreeing—we can overcome differences and finally see that all perspectives had a contribution to make."[8] This takes us into the next dimension—humanity.

Humanity

There is one thing I have observed across all cultures, nations, and organizations I have worked in: When people see the story behind a tense situation or difficult-to-understand behavior, when they see the humanness in another person, they develop compassion that often leads to revolutionary change. Paul Polman, CEO of Unilever, admitted that his inspiration for his company's ten-year Sustainable Living Plan—itself a revolution in the way large corporations work in the world—"came from looking into his children's eyes and recognizing he would be failing them if he did not do all he could to ensure their future wellbeing."[9] Jochen Zeitz, the former CEO of Puma, openly talks about his experiences in a monastery that made him introduce a transparent environmental profit and loss accounting for his company. But it is not only CEOs who have revelations and access their humanity. It is you and me, every day.

How can we enhance the dimension of HUMANITY? We can acknowledge that humankind is diverse in every respect, and then we can harness this to develop a culture of mutual respect in our organizations and collaboration efforts. We can pay attention to our inner world and to the balance we create in our personal lives that can help us become more human. Both individual and collective reflection contribute to seeing the person behind the task, the story behind something unexplainable. If we suspend our prejudices or our frame of reference in judging others, an entirely new world opens up. As we come closer to others, we come closer to ourselves.

At times, accessing the humanity in another person is hard work. Glenda Wildschut, a member of the Truth and Reconciliation Commission in South Africa—a group installed after apartheid to facilitate restorative justice—told me: "It was emotionally very, very hard work. You had to deal with people who had committed atrocious crimes, and still you had to see them as human beings. They may have been loving fathers or serving priests in their community—and they had this other extremely negative side. I worked with people who seemed to have no humanity at all. When we showed them the videos of their killing of soldiers of the liberation movement they seemed to feel nothing, absolutely nothing. And I realized, that they did not have any emotions, because they had to deny themselves their own humanity. This is what I learned. People can cut themselves off from their own humanity. And still, you have to reach out to the trace of humanity that you can find."[10]

Can consciously accessing our humanity make a difference in complex situations? In 1999, when—after years of the most brutal civil war—a peace agreement was under negotiation in Sierra Leone, Glenda Wildschut went on behalf of an international church into the war-torn capital, Freetown. People from international NGOs and peace workers had approached her, because Foday Sankoh, the rebel leader of the Revolutionary United Front, known for brutal practices such as mass rapes, amputations, and recruiting child soldiers through horrific methods, would not let them behind the rebel lines to help the child soldiers. Her team was asked if they would be willing to approach Sankoh and ask him to allow the aid workers to operate behind the rebel lines.

She vividly recounts: "We approached him and he agreed to meet us, but let us wait for 48 hours in his house, of which people said that every brick was stained with blood. But I told myself, I will not move before I have seen this man that was known for unspeakable atrocities. When we were let into his room, I could see that he was a mad man. And the only thing I said to him was: 'I know you are a father. And you love your children dearly, and I am sure you would do everything to get the best for your children in life. I know that you have recruited a lot of young boys and young girls and they all see you as their father and you see them as your children. And I am sure you want the best for them. And the best is that they get good nutrition, medical support and immunization. And there are many organizations outside that are willing to help you.' No judgment. Straight into humanity. The next day 800 child soldiers were allowed into the capital Freetown and the organizations could help."[11]

Developing our own humanity and taking care of the needs of the planet as a whole mutually reinforce each other. This is a strange equation: When we access our own humanity, we open up to the underlying humanity that connects us all across the world. Our personal leadership journeys may differ and the intentions that define our pathways may reflect enormous variety, but what connects us is the fact that we once set out on a journey with a passion for making a difference, for excelling and contributing to the world. In that way, each leadership journey is a process of unearthing our true nature in a gesture of responsiveness to what needs doing in the world. We can contribute our individuality, our gifts, and our experience to the world with increasing awareness of the need for exchange with other people about the many paths to sustainability.

Collective Intelligence

We cannot travel the path toward sustainability alone. No matter how important our own contribution may be, we exist in a web of relationships. We have seen that focusing on future possibilities frees the energy we need for the challenges ahead, and that we need to learn the art of engagement so that stakeholders can help shape goals and subsequent action plans. While we keep ourselves busy progressing we need to tend to creativity, excellence, and our ability to adapt—as these are cornerstones of innovation, which we need if we want to journey successfully. Yet the access to humanity tends to get lost when we become busy pursuing our goals, and we need to bring it back—straight into our workplace, our professional lives, our sustainability initiatives.

Let's assume we have mastered all that—and all of a sudden we get stuck in conflicts. Wouldn't it be so much easier if everyone shared our opinion and followed our path? But that's not how life works, and not how people work. Life thrives on diversity, and so do human societies. All historical attempts to silence oppositions—even the most severe forms of dictatorship—have failed in the long run. It is a human competency to differ. That's where progress comes from. If we exclude opposition it will come in through the back door. If we do not listen to people with different worldviews, they will get angry and possibly violent. Opening up to collective intelligence is what will help make the difference. Some people may think collective intelligence is a result of a harmonious conversation with all in agreement—in fact the opposite is true.

How can we develop our competency in the dimension of COLLECTIVE INTELLIGENCE? We can do it through actively encouraging difference, acknowledging it, and suspending judgment about it. We can create an atmosphere, a "space," in which the appreciation of a person as a person is present (see the dimension of humanity). In such a climate it is easier to develop the willingness to encounter difference and difficulties without building walls against one another, defending one's own identity, imposing one's conviction on others, and dominating or annihilating one another. Less time is invested in self-protection or fighting for one's exact vision. More time can be invested in finding and fostering the collective intelligence.

The art of dialogue is at the core of harvesting collective intelligence, and at the core of dialogue is the art of listening.[12] We can develop our listening skills and give one another "time to think," as leadership consultant and author Nancy Kline calls it.[13] Listening creates a "thinking environment," which Kline describes as a powerful but undervalued contribution to better co-creation—and, more practically, to the efficiency of our meetings, the quality of our relationships, and the success of collaborative initiatives.

Not listening can be dangerous. Consider the 1986 launch of the Challenger space shuttle, which ended in a disaster killing seven astronauts. All meetings leading up to the launch had been recorded. When reviewing the tapes of a teleconference held before the launch, investigators heard one of the engineers repeatedly mentioning that a certain metal ring had not been properly tested under the expected temperatures.[14] His intervention was overrun several times, until he gave up. There was too much political pressure to launch.

We can enhance our competency in harvesting collective intelligence when we respect difference and invite diverse perspectives, experiences, and viewpoints. This requires a genuine interest in diversity, the art of structuring outcome-oriented dialogue, genuine listening, and a habit of iterative learning. Then collective intelligence becomes a pathway into future possibilities. In her thought-provoking book on leadership and the new sciences management, consultant Margaret Wheatley writes, "Why would we stay locked in our belief that there is only one right way to do something, or one correct interpretation of a situation, when the universe demands diversity and thrives on a plurality of meaning? Why would we avoid participation and worry only about its risks, when we need more and more eyes to be wise? Why would we resist the powerful visions and futures that emerge when we come together to co-create the world? Why would we ever choose rigidity or predictability when we have been invited to be part of the generative dance of life?"[15]

The exposure to different constructions of reality is paramount for our capacity to master the challenges of sustainability. In the international initiative for sustainable coffee production, a lady from a radical international NGO tested the patience of all participants, particularly those from industry. When an agreement had almost come to a closure, she would predictably raise her hand and ask: "Are we sure we're not disadvantaging small-scale farmers with this?" You could observe industry participants rolling their eyes in despair. Yet it was her consistent opposition that made a considerable contribution to developing two cornerstones of the initiative's approach—a system of verification that would not burden small-scale farmers with auditing costs, and industry funding for building sustainable farming capacity. The underlying intention of opposition is often correction, and this provides an entry point to seeing a larger picture. That's why our collective move toward sustainability needs to be embedded in our ability to sense wholeness.

Wholeness

What does wholeness mean? Rusty Schweickart, one of the astronauts who went to the moon in 1969, had a life-changing experience when he was circling our planet. "Up there you go around every hour and a half, time after time . . . and you begin to recognize that your identity is with the whole thing. And that makes a change . . . You look down there and you cannot imagine how many borders and boundaries you crossed again and again and again. And you don't see them. At that wake-up scene—the Mid-east—you know there are hundreds of people killing each other over some imaginary lines you can't see. From where you see it, the thing is whole, and it's so beautiful. And you wish you could take one from each side in hand and say 'Look at it from this perspective . . . What is important?'"[16]

Few of us will have the chance to experience what Rusty Schweickart did, but his account gives us an important insight—sensing wholeness requires perspective. If we look at things from a distance we come to new insights, we may see things differently, and we understand the coherence of a situation. So wholeness is about seeing things in a larger context. This may be relative, because if we do not want to drown in complexity, we may need to choose only the next level higher for context. That is where the dimension of collective intelligence helps—through dialogue and diversity we ensure that we do not overlook crucial aspects of the larger picture. Sensing the whole and leading toward sustainability are closely connected. We are often trained to focus on fragments of reality, on our narrow part of a larger story, our field of expertise. Our selective perception concentrates on difference between us and others. We may think that if we can somehow connect the parts, we will achieve a sense of wholeness.

But there are many ways to gain perspective. Unilever Hindustan sends their most qualified young high-potential employees to live for one year in a rural village—a significant change for those who have risen through university and acquired one of these coveted jobs.[17] Why does this investment count? Because it is an exposure to the way a large part of the world (their client base) lives and the issues of poverty they face. It pushes people to do business in a different way, and it hints at another aspect of wholeness—meaning. When we see our action in a larger context, and if we commit to something larger than ourselves—we gain enormous energy.

Many of today's managers get lost in a world built on shortsighted quarterly reports—they lose their connection to meaning, to the larger potential of their contribution. Yet the longing for meaning is an essential human capacity and, if fulfilled, contributes to happiness. How then can we develop our competency in the dimension of WHOLENESS? We can make a commitment to place our action plans in a larger context—by listening to stakeholders (COLLECTIVE INTELLIGENCE), checking what are the best practices in our field (INNOVATION), exposure (WHOLENESS), and inquiring into the underlying story, if we do not understand something (HUMANITY).

The revelations that inspired Unilever's Polman or Puma's Zeitz are evidence of a deep connection between accessing our own humanity and sensing wholeness. Often, this combination leads people to enact future possibilities in a different way—even shifting multinational companies toward sustainability. The combination of accessing our humanity and sensing a larger context can be very powerful—and useful. When I was supporting a provincial ministry in South Africa on its way to better service delivery, we had a management retreat that started with a list of complaints by the top management about their staff being corrupt and underperforming. One minister, quite closely involved in the operational road to improvement, suddenly asked: "What if the way our staff operates has a direct relation to how we are with one another as a leadership team?" The question was met by a long silence—and it entirely changed the discourse. It placed the problems in a different context, and opened up a fruitful and new conversation about developing a winning top management team that led future possibilities by finding ways of empowering their staff to see the vision of service to a country so desperately in need of good governance.

Attending to wholeness is more than seeing a collection of parts. We can gradually understand that everything on our planet is interlinked. Globalization demands that we redefine our relationship with the world and our action for sustainability in a larger context. If we refuse this journey into our interconnected world, social media will take us there, making the connections visible. The Internet does not substitute for the experience of Rusty Schweickart, but it helps us take the first step into the direction of his revelation. We can begin to see how the six dimensions of collective leadership invigorate the potential of these connections. They support one another, and also provide checks and balances so that we do not get lost in one dimension. So how do they work together?

Back in 1962, Martin Buber diagnosed the crisis of humankind as a crisis of the shared space between human beings.[18] This "space in between" he considered to be dramatically neglected and desperately in need of cultivation if humankind wanted to embark on a more human future. More than sixty years of human history have passed and his argument is still valid: The "space in between" will only change and lead to a different form of human co-creation if people live, act, and communicate with an inner posture of unconditional acknowledgment of the humanness of the others around them. Without humanity our change efforts are futile. While my experiences in collaboration processes show that there can be other entry points for fruitful interaction among the human competencies in the six dimensions, I will illustrate how they work together with an example in which the access to humanity, combined with people's capacity to sense wholeness, made all the difference.

The Magic of Story

The very first stakeholder meeting of the coffee initiative described at the beginning of this book turned into a commitment for collective action. What made the extremely skeptical stakeholders from coffee-producing countries, industry, NGOs, and development organizations overcome their doubts and mistrust? They did not entirely drop their skepticism, but they took an essential step toward collective leadership; they were prepared embark on a journey with an uncertain outcome and they committed to traveling together. How was it possible to get from severe mistrust to joined commitment in thirty-six hours? How did the dimensions work together? And which competencies did this group of actors develop? This was not an exceptional group of people. Nor were they exceptionally lucky.

The meeting had its challenges. I had been asked to facilitate it just a few days before it took place. Invitations had already been sent out, the program was fixed, and no preparatory calls with important stakeholders were possible at this late date. For me this was already a worst-case scenario. But things deteriorated. As I arrived in London the representative from the coffee industry told me upfront that she would not accept any seating arrangement other than a U-shaped table with microphones, because this was what industry was used to. As mentioned before, that

setup, a facilitator's nightmare, encourages positioning and long statements and discourages listening because everyone's mind is occupied by
preparing their own comments instead of listening to other speakers. In
addition the representative from the financing development organization
made his stance very clear: He would withdraw finances if the stakeholders
did not give their clear commitment and the industry did not contribute
funds. Such stringent opening positions are not unusual for collaboration
initiatives. It almost made me book an immediate flight back home.

But I stayed, listened carefully to all the demands, and was clear on
one thing: I needed to take a stance as an expert on co-creation. With strict
decisiveness I conveyed that there were certain conditions for success—
that I would choose my preferred table setting, have the freedom to change
the program, and reduce the expectations of any written commitment to
"we are prepared to continue together." So I tuned myself in to future possibilities by being focused on wanting to achieve the best possible result.
What I did not say was that my mind was working hard on how to get this
conflict-ridden group to experience at least a tiny bit of a possible future.

My first challenge was how to start. I chose humanity and wholeness
as a joint starting point, thinking this would create the minimum level of
cohesion we needed to shift into a collaborative space. What did this look
like? When the host had given his introductory remarks and handed over
the meeting to me, I did not go through the program. Instead, I told a
story about my relationship with coffee, about our family ritual on Sunday
mornings when one of us three kids would secretly get up and prepare a
lovely coffee for the whole family. We would then wake up our parents and
all sit in bed and have coffee. I remember these events as very special—
moments frozen in time. It was those mornings when we had the most
interesting and touching family conversations.

Then I asked the meeting participants to chat at their tables, telling
other participants where they came from and what their story was about
coffee. Rational observers might ask what I was thinking. It did the job,
though, of going straight to participants' humanity. These seasoned industry
managers, high-level NGO representatives, and top marketing managers
from coffee cooperatives connected as people. It was an eye opener. While
some managers openly admitted that they could not survive with less than
ten cups of black coffee a day, some of the producers said they harvested
and washed coffee, but had never had a cup. Every story was different.

When the ten minutes of storytelling were up, there was a different atmosphere in the room. I used the changed mood to connect with the objectives of the meeting. I reminded everyone that all over the world, coffee and tea are the means for human dialogue—a ritual so much embedded in most cultures that many have developed their own very special way of preparing coffee. Coffee connects us and yet shows us our human diversity. Now imagine if all the coffee consumed around the world were produced in a sustainable way: environmentally friendly, socially just, and economically empowering. Wouldn't this be a pioneering step into a better future? It did not take more than a few minutes, but I could see that suddenly the visible differences in the room—smart industry managers in suit and ties, NGO representatives in old jeans—became meaningless for the few seconds that they could all sense wholeness and the larger context this initiative was embedded in. They could feel the potential.

From there it was easy to step into future possibilities. People did not drop their reservations and criticisms toward the approach; they did not hold back with their concern that industry is taking yet another step to exert power and greenwash. They did begin to genuinely listen to viewpoints of others. We channeled this listening into a structured dialogue where every voice, no matter how encouraging or how discouraging, could be heard—a prerequisite for enhancing the dimension of COLLECTIVE INTELLIGENCE. This contributed to trust building—not necessarily agreements, but the capacity of all participants to see the differences yet keep the possibility of a larger contribution at heart.

If we had let the beginning position statements play out, people would have been lost in fighting one another's worldviews. Now, with humanity, wholeness, future possibilities, and collective intelligence present, the project team was finally able to focus on innovation. What might they contribute to existing sustainability standards?

This was a contentious question, as some believed that this mainstream initiative would endanger other sustainability standards. The increased level of trust and mutual respect, however, allowed us to explore these differences in views. It became clear that the initiative had to prove that it would not compete with other standards, but would embrace them. From there the steps into engagement were almost easy. We suggested that all participants who decided to become part of the steering committee co-design the initiative's road map. That was the moment when people realized this was not just another consultative talk shop; it was about working together and making a difference together through collective action.

The climate in the room moved toward a spirit of mutual support, and the participants began to enact wholeness themselves. They started thinking about their networks, about who else needed to participate, which expertise they had access to that would be of help, how to convince funders to join, and in which industry meetings one would have to address the issue of additional finance. People volunteered to connect the project team to their network of influential actors. When, at last, I asked people to pin a card with their name on one of the two boards, I AM JOINING THE INITIATIVE or I AM NOT JOINING THE INITIATIVE, only one card hung on the latter. The lady who pinned that card explained that her organization could only be a friendly observer. Yes, I managed the pattern of the different dimensions, but was I doing anything more than reviving the latent potential of this group and giving a bit of structure for the human competencies to emerge and interact? That's one way of working with the Collective Leadership Compass.

The Magic of Transformation

Let me take you into a different world and into a story of a leader who truly invoked the capacity for leading collectively.[19] The time was 2012, and it had been eighteen years since Nelson Mandela had been installed as the new president of South Africa. The University of the Free State used to be a stronghold of white Afrikaaner culture, and even after nearly two decades this had not fundamentally changed, although more and more black lecturers arrived and, of course, many black students accessed the university. There was an unspoken claim among the white academic university staff that this was "their" university and that the academic standards could only be preserved if the culture went unchanged. Hence, the arriving black lecturers and students felt as if they were guests in the house of somebody who had not invited them.

In 2008 a group of white students humiliated black cleaners in a terrible racist incident that left the entire university in shock. The following year Jonathan Jansen was appointed vice chancellor of the University of the Free State; he was the first black person holding a high office in the school's

105-year history. At that time, the vestiges of apartheid were still visible, mostly in the segregated student accommodations. When Pumla Gobodo-Madikizela arrived as a senior researcher in 2012, she found a profoundly transformed university with senior management, senior academic staff, and student leaders jointly driving the transformation toward a fully integrated and academically thriving university. And at least 80 percent of staff and students had actively engaged with the vision.

What had happened between 2009 and 2012? How did Jansen approach the change? His personal starting point was firmly grounded in future possibilities; he had a clear vision for a deeply transformed university—integrated and with high academic standards. He had launched two intertwined initiatives—the "human project" and the "academic project." But his starting point for the change was humanity. "It is really about 'love' rather than the regulatory, administrative and managerial kind of stuff; that is necessary, but secondary to the heart of a leader in a difficult place," explains Jansen. "You can't be tough unless you have shown love first."[20]

He not only reached out to students, but very consciously embarked on a restorative kind of transformation in which the mistakes of the past could be brought to the table and discussed in honesty rather than swept under the carpet. He firmly believed that only a restorative approach would contribute to wholeness and create an atmosphere in which the white conservative lecturers could come to terms with their complicity in the history. The white faculty wasn't excused for its misdeeds, but they did feel acknowledged, and this was the pathway to engaging them in the vision of a transformed university. He extended this engagement process to the student leaders when—after a heated discussion with them on the best way forward—he handed to them the responsibility to lead the integration of the student accommodations, without setting firm integration targets.

Jansen himself was not only open to learning, but also prepared to take risks and provoke critical thinking, modeling the competency for innovation that he considered key to the future of the school. Part of his strategy to promote open-mindedness was to establish internal university platforms where people could speak openly and learn to understand one another. Members of the university community began to see one another's differences as potential, which galvanized collective intelligence through networking and an environment of dialogue and debate. He instituted a compulsory critical thinking program, increased exposure to the world of thought, and named the dragon—the apartheid past that was still haunting society, even young people.

Slowly, the university changed. A climate of mutual respect and nurturing emerged. Rather than focusing on their fragmented worlds and territorial boundaries, people could see the university as a whole on its way into a better future for all. They joined the journey into transformation and started leading it at all levels.

Chapter 6

Becoming a Collective Leader

When all six dimensions of the Collective Leadership Compass are working in concert, it can be invigorating without kindling false hopes for a world without complexity, emotional tension, or disagreements. In human collaboration there will always be hurdles and pitfalls. But strengthening a pattern of human competencies in interaction increases the resilience of the system of actors and their capacity to better co-create.

The examples show that starting points for change can be different, for the individual leader's personal development as well as for the first move into changing the status quo. We are all unique. Have you ever caught yourself arguing that a problem must be solved in the exact way you think it should be? Likely, you were limiting your view of the situation to one angle, based on your expertise and experience. You were probably right, and yet there were probably other ways of dealing with the issue at hand.

As Steven Covey writes in *The 7 Habits of Highly Effective People*: "We see the world, not as it is, but as we are—or, as we are conditioned to see it."[1] We narrow our worldview to cope with the complexity of life; otherwise we would not be able to *act*. But the downside of our competency to simplify reality is that we may believe everybody else should have the same view we do. A way out is to see the world through our simplified structure while also becoming aware that the way we simplify shapes our understanding of and outlook on reality.

Let me take you into my journey. My strength is wholeness. I tend to see the larger picture of a situation and visualize the future state. I love to begin with the goals in mind. And I really *see* them. This enables me to work with groups of collaborating actors and quickly grasp what it is all about and how we can map the best possible path to reach those goals. But strengths are weaknesses in disguise, and vice versa. I cannot always translate what I see into a conversation with the people I want to help. What I can see may not be visible to them. My explanation may sound ephemeral because it is grounded in a different view of reality. To follow my thinking, someone would need to bridge the same ideas in the same way. So I need to provide step-by-step translation, which requires other competencies.

In the coffee collaboration I listened carefully before I redesigned the program—a competency furthering the dimension of COLLECTIVE INTEL-LIGENCE—and I took a stance for the quality of my work by explaining the conditions under which I could guarantee results. It is important to notice that the starting point for change is not always our area of strength. We need to expand our range of competencies and observe what the best possible first move requires. What a great opportunity!

Understanding Our Personal Pattern

Let's look at how our fellow travelers saw their strengths and the potential entry points for their change initiatives. They all noticed that they needed to expand their own leadership competency to create a climate in which many could take up the challenge. They needed to inspire and empower different actors to lead collectively, as their tasks were way beyond any individual's reach.

When Tina, the social entrepreneur who wanted to build a mentoring movement for disadvantaged young people, revisited the Collective Leadership Compass, she immediately spotted HUMANITY as her strong point. That was what her friends had always told her: She could easily connect with people, reach their hearts, and live in spontaneous empathy. This was her natural way of being. That was why she could not listen to the panel discussion on educational inequities without thinking about how to alleviate the problem. She had a very strong creative urge and often came up with brilliant ideas, which she did not always implement. They popped up and disappeared. That's why she identified INNOVATION as another strong area.

She realized two things. The first was that her strength was also her weakness. She knew she had been a dreamer dreaming of a better world, and was still afraid that attending university and working as a professional would kill her dreams. She considered dropping out of school because she could not handle her dreams and her heart. For her, the world was a mess, unjust, unfair, ripping off people's life energy and exploiting many for the benefit of a few. She did not want to be part of this world; she did not want to get educated into a world she did not want to live in. She felt empathy with the outcasts of society. That's where she thought she belonged. It was the gentle guidance of her cousin that helped her gain the confidence that she could possibly change the world if she acquired professional skills. So she went back to school.

The second insight she had from the Compass was that HUMANITY and INNOVATION alone would not create a mentoring movement. As her immediate development area she spotted FUTURE POSSIBILITIES—realizing that even creating a movement was about having a clear goal in mind plus having the decisiveness to follow through. But it would not make sense to talk about ambitious plans with fellow students right from the start. It dawned on her that her first steps had to be around HUMANITY and ENGAGEMENT, by awakening the empathy of her fellow students and involving them quickly in *collective action*, encouraging them to go out and actually do the mentoring. With that experience in hand, they would then be able to plan the next steps together.

Nadeem knew that an elaborate project plan with milestones, indicators, and allocated tasks for each of the partnering agencies did not guarantee success for the project to empower small African farmers. On the contrary, he noticed that the partners tended to hide behind their tasks, focusing on their clearly defined roles and only reporting back about those items that were referenced in their specific milestones. Nobody seemed to care about the larger picture, and they were detached from the actual goal—empowering farmers—while they concentrated only on indicators. Meetings were very formal. When Nadeem took over the project, implementation had already started. He was shocked by the lack of alignment and coordination that the successful delivery of results would require.

In reviewing the Collective Leadership Compass he identified his strengths as WHOLENESS, HUMANITY, and COLLECTIVE INTELLIGENCE. His personal mission had always been to contribute to a better world and, having been exposed to Buddhism at an early age, he saw humankind as having one consciousness—WHOLENESS. His colleagues appreciated his compassion and his wisdom to easily cut to the core of an issue, yet also keep people aware of the larger picture. He was a brilliant facilitator who felt most at ease when he could help people have a fruitful dialogue and better interactions. Yet a few weeks into his new position, he realized that a new challenge was awaiting him—the actual management (not facilitation) of a complex project with high funder expectations, a private sector requesting key performance indicators, and implementing partners that were not used to being tightly managed. He identified FUTURE POSSIBILITIES as his personal development area as he saw that the challenge was not only facilitating, but also getting the job done and being accountable for the ambitious targets set. He gave himself a grace period to listen to the different actors, including funders and private sector players, before deciding what the entry point would be to get this complex collaboration project set up in a way that would actually benefit small-scale farmers.

Six months after Celine took over her post as a chair of the coordinating committee on water she knew that what lay ahead of her was nearly impossible. She ensured that regular meetings took place among the three ministries involved in drinking water issues in the DRC, but different people turned up at every meeting, if people came at all. It was clear that there was no one person driving the work, there was no energy, and there was no genuine interest. Yet when she started talking to various actors in the water sector, including donor agencies, NGOs, and international organizations, she had the impression there was nothing more urgent than drinking water in the DRC. Each actor looked at a small piece of the problem and was faced with insurmountable challenges. Each was desperate to get *something* going, so activities were uncoordinated and unsustainable.

When she looked at the Collective Leadership Compass she saw that her greatest strengths were FUTURE POSSIBILITIES and WHOLENESS. Celine was known as a determined person; once she had made up her mind, she followed through—FUTURE POSSIBILITIES. Her training as an engineer helped her plan and monitor. And one thing was for sure: Nothing got lost from Celine's to-do list. The downside of being so organized was that she often ran meetings in a very formal way. She noticed that people did not engage.

WHOLENESS was Celine's second strong area, because it was easy for her—with her international experience—to see the larger picture, the global context in which she acted. She always made this clear during meetings: "It is about DRC, but as a committee we are operating in a wider context—our success and failure contributes to water issues globally." She noticed, though, that people did not always understand what she meant.

Looking at the Compass, she realized she would not get anywhere with only these two dimensions. She needed to develop her skills in ENGAGEMENT and COLLECTIVE INTELLIGENCE.

Peter was aware of the reservations his senior staff members held about him. The founder of DiverseAct had allowed the staff to develop their own territories, autonomous projects that included independent relationships with funders. When Peter arrived, there was little interaction among projects or even exchange of ideas. The staff assumed that Peter, coming from the private sector, would not really understand their organization's mission and history. In addition, they were afraid that he would introduce a command-and-control management style. He saw that the task of leading DiverseAct was more challenging than he had anticipated and that he would need to take his organization to the edge of chaos to enable a breakthrough into a new way of working.

When he reviewed his areas of strength from the Collective Leadership Compass, he chose ENGAGEMENT and FUTURE POSSIBILITIES. In his former company, he was known as somebody who could brilliantly align people behind a goal, get commitment to a well-defined and structured process, and play his networks within the company to produce alliances—all aspects of ENGAGEMENT. What counted for him, though, were results. Peter was known for setting clear goals and following through until they were achieved. More recently he decided to take a stance for sustainability, because he felt a longing for meaning. That's why he joined DiverseAct.

But he knew the organizational culture was entirely different from his earlier experiences. He had never been questioned as a leader in his previous company, but it seemed to be part of the culture here. Not only did he receive upfront opposition from his senior staff, but the project managers were not shy about openly criticizing the senior staff. Everybody seemed to be an expert in something and willing to criticize the lack of expertise in others. Peter's expertise was in management, not biodiversity or natural resource management.

After contemplating what would be the first move to shift his organization toward the future, he decided for COLLECTIVE INTELLIGENCE. Even though his predecessor had not invested in joint learning, he felt that this was the hidden strength of his organization and would build on his own strength in ENGAGEMENT. First, he simply wanted to listen without judgment to really understand where people were coming from and appreciate the past. Next, he made an intuitive move to build on the dialogue and debate culture of his organization and get people into a conversation around what they, as a team, could learn from biodiversity.

Andrea was quite conscious that she needed to manage her own ambivalence between working at a company as old-fashioned as EnergyTech and her passion for renewable energies. She needed to find a way to quiet her doubts as friends questioned her about working for one of Germany's energy monopolists—one that was still heavily involved with coal plants and nuclear energy. But she actually enjoyed going to work. The people in her corporate social responsibility department were ambitious and had interesting careers. She got along very well with her boss and, above all, she had lots of exciting conversations about the future of energy. What she had difficulty explaining to her friends was that the people in her department were not interested in greenwashing; they really wanted to see the company shift. They were also very realistic that a megaton-vessel like EnergyTech would only change its direction in very slow movements.

Looking at the Collective Leadership Compass, Andrea initially thought she was strong in all dimensions, but with a bit of hindsight agreed that COLLECTIVE INTELLIGENCE was her primary strength. She was somebody who would find herself moderating a conversation, rather than taking a stance. Early in her life she played the role of moderator at home, having "rescued" her parents from a divorce. She was a formidable listener. Her female friends, particularly, knew and appreciated this. She would inquire without judgments. When asked what she thought would be a starting point for change at EnergyTech, she could not say what would move the company toward more responsible business. That's why she decided to first draw on her strength—COLLECTIVE INTELLIGENCE. She wanted to find out how people at EnergyTech, and particularly the three top layers of management, thought about the future.

Mike knew that he needed a two-pronged strategy: changing TrendWear toward responsible supply-chain management and seeking an alliance with competitors to tackle the vicious cycle of price pressure from buyers and bad worker conditions at their supplier base in Asia. Mike was a man of fast decisions and action. That's why he sent two senior managers on the incognito mission to Bangladesh, so they could see the conditions under which people worked to produce TrendWear clothes. He loved exposure trips, and this one worked well. It was the first time since he'd started at

TrendWear that he had an open conversation about the real issue. The two managers immediately suggested a top management retreat where they would confront the entire leadership with the consequences of not acting responsibly in the supply chain. They saw that TrendWear had no option other than to shift toward more sustainable supply-chain management.

Mike's own strength was in FUTURE POSSIBILITIES, but he also saw the larger picture and had a second area of strength in WHOLENESS. Inspired by the CEOs of Unilever, Nike, and Puma, he saw sustainability not as a threat but as a business opportunity. The change needed to go deeper, yet he wasn't sure how to start. Reluctantly he admitted that his most important development area was HUMANITY, closely followed by ENGAGEMENT. He tended to be a lonesome rider, a warrior fixed on a mission. Reaching out to people was not his strength. His gut feeling was clear; he needed to start his inner journey to expand his leadership skills exactly where he needed to start his outer journey, in the dimension of HUMANITY through reaching out to people. He asked himself a scary question: Was the lack of responsibility of TrendWear in the supply chain mirroring a culture within TrendWear, where the focus was always on figures, not on people?

As you can see, the Collective Leadership Compass opens up conversations and thinking processes that lead to seeing ourselves, our colleagues, and our situations holistically. It becomes easier to spot what needs to be strengthened, either in ourselves or in our team. The Compass offers a tool for observing the connection between our inner journey—the broadening of our leadership skills—and the outer journey—our pathway to enacting the change we envision. The starting points for inner and outer change are as different as the challenges and the people involved. The Compass provides an orientation that frames both the inner and the outer paths.

Chapter 7

Navigating Collaboration

There are many different ways to enact the six dimensions of collective leadership—depending on the context, on our own story, and on the preconditions with which we start the journey. But the underlying principle remains the same: Each dimension is enacted through conscious attention to human competencies. When we choose to embark on an inner journey to enhance our competency and an outer journey of empowering people, it is helpful take a deep dive into each of the dimensions of collective leadership. What helps us to enact these dimensions?

If you have ever had the opportunity to sail through an area with a lot of rocky outcroppings, you know it is a challenge. I once joined others sailing along the east coast of Sweden, a beautiful area with many rocky islands. With our seventy-five-foot-long traditional sailing boat, we could not afford to hit a rock. We had an experienced captain, but we all took turns steering and charting the route. One task the captain would only reluctantly delegate was looking out for navigation marks. This was a serious job; we had to stand up while the ship was moving up and down through the waves, and fix our eyes through the binoculars on the horizon to find the faraway marks that would show the route. We then compared the observed location with the map. The marks, like an agreed-upon language, gave us orientation and made a difficult journey safer.

Each dimension of collective leadership has three guiding aspects that function like these navigation marks, as table 2 shows. They become orientation points on our compass, shown in figure 2, and begin to round it out into a comprehensive tool for our leadership journey.

So how can we use these new points on our compass to more consciously strengthen our competencies in all dimensions?

Table 2. Guiding Aspects for the Collective Leadership Compass

Dimension	Competency	Aspects	Attention
FUTURE POSSIBILITIES	Take responsibility and consciously shape reality toward a sustainable future	*future orientation*	Focus on potential or opportunities and drive change for the better.
		empowerment	Inspire, enable, and awaken passion and options for change.
		decisiveness	Commit, focus, follow through, and measure progress.
ENGAGEMENT	Build step-by-step engagement toward effective collaboration ecosystems	*process quality*	Build step-by-step and structured engagement.
		connectivity	Foster cohesion and build networks.
		collective action	Drive joint implementation and delivery of results.
INNOVATION	Create novelty and find intelligent solutions	*creativity*	Nourish sources of creative energy and collective generation of ideas.
		excellence	Pursue mastery and grow knowledge.
		agility	Move through crises, stay open to change, and cultivate risk taking.
HUMANITY	Reach into one another's humanness	*mindfulness*	Deepen our awareness of reality in all aspects.
		balance	Integrate personal and professional aspirations.
		empathy	Embrace the perspective of others and open gateways for reconciliation.
COLLECTIVE INTELLIGENCE	Harvest difference for progress	*dialogic quality*	Attend to the structure and quality of conversations.
		diversity	Foster diversity in thought, viewpoints, background, and experiences.
		iterative learning	Develop cycles of reflection into action.
WHOLENESS	See the larger picture and stay connected to the common good	*contextuality*	Connect with ourselves, one another, and a larger context. The way we explore the larger context and place our action in it.
		mutual support	Enhance one another's strengths.
		contribution	Use our gifts, assets, and capacity to make a difference toward a sustainable future.

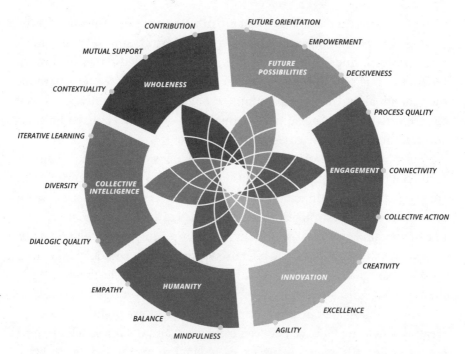

CONTRIBUTION
FUTURE ORIENTATION
EMPOWERMENT
MUTUAL SUPPORT
FUTURE POSSIBILITIES
DECISIVENESS
CONTEXTUALITY
WHOLENESS
PROCESS QUALITY
ITERATIVE LEARNING
ENGAGEMENT CONNECTIVITY
DIVERSITY
COLLECTIVE INTELLIGENCE
COLLECTIVE ACTION
DIALOGIC QUALITY
CREATIVITY
EMPATHY
HUMANITY
INNOVATION
BALANCE
EXCELLENCE
MINDFULNESS
AGILITY

Guiding Aspects for Each Dimension of the Collective Leadership Compass

Driving Future Possibilities

We lead in the FUTURE POSSIBILITIES dimension when we bring our unique potential into the world and learn from the world's responses—as individuals and as a collective. Leading is a creative act, no matter how structured the task appears to be. The creative energy needs regular and conscious renewal. It is our passion for the future that enlivens what we do. The signposts on the road to developing our competency for leading FUTURE POSSIBILITIES are *future orientation, empowerment,* and *decisiveness.*

Future Orientation

Have you ever experienced a group that was locked in problem analysis and could not move into solution finding? I call it the "Yes-But" syndrome. Yet, we do have choices; we can change our mind-set toward a "Yes-And" mentality. The situation is as it is and still we can move into the future. Tuning in to possibilities can become a helpful habit. Small or big, almost every problem finds a solution. Once we have oriented ourselves toward the future, goal setting helps. There are many techniques for that, both for the individual and for organizations or collaboration initiatives. We can choose whatever we find suitable to our needs or culture, but setting goals and creating a vision are essential.

Starting with the end in mind and noting our vision of the future helps us focus. But there is an important addition—we need to balance planning with emergence! Setting the intention clearly and getting the picture painted is paramount, yet even the strongest vision needs to give the life around it a chance to be spontaneously creative. I admire entrepreneurship scholar Saras D. Sarasvathy's word *effectuation* to refer to enacting a future without predicting it through fixed goals: "Effectuators see the world as open, still in-the-making . . . they work to fabricate, as well as recognize and discover opportunities."[1]

We can cultivate our sense of possibilities and gradually get better at creating a delicate balance between clear goals and openness to emerging opportunities. If the goal is too fixed, we tend to overlook opportunities. If the goal is too vague, we get lost in the complexity of myriad options. I often recall the quote from Robert Greenleaf, a pioneer in developing the concept of "servant leadership": "Behind every great achievement is a dreamer of great dreams. Much more is required to bring it to reality; but the dream must be there first."[2] There is a potential in almost everything and every person. When we take this orientation as a mind-set, the world changes. Here are a few questions that help to tune in to *future orientation*:

- How do I explain my biggest dream to my best friend?
- How does the vision of my organization revive the passion of the people working there?
- In what way are partners in my sustainability initiative emotionally engaged with the goal?

Empowerment

We tend to empower others and disempower ourselves. This is particularly true of women, but both sexes suffer from the disempowering habit. If fear is keeping us timid or if we have internalized the parental critic, we aren't able to help the world. Discouragement reduces our potential, our strength, and our contribution. Again, we need to change our mind-set; self-empowering is not only okay, but important. When we have developed trust in our ability to make a difference, we need to claim the power to do so. We need to drive a direction, even if we are being pushed back by different opinions.

We can't do this if we hold back our opinion, our expertise, or our experience. Finding ways to empower ourselves is a prerequisite for empowering others. There are many techniques that can help, including affirmative thought, pursuing our dreams, and setting small attainable targets. But there is nothing more empowering than accepting reality as it is and knowing that if we got us here, we can also get us somewhere else. We become the artists of our life. Naming injustice is absolutely crucial, but being locked in a feeling of victimization takes our life force away.

There is a strange equation: The more we feel empowered, the more we begin to empower others. Hence what applies to us as individuals also applies to groups, teams, organizations, and collaborating stakeholders. We can severely disagree, but if we disempower one another, we derail our path into the future. Talking behind somebody's back, launching intrigues, ganging up against one person—we all know the techniques of disempowerment. This is human, yet awareness of the impact helps us avoid the behavior. Disempowering others is a boomerang.

One of the most fascinating techniques for mutual empowerment I have come across is FeedForward—designed by the well-known coach Marshall Goldsmith, who discovered that most forms of feedback focus on the past, while it would be much more empowering to focus on future recommendations.[3] FeedForward can be applied to personal questions as much as strategic questions. You can also use it as a tool to improve ideas, projects, plans, and processes. The technique is simple: State a challenge, phrase a question, or explain a plan. Then ask the person who gives you FeedForward to make suggestions for improvement or solutions or answers. Reasonable or unreasonable—anything counts. You simply listen and take notes without commenting, defending, questioning, discarding, or judging what you hear. After just a few minutes you say thank you, and evaluate your list of ideas received. Chances are this has helped you think of possibilities you did not come up with before.

This technique taps into our human desire to help, to empower. It invigorates creativity and leads to innovation. The inspiration received nourishes a feeling of empowerment, which in turn can awaken our passion for change. In such an atmosphere of inspiration people find their own creativity and thus contribute their best.

Yet empowerment is also about enabling self-reliant action, not distributing tasks but delegating and decentralizing responsibility. What helps collaborating partners in sustainability initiatives are transparent agreements about the scope of self-reliant action. These agreements build clarity in four areas: a joint understanding of framework conditions (external factors, risks, potential conflicts); agreed-upon milestones (goals, targets, key performance indicators, and so forth); an outspoken agreement on what can be implemented without consulting other stakeholders (this includes how to communicate about the joint initiatives); and an open commitment to how and when joint progress review will take place.

Here are a few questions that help guide us toward *empowerment*:

- If I could not fail, what would I do in the next six months of my life?
- In what way do we as a team inspire others?
- What is our jointly agreed upon frame for self-reliant action in our organization or sustainability initiative?

Decisiveness

As individuals we thrive on putting insights into action. There is nothing more disempowering than New Year's resolutions that we abandon before the end of January. The failure stays with us and reduces our self-confidence. Not surprisingly, the same happens for a group of collaborating actors. If meetings do not take place at the announced dates, if decisions jointly made aren't followed through, if agreed targets are not met, if no joint success can be celebrated, then the collaborating stakeholders lose confidence in the initiative. Have you ever experienced how a team repeatedly decides on a certain action, only to discover months later that the action never happened because too many other urgent matters came up? This deteriorates the confidence, and subsequently the happiness, of the team. We'll never be perfect, but persistence and patience are crucial in leading future possibilities.

The route to improving our rate of return for action decisions is *focus*. There are many people who have developed techniques for focus.[4] I have made good use of my fifteen-minute, Sunday-evening ritual: I review my past week in relation to my goals and focus areas, and then set the focus for the coming week. We each need to find the approach that resonates with us. The mind is a monkey, and it needs to be trained to focus.

Taking steps toward a goal or vision collectively also requires us to identify focus areas. When we tumble in the complexity of our endeavors, focus becomes our guiding force through the jungle of daily demands. The essential question is: *Does this contribute to the focus?* That's how goals get achieved. What if we become too narrow-minded by focusing? What if we lose out on opportunities, because we ignore the jungle and only concentrate on the path? That is where it helps to tend other dimensions. COLLECTIVE INTELLIGENCE helps us take stock of the issue at hand and tend to different perspectives; INNOVATION allows us space to think beyond boundaries; WHOLENESS helps us set our goals and focus in a larger context and revisit our contribution to a more sustainable world.

Decisiveness is both a mind-set and a technique. It is a mind-set, because it's the testing ground for how important our goals are to us. It requires us to take a mature stance on an issue and show that we feel accountable to a goal, a vision, our team, our organization, and our collaborating partners. It is also a technique, because there are many helpful tools that support us in developing decisiveness—the process of putting ideas into action.

Decisiveness is also driven by measurement. On an organizational or project level, the tools that help us measure progress (key performance indicators, milestones, balanced scorecards, project-planning tools, monitoring tools, and so on) support our competency to lead future possibilities. What gets measured gets done. We only get lost in measurements when we neglect other dimensions of the Compass—ENGAGEMENT, INNOVATION, HUMANITY, COLLECTIVE INTELLIGENCE, and WHOLENESS.

Here are a few questions that help guide us toward *decisiveness*:

- What have been my most positive experiences in following through and what was the impact?
- How would our team rate the percentage of jointly made decisions that got implemented?

- If I picked six key stakeholders from my collaboration initiative and stepped into their shoes, how would they rate (1) the appropriateness of planning indicators, and (2) the achievements according to plans on a scale between 1 and 10?

Strengthening Engagement

We have mastered the art of engagement when people commit, when they actively drive implementation, and when new people ask to join the journey. Tuning in to the future, inspiring others, and empowering them to lead—all competencies in the dimension of FUTURE POSSIBILITIES—go a long way toward engagement. But reaching the hearts of people is crucial, too. That is why humanity is also important for engagement. Inspirations fade if they are not sustained; relationships turn dry if we do not take care of them; processes derail when stakeholders aren't regularly brought back on board; a sense of ownership gets lost if people do not see results. We need one another's caretaking. In my experience, engagement requires much more attention than people realize—especially when they plan and fund collaboration initiatives. We can spot signposts on the road to developing our competency for engagement: *process quality*, *connectivity*, and *collective action*.

Process Quality

In his introduction to the book *Leading Change*, James O'Toole explains the new challenges for leaders by referring to an eighteenth-century painting showing a rather chaotic crowd of people reminiscent of a political demonstration.[5] Christ is somewhere in the middle of the crowd, but not easily found. He is not obviously leading the crowd and is not in a particularly powerful physical position. O'Toole points out the parallel between the painting and the situation of leaders in the present chaotic and transformative environment inside or outside of businesses. He provokes the reader with the assumption that the artist had, somehow, foreseen that "leaders would face the challenge of having to lead without the traditional powers of station, sanction, or threat of suppression. Instead, like Christ, leaders would have to appeal to the minds and hearts of the followers . . ."[6] He concludes that, looking at the painting, we might ask ourselves how "anyone could lead from the middle of an inattentive crowd of individualists."[7]

Those of us who need to get collaboration initiatives going can recognize this phenomenon. That's why engagement is a mind-set as well as a technique: We need to acknowledge that human beings need caretaking and attention. So how do we create the case for change? What would Christ in the painting have done? He might have taken the most crucial step that Margaret Mead hints at when she talks about "a small group of thoughtful, committed citizens."[8] Change starts small, but not too small. Christ alone will not be successful—he needs to gather around himself a group of thoughtful, committed citizens. So do we, when we want to bring about change in our organizations or across institutions, nations, and expertise in our sustainability initiatives.

The term that best expresses the quality of such a group is that it is a good *container*, and such a container has three key traits: (1) It involves people who can drive change in their operational or decision-making role; (2) the people mutually respect one another; and (3) they are emotionally engaged with an envisioned future state. Change processes that have an impact work with good containers. When you analyze failed change processes or unsuccessful collaboration initiatives, look for the existence of a good container. Most likely it was missing. When we have a good container people lead collectively, often first across institutions and then gradually involving more and more people. We enact the six competencies. It is an art to design and implement structured processes that build *containers for change* and grow them into *communities for change*.

High-quality collaboration processes hinge on step-by-step engagement, reliability (where all parties act as agreed), sufficient caretaking, and communication designs that orient people toward results and also build relationships. There are many brilliant process consultants, change management experts, and facilitators around the world who can create high-quality processes. It is worth getting their advice, and it helps to check whether they attend to all six dimensions. If so, it will create trust (the oil that makes process designs work) and vitality (the force that shifts a system toward better co-creation). We will hear more about this when we follow our fellow travelers into their challenges.

Here are a few questions that help guide us toward *high-quality processes*:

- What must somebody else do to engage me successfully?
- When does my team engage—both with one another and with the goal?
- If I look at my collaboration initiative, what are my indicators for a high level of engagement of the key actors?

Connectivity

Shifting our world toward sustainability requires massive changes in the behavior of many people. If we see the change ahead not so much as a strenuous attempt to convince and push people but as creating dynamic movements and invigorating networks that people can happily join, we remove a burden from our shoulders. Connectivity is a mind-set—a way of seeing the world as a web of relationships that need to be appreciated and enhanced. I love the way Joe Jaworski captures the potential of connectivity in his famous *Synchronicity: The Inner Path to Leadership* when he states that in our world "relatedness" is much more important than "thingness."[9] That's why we engage: Meaningful relationships are a cornerstone for better co-creation.

Trust is the glue creating the cohesion that takes us from good containers to communities for change. We may start small with a step-by-step engagement process, but whatever we intend to achieve, we eventually need to grow a movement that will have an impact when it stretches along network connections. As initiators we become nodes in the network, connected with other leaders who take up the movement. Like the cross-sector community in the coffee initiative, these can be networks of people who identify with an issue and enact the agreed-upon change in their wider community. Often the impact is higher when the community for change reaches across boundaries of institutions—across the silos of public sector, private sector, and civil society.

Once the networks are established, it becomes easier to plan change, to inspire and initiate. Connectivity is a response to the human sense of belonging and the desire to contribute. We need to harvest these human competencies more consciously. That is where connectivity is also a technique; the way of building networks can be learned. It is more than handing out our business cards or engaging people because we need them; it is the attention to humanity that counts. How do we enhance networks for change? By showing authentic interest in the person we want to engage, by offering our contribution to help, by appreciating people's expertise, by being open to learning from others, and by genuinely caring.

Here are a few questions that help guide us toward *connectivity*:

- How did my most stable and fruitful business relationships come about?
- If I drew a map of my team's network connections, what would it show?
- If I had to rate the cohesion of my wider network of collaborating stakeholders on a scale between 1 and 10, what would be my assessment?

Collective Action

Collective action is the coordinated or self-organized collaboration among different actors that leads to tangible results toward a common objective. There is nothing more invigorating for people who collaborate than the experience of a visible outcome from the joint effort, especially if they see how their effort positively contributes to others. Yet many sustainability initiatives require a lot of patience and persistence in sustaining collaboration before impact becomes visible. Because people thrive on achievements, we must celebrate our successes and attend to joint results even if they are small. Using the step of prototyping, we can cut through the complexity of an issue by focusing on how to make real one example of the impact we envision.

Maintained engagement of stakeholders is a result of collective action that works. We need to see reality changing to strengthen our commitment. If we deprive ourselves of tangible results, we get tired and distracted. It's almost like climbing a mountain. It helps to turn around once in a while, enjoy the changing view, and see how high we've climbed already, instead of constantly looking at the mountaintop and measuring the distance to the goal.

I am not talking about false success stories. Truly sustainable development will only happen when both strategic decisiveness and collective action on the ground come together. Having contributed to an impact is what keeps us going. Collective action is a mind-set that must become a habit. The key question is: *What will be different after we have met or implemented our plans?* If you remember the stories of times when the costs of non-collaboration were too high, you know that people can get lost in their little territories if they lack an orientation to the joint outcome. Collective action is also a technique. The keys to achieving tangible results are: (1) true co-design of initiatives and joint planning, (2) focusing on the first easily achievable successes, (3) creating prototypes'—examples of future broader results—as well as (4) joint evaluation of results and celebration of successes.

Even in the beginning of collaboration efforts collective action can be present. During the successful launch meeting of the coffee initiative in London, a joint diagnosis of the then current coffee-supply-chain reality made all the difference. Suddenly we had a collective picture—a result achieved together that helped people to commit to the initiative, even though they still had entirely different opinions about how to change the situation.

Here are a few questions that help guide us toward *collective action*:

- Can I remember a situation I was involved in where collective action worked? What was present?
- If I asked my team what the most successful collaboration habit is, what would the answer be?
- What are the small prototypes we need to implement that would help our stakeholders see quick results?

Scaling Up Innovation

Innovation is a culture, not the skill of a few rare people. It is a force each of us has inside, as well as a phenomenon that happens as a result of human interaction. Yet we are different; some of us are quintessential inventors while others are slow to generate new ideas. For innovation, we need both the creativity of the brilliant inventors and the keepers of the current reality. In collaboration they can successfully implement new ideas.

We must recognize that people do not always favor innovators. Brilliant new ideas often meet massive resistance before they finally are taken on as natural and self-evident. But sustainability really needs innovation, so we need to more consciously cultivate it. We know we are moving toward a culture of innovation when we have spotted these three aspects: *creativity*, *excellence*, and *agility*.

Creativity

Often people tell me they are not creative—particularly when they have been asked to paint a picture during a workshop. I sympathize with them, because I also hate to be forced to be creative on command. But their statement isn't true—even if they hate painting and do not play an instrument. We are born with this competency; it is a human skill nobody has been exempted from. But we can unlearn creativity, we can deprive ourselves of our own creativity, and we can deaden creativity in our professional context. Setting it free is a process of unblocking or reviving.

We can relearn creativity, and we need to, as we will not master the challenges of sustainability without creative solutions. This is why creativity is a mind-set, which, if we tune in, helps us become more confident that there will always be a solution to problems, a better way of doing things, a breakthrough invention that can change millions of lives for the better. If we are serious about the mind-set, we cherish ideas and do not immediately disregard them because they disturb our way of doing things or go against established procedures or seem to make our life more difficult. Check out the potential for innovation in an idea before you drop it.

Creativity is also a technique, as there are many ways of enacting our creativity. I can only touch on a few. Nourishing sources of creative energy for others and ourselves can become a useful habit. I have mentioned the art of not-doing, which is why creativity and mindfulness are good friends. Creativity often pops up through gaps in our busy schedule, as if the creative urge has just been waiting for a small window to open. The useful habit is about becoming aware of our own pattern of creativity, and then nourishing it with utmost decisiveness. I know people who always carry a notebook around with them so that they can record ideas popping up. Other people need nourishing conversations; they need to feel listened to—and suddenly pathways to solutions open. Empathy and dialogue can further creativity. Some organizations deliberately create "spaces" in which people can casually meet, nourishing their creative energy. A well-known German software company made a conscious choice for informal interaction to stimulate creativity. Many people love the city of Berlin because there are many places where creative people meet. Creativity is contagious and has a self-reinforcing effect. Exposure to creative spaces and creative people helps. Some organizations bring in artists to loosen the creative force of managers; others take them into a different world. People who run leadership programs have suitcases of tools for reviving the creative force.

And what is the role of creativity in sustainability initiatives? They would not be in existence without one or a few people having had a grand idea of how to change the world. When collaboration becomes too administrative, it helps to remember that we are here because we want to better co-create. If we foster informal interaction among stakeholders and attend to all aspects of engagement, it will enhance creativity and improve collaboration results.

Here are a few questions that help guide us toward *creativity*:

- When do I feel energized? If money were not an issue at all, what would I love doing most?
- Can we remember three incidents when our team had especially creative moments? What contributed to this happening?
- In what way do we schedule space for informal interaction into our stakeholder meetings?

Excellence

When I was still at school, I never had difficulties performing well—and I mean well, not excellently. I made it my habit to set the easy goal of "do well" but not "become the best." That worked until I learned a craft—joinery. The moment of revelation came when I noticed that it makes sense to cut a piece of wood exactly in the middle of the thin pencil line, because only then will the pieces fit together perfectly. Good craftsmanship is about that sense of perfection. We feel it when we see an old piece of furniture where all the joints still fit tightly. It takes love to get to that level of perfection, and it creates justified pride in the heart of the craftsman (or -woman). We strive for the perfect cut, not because other people will appreciate it, but because we feel this is the way it has to be. It is a matter of honor. It is about mastery. We owe this perfection to the piece we are creating.

The experience changed my attitude toward quality. I now understand that high quality is an inherent possibility of whatever we create; lacking quality is dishonoring that possibility. It has nothing to do with getting praise. Have you ever noticed in great artisans that excellence and humility belong together? That is why excellence is a mind-set. Delivering the best possible quality is a way of honoring life. Looking out for the best expertise, the best people, the best knowledge is an obligation, a commitment to serve, because with high quality we enhance the generative force of life.

Excellence is also a technique that starts with learning. We can always get that little bit better in what we do, even if we are already good. Striving for excellence will help us deliver better results. The search for innovative solutions to sustainability issues requires us to develop excellence in our expertise. This is both an individual and a collective pathway. It invites us to see excellence as a gateway to innovation. We want to bring creative ideas forward so that they can help the world. The purpose of competition is enhancing excellence, not outmaneuvering others, so that we encourage one another to continuously find better solutions. Our individual expertise counts as much as our ability to bring in additional and complementary expertise and acknowledge when others know more or can do things better. Benchmarking, knowledge and exchange of best practices, as well as professional networks of excellence can greatly support our pathway to innovation. It is important to remember, though, that life is not perfect, but it strives toward beauty and better solutions all the time.

Here are a few questions that help guide us toward *excellence*:

- What is it that I am really, really good at?
- What is our team's way of acknowledging the high-quality delivery of a result?
- What are our ways of making sure that we utilize all available knowledge and expertise for our sustainability initiative?

Agility

When I was working in a large institution, I attended a leadership development program. During one of the modules we had an outdoor training in which we were asked to stand on a bench and fall backward into a group of colleagues who would (we hoped) catch us. I know people who love these exercises, but I hated them. Not because of my lack of trust in my colleagues, but because I didn't like to follow the instructions somebody else gave me. I tended to question instructions. What did I learn? I noticed the boundaries of my comfort zone.

There are as many different comfort zones as there are people in this world. It is helpful to become aware of them to push them bit by bit—every day. We discover the world and we strengthen our capacity to adapt to new situations. Habits are important—and so are our abilities to question them and create new ones. Agility—the ability to adapt—is a mind-set that we can take on. Since the only constant in life is change, we might as well become its partner.

Yet agility, too, is also a technique. Some people journal every day; some people regularly take stock of their life and professional advancement. Some people use a coach who becomes the guardian of their agility. This is a great support for leading future possibilities. Reflective leadership retreats can make a difference to the strategy of an organization. And what about sustainability initiatives? My experience is that there is a lot of time spent on reviewing plans and milestones, yet little time invested in a deeper collective reflection that lets experiences, thoughts, and feelings sink in. We seldom talk about the relationship between our inner change and the outer change we seek in the world. Yet it would increase our resilience as we learn about the stories of others, the longing, and the search for meaning.

Collective reflection can help to mutually strengthen us in venturing into the unknown, taking risks, and overcoming boundaries that seem too high to climb. I like the way leadership coach Robin Sharma says it: "The impossible is generally the untried."[10] Yet for innovation we need to try, fail, and try again. Giving up on sustainability issues is not an option.

The world is made up of territories, internal and external, but the challenges of sustainability do not stop at territorial boundaries. They cannot be reached within the confined space of a nation, a certain expertise, one institution, or even one societal stakeholder group. We need to transcend boundaries and open up to collaboration. Going beyond our comfort zone into new territories with different thinking, different ways of seeing the world, and different interpretations of the same reality is paramount for the collaboration journey.

One way to steer us toward agility is inquiry. This requires being willing to look into what we do not know or understand, and to search for the coherence of a situation that we dislike. Within each difficult-to-answer question is a request to open beyond the old interpretations and take a fresh look at what we think we already know. What has worked well for me in crises (the typical events that ask us to adapt) is asking the most difficult question: What if this (what happened) is the best thing that could have ever happened to me? Why would it be so?[11] If I carry this really annoying question around with me for a while, then—after hours, days, sometimes weeks—an answer will emerge that opens up an entirely new gateway to success. Our minds love such questions; they must to be answered at some point. Everything is possible.

Here are a few questions that help guide us toward *agility*:

- What has been my best experience in overcoming a crisis?
- In what way have we established collective reflection in our team?
- How do we get to know the dreams, the stories, and the life experiences of the people we collaborate with?

Fostering Humanity

When I traveled in India in 2003, I stumbled upon a little bookstore somewhere in the center of Mumbai. It was one of those stores that immediately take the astonished customer into a world of dreams, almost like Ruiz Zafón's graveyard of the forgotten books.[12] The shelves were loaded with booklets made of inexpensive material, a testament to the human desire to transform thought into words so they can be shared with like-minded spirits. I searched the shelves as if I was waiting for a book to find me, and suddenly I held in my hand the little booklet that would change me: *The Future of Humanity*, recording the previously mentioned conversation between philosopher J. Krishnamurti and physicist David Bohm.[13] I sat down in a quiet corner and within half an hour I had finished the booklet, which concluded that humankind's biggest problem was the human thought process itself, because it created unnecessary separations between people, denying each other their deeper humanity. I left the store more aware, pondering about what my contribution could be to help shift human awareness.

Our heart knows that we cannot win the struggle for fulfillment in isolation. Nor can we master the challenges of sustainability alone. There are many routes that take us to our humanity. Among the abundant choices it may help if we spot these three aspects: *mindfulness*, *balance*, and *empathy*.

Mindfulness

As we have seen in agility, awareness can be curative. When we reflect, we draw meaning and coherence from a stream of experience that is riddled with incoherence. We gain the distance needed to observe reality without judgment. This is the time when insights emerge. Pieces begin to fit into a bigger picture. We get back into the driver's seat of our life. Awareness begins with observation and reflection. In whatever way we integrate phases of stillness into our leadership journey, it helps us to slowly cut through the chains of habitual thought patterns or preconceptions and their subsequent actions. We become more human as we become more mindful of who we are and how we have come to be.

This is not self-indulgent introspection for its own sake. It is a gateway to transformation. We do not disengage from the world; we are more present in it. We become more responsive. As we connect with our own story, we connect with the story of humankind. In this story, tending the common is not an additional voluntary service but the deeper meaning of our being here. There are techniques helping to develop mindfulness, and they can be learned. One of them is meditation, the art of working through differences. Research shows that meditation in our personal lives leads to general contentment, more creative thoughts, and improved relationships. There are clear benefits for business, too, ranging from better productivity to reduced staff turnover.[14] Not surprisingly, some larger companies are offering meditation practices to their staff. But is this all that can be said about mindfulness?

There is a more important role of mindfulness, and meditation can take us a long way toward it. The moment the mind finally becomes quiet, it sets free other competencies—compassion, gratitude, humility—as if these elements were waiting to be unleashed. The key technique for mindfulness is mastering the mind and understanding that at the core of the human heart is love. If we access this place more often, we become more attentive to the human encounter and the depth of a situation—essential to better co-creation. If we become aware of our own fears, our need for self-protection, or our desire for recognition, it frees our perception. We can see the same struggle in others. It helps us to relax, respect difference, and deal with conflicts and difficulties in a much more mature way.

If all this sounds too philosophical, I invite you to use a simple and mundane piece of mindfulness: Introduce a check-in to all your meetings, and then observe the difference that it makes in getting to results. How do we do this? Start every meeting with each participant sharing just one sentence about what is on his or her mind. This simple act can make all the difference to people being present. Remember the launching of the coffee initiative in London? It was the sentence about the relationship to coffee that was the starting point for an effective result-oriented meeting.

Here are a few questions that help guide us toward *mindfulness*:

- How do I integrate phases of stillness into my days?
- In what way have we established a check-in ritual for our team meeting?
- When we think about our next stakeholder meeting, what would be a way of allowing people to meet as people in the beginning?

Balance

Our lives tend to be unbalanced, sometimes for long periods—too much work, the discontent of not attending fully to family life or relationships, and often a lack of the stillness that mindfulness requires. We all know the symptoms of dwindling relationships, a sudden lack of passion for life, or the first signs of burnout syndrome, when everything seems to become too much.

My experience is that there is a deeper force that pulls us back into balance: a broken arm that forces us into not-doing, a good friend who turns away, a child needing attention, a crisis at work that we did not expect. Not that we always understand the message, but if we observe the hints more closely we may gradually find a better rhythm of balance. Why is this important? Because if we get the rhythm of balance right we become more effective, we're happier, and—important for sustainability initiatives—we have more clarity in walking our path.

Balance is not an additional "nice-to-have"—it is essential in staying more relaxed in complexity. Hence it's a mind-set, because if we render it important, it gets the attention it requires. It's a technique, because there are many ways to get it right—from the regular workout at the gym, to meditating, to playing with our kids. Yet I believe we can go one step farther in understanding how it works and why. Can we simply learn from life?

We need three different energies to bring forth life, maintain its growth, and take it to the next level. The first energy is our *passion* for life, for what we do, for how we relate to others—a prerequisite for creativity. If passion is remote, our contribution is manifesting far below its potential. If we cannot answer the question of what we are passionate about, it is worth beginning a search. We need to renew our quest. There is a journey waiting for us.

The second energy is *commitment*. It is the decisiveness and perseverance our endeavors require to become successful; the caring and nourishing our projects need to take root and grow. If we lack patience or become bored too easily, we might sabotage our own success. If we drown in obligations, we jeopardize our creativity. Then it's time to ask inconvenient questions like: *What's really important to me?*

This takes us into the third energy—*renewal*. Reflection always finds us, whether it is our yearning for stillness or our move into slightly disenchanted self-doubt. There is nothing wrong with it. It is a circle turning and helping us to make sense of experience or to reconnect with what we really want, with the core of our intention, with new possibilities in life.

How does this play out in collaboration initiatives? They follow the same rhythm. We need to revive passion when we notice that it dries up; we require sustained commitment to get to results. Even as collaborating partners we need to attend to renewal—a mix between collective reflection and having fun together. It can be an enormous energy boost to schedule fun into collaboration initiatives, and it contributes to better results.

Here are a few questions that help guide us toward *balance*:

- What does my pattern of passion, commitment, and renewal look like?
- What helps our team to follow through and sustain our path?
- What are our ways of scheduling fun into our collaboration initiative?

Empathy

Do you remember the habitual opposer from the radical NGO in the coffee initiative who constantly questioned whether our proposed actions would benefit small-scale farmers? Her empathy with the poor might have been regarded by some industry representatives as not only exaggerated, but also slowing down results. It demanded enormous patience from them. It was a reminder that no matter what we did at the international level, we had to step into the shoes of small-scale farmers. There is an African proverb: Don't judge people unless you have walked for a couple of miles in their shoes. Yet judgment is human. We often need it to walk our path with clarity. Can we learn to judge and also learn to suspend judgment? Let me tell you a story that taught me a lesson.

When I was a young development worker in Zimbabwe in 1991, I was invited to a party where I met a young man from South Africa who fit all my politically motivated prejudices about apartheid South Africa—a handsome, young white man arriving in a Land Rover with fuel and water tanks on the roof and exhibiting the confident gestures and movements of somebody who feels superior. My judgment was clear: He's one of those privileged white people in total ignorance of the struggle in his country for the release of Mandela and the transition to a post-apartheid society.

Somebody introduced me to him and we got into a conversation, and then I listened to his story. He was American in origin and had joined the anti-apartheid struggle in South Africa. His grandfather had been involved in the development of the first nuclear bomb. This legacy in his family made the young man decide to commit his life to the South African freedom movement. He had arrived at the party still traumatized, because he had miraculously survived a letter bomb from the apartheid regime just a few days before, and was looking for a place to hide in the mountains for a few months—still afraid that the South African Defence Force would track him down and kill him.

Judging inappropriately and denying ourselves our humanity is a tendency we all have. It shows up in the inner struggle to walk past a beggar in the streets or in the important question we do not ask our staff—how are you? Empathy is a mind-set, because it can become a value that we live by—seeing the person behind the task, seeing the story behind the person, reaching out to the humanness in other people. It is also a technique that we can learn or consciously implement. After the incident at the party I trained myself to become more aware of my judgments, and then inquire into them. Asking questions from genuine interest goes a long way to keeping our humanness alive and acknowledging that of the person we live or work with. It is the oil that makes collaboration work—in conjunction with mindfulness and genuine listening. If we want to ensure high process quality, we can engage every person we want to have join the initiative in one-on-one conversations that are half formal, half informal. This is about appreciating the human being, the interests, the passion, the dreams, and the story. Then we can talk about the issue.

Here are a few questions that help guide us toward *empathy*:

- When I focus for one hour on noticing my judgments, how often do I judge?
- How do we consciously schedule time for storytelling into our teamwork?
- In what way have we planned for inspiring and informal preparatory conversations before actual stakeholder meetings?

Harvesting Collective Intelligence

The sustainability challenges in our world undoubtedly require collective intelligence. As collective wisdom expert George Pór has noted, success will be based on different stakeholders bringing in their expertise, experience, and perspectives as we move to higher orders of complexity in our world.[15] But how do you turn those diverse viewpoints into collective intelligence?

What helped me most was being introduced to the art of dialogue by my colleague Peter Garrett when we worked with a group of twenty engineers from an international oil company.[16] He said something like this: "You have probably all come here because somebody thought it would help your career advancement for you to learn some soft skills. I must disappoint you. This is not about soft skills. This is about saving time and getting to better decisions faster." That's the way he got them hooked. The issue was real—they had come to the workshop because of a sequence of near casualties in their refinery, and it had become clear that their usual command-and-control style of management had not worked. The plant was considered high risk, and they needed to find a new approach to safety. Human beings dwell in the house of language—online and offline. It is diversity of thought that gets us to better solutions for sustainability. Yet we can waste a lifetime in ineffective communication patterns—privately and professionally. It helps when we put some structure to our way of talking and being with one another. There are three pragmatic signposts that need attention: *dialogic quality*, *diversity*, and *iterative learning*.

Dialogic Quality

It is not only our conversations that matter, but also the quality of our conversations. We engage when we experience meaningful conversations that tap into our desire to make a difference. We feel satisfied when a meeting leads to clarity and results. The intention of stakeholder engagement in collaboration is, in essence, dialogic: to get people from different walks of life and with different perspectives into a conversation that will lead to a practical outcome. Dialogue allows for the integration of different perspectives, standpoints, and interests into planning and implementation processes. That's the theory, and it's a good approach to accepting dialogue as a mind-set. We open up to the conversations with others that may influence our strategic path, because we are convinced this will enhance the quality of our collaboration endeavor. And then we stumble. People do not listen to one another, one person talks a lot, others never talk in public but during the coffee break express severe criticism, and we feel the real issues are never bought to the table. Welcome to human incompetency in interaction.

But in the midst of such difficult conversations we often can find shining examples of human competencies—somebody listens intensely, somebody else asks a question, another one says what she really thinks is important. What can we do to enhance dialogic competency? Dialogue is as old as humankind, and it's both a mind-set and a technique—an attitude and a structure put in place that helps people build their competencies in communicating and being with one another. I admire the great thinker and pioneer in process consultancy Edgar Schein, who in 1993 rendered dialogue a pragmatic necessity: "If we did not need to communicate in groups, then we would not need to work on dialogue. But if problem solving and conflict resolution in groups is increasingly important in our complex world, then the skill of dialogue becomes one of the most fundamental of human skills."[17]

If we need circles of reflection and dialogue, on a small scale and on a large scale, to increase our agility and learn iteratively, how can we improve the dialogic quality of our conversations? What are effective ways of engaging stakeholders to ensure that collective knowledge, individual experience, and expertise can be sufficiently harvested? The good news is that it starts with us. Becoming aware of our own communication patterns takes us to observing the communication pattern in collaborative groups, and this inspires us to bring in what is missing.

There is a whole body of work on the art of dialogue, yet in my experience one simple tool goes a long way toward improving dialogic quality: attending to the balance of *advocacy* (seeking to be understood) and *inquiry* (seeking understanding).[18] I owe this insight to my work with William Isaacs, a pioneer in getting dialogue on the agenda in large corporations. Inquiry needs the skills of listening and the ability to suspend judgment. Only then can we gain a deeper understanding of an issue, a stakeholder position, or a way forward. Advocacy requires the courage to speak our voice or to speak on behalf of others, to convey a purpose and defend a course of action, and at the same time to underscore our position or criticism of other positions while respecting difference. Balanced advocacy and inquiry is effective in helping us to see the whole picture of a situation and the best possible way forward.

Here are a few questions that help guide us toward *dialogic quality*:

- How would I describe my own pattern of advocacy and inquiry?
- How can we bring the awareness of advocacy and inquiry into our team?
- In what way can we design our stakeholder meetings to offer a balanced pattern of advocacy and inquiry?

Diversity

We know collective action toward sustainability requires bringing actors with different perspectives and diverging interests together. Agreements and achievements must be reached through consensus and collaboration. This will allow us to use communication constructively, create lasting trust, avoid or overcome crises, and maintain a shared orientation among different actors. So far, so good, but what if diversity becomes a threat?

In my work with collaboration initiatives there is always an important step in the beginning that cannot be skipped—doing a stakeholder analysis. It is amazing how people handle the same task in entirely different ways. Some list up to two hundred stakeholders and drown in the complexity of the task; some reduce the list to those stakeholders they already know and get along with, deliberately ignoring those they don't like to work with.

How do we deal with the complexity of diversity? It is very human to assume that everybody is like us and, if not, should become so. Take a deep dive into complex collaboration initiatives for sustainability and you will observe this phenomenon. It is a constant learning curve of processing difference into progress. I think we can learn from large multinational companies operating on several continents. There always seems to be a point when they notice that sending their national staff to foreign countries to manage affairs stops working. It endangers business. They need to employ people with different cultural backgrounds. It's scary in the beginning, because the new staff will inevitably run operations differently, no matter how strict the current procedures are. Management needs to strike a balance between binding rules and permission to create variations. Yet if this is done consciously, they notice that the variations enhance business. That's when diversity becomes an opportunity, not only a value.

Life would be easy if cultural difference was equal to diversity, but it isn't. Even within one culture, we are different. There is a reason for this: We need the differences. In a leadership program I ran for young professionals, I asked participants to think about how they would most likely approach change and then urged them to focus exclusively on one of the following options:

- Only addressing the awareness of individuals.
- Only bringing about behavioral change through information.
- Only addressing the relationships.
- Only putting regulations and procedural structures in place.

The participants were distributed evenly across all four options. They began fighting about what would be the right approach. Instead of letting them argue indefinitely, I deliberately asked them to caucus around their chosen approach and quickly form a made-up consultancy company that would focus solely on this particular approach. The task was to define ten major recommendations to German chancellor Angela Merkel on how she could successfully manage the country's move to an energy supply from renewable sources only. The result was encouraging—brilliant ideas emerged from the seemingly irreconcilably different approaches! The most striking insight for all was that if the chancellor integrated all four consultancy approaches, success in mastering a hugely complex and difficult challenge looked amazingly likely.

Here are a few questions that help guide us toward *diversity*:

- If I think about somebody I really don't get along with well, what are three little things that I can learn from this person?
- How would we describe the differences in strengths and competencies in our team?
- In what ways are approaches to change different among the stakeholders we are collaborating with?

Iterative Learning

Collaboration initiatives for sustainability are collective learning journeys with no final answers to the challenges ahead. As the example of sustainability standards revealed, moves we make in the right direction may turn out to be not beneficial in the long run; we must adjust our strategies by trying to find higher-level solutions that probably require more complex collaboration structures.

Let me invite you to the complexity of the German Energiewende. The bold move by Chancellor Merkel in 2011, based on her emotional and rational insight into the potential danger of nuclear energy, threw the country into an exciting and difficult learning journey. Government subsidies for renewables had already led to increased production of electricity from renewable sources. Each federal state drew up its own strategy with targets and governance structures to navigate between public needs and private investments.

But there was very little exchange of experience among the federal states. Farmers in Germany began to become energy producers. Increasingly, you could see photovoltaic fields taking over farm fields along the highways. The number of windmills expanded so that they became a common feature of the German landscape. Small investors felt empowered and created energy cooperatives. These were dynamic and wonderful developments, but some locations already produced more electricity than necessary, while others continued to depend on nuclear energy. At the same time, people began to fear energy cuts, and energy companies happily used the fear to promote doomsday scenarios. A debate began over how the highs and lows of energy production could be leveled and energy could be properly distributed throughout the country. This would require expanding the grid and building large transmission lines—the one landscape feature that Germans hated more than windmills.

Is this a complicated German case? No, it is just one example of how the challenges of sustainability will force us into setting up iterative learning structures. It is the mind-set of iterative learning that helps. We don't want to gallop in one direction without checking what other people are doing at the same time. But iterative learning is also a technique that helps support agility. This is not new; sustainability initiatives require strategic and operational planning like all other change activities, and this planning includes observing outcomes, impacts, effects, side effects, and implications. The crucial point here is to empower collaboration structures to learn—collectively. That is why governance structures in stakeholder consultation and collaboration initiatives are first and foremost learning structures. Research, evaluation, and assessments help, but diversity is a must. If Germany looks at its Energiewende initiative from just one point of view—political or corporate or any other—the process will derail.

Here are a few questions that help guide us toward *iterative learning*:

- What is my method of regular personal stocktaking?
- What are the iterative learning structures that we have established in our team?
- What is the form of regular collective learning that we have chosen for our stakeholder initiatives?

Creating Wholeness

People often compare the role of a leader to that of a conductor in an orchestra. I love the image; it shows the essence of collective leadership, but I often ask myself if people really know what it means to play in an orchestra. I had the privilege to grow up with occasional visits to the world-famous Berlin Philharmonic orchestra for a reduced fee, as a close family member was playing the bugle. If you listen to this orchestra's sound, you most likely know what I mean when I call it magic. Not only do the musicians play well, they live the piece of music. The result is that they play straight into the heart of the audience. I know people who say it has a healing effect.

You feel larger, more whole, when you leave the concert hall, as if you had become part of the collective sound.

What fascinated me was how the musicians could strike such a delicate balance between being responsive to the music and responsive to the other musicians. In the movie *Trip to Asia*, we are taken behind the scenes of this special orchestra. The musicians talk about how they perceive their work not as the performance of perfectly practiced pieces, but as a form of interaction among otherwise very special and peculiar people with profound egos. They are deeply aware that they all have an influence on the course of the orchestra, yet they succumb to the togetherness that creates the magic. Simon Rattle, the current conductor, summarized the essence of the experience: "The idea of that many egos coming together for that moment and saying, *It doesn't go there, it goes there*, is an astonishing thing. But the minute you start thinking it is about *you*—you are in crisis! If you don't believe that the music is a much greater thing, then you are in trouble."[19] Can we spot signposts that show us a pathway to developing our competency for WHOLENESS? If we attend to these three elements, we are heading in the right direction: *contextuality, contribution*, and *mutual support*.

Contextuality

The musicians in the Berlin Philharmonic Orchestra play the compositions with three parallel levels of attention: (1) to their fellow musicians and how they play as a whole; (2) to the quality and heartfelt intensity of their own playing; and (3) to the music. The purpose of playing is to allow the utmost potential of sound to emerge. And what about the conductor? Can the orchestra play without the conductor? Likely they can, yet there also is magic around Simon Rattle: They play even better with him. He holds the orchestra by creating a space characterized by his deep dedication to the piece of music, to enhancing the spirit and exceptional giftedness of each musician, and to the way they interact. He brings in his own interpretation of how the music should sound—committed to the potential that is hidden in the notes. This is collective mastery!

What can we learn from it? First, if the musicians played in competition, the result would be terrible. Second, without each player bringing strong individuality to the performance, there would be no magic. Third, the combination of individual excellence, intense differences, and togetherness has a healing impact.

I have observed the opposite in many professional environments, in organizations, and in collaboration initiatives for sustainability, no matter whether people came from the corporate world, the public sector, NGOs, or development cooperation projects. Participants may act with no synchronicity, and in ignorance of other parallel activities in the same field. Remember the cost of non-collaboration?

In the collaboration world I know there are enormous efforts conducted in parallel; they are isolated and uncoordinated. They often leave customers, beneficiaries, or the so-called target group disoriented. That is why contextuality is a mind-set. It frames how to attend to our fellow musicians and what the larger piece of music is all about. It is a technique, because there is a lot we can do to improve contextuality. The question of who else is operating in the same field and what their experiences are is a good starting point. Look at the system of actors that could potentially play better together to create an impact. This can start as a simple stakeholder mapping and grow into an elaborate diagnosis of intervention patterns that could enhance impact. Observing trends and developments and maintaining dialogue with one another and with the people we serve all improve results.

Sustainability initiatives often channel social change. Finding a collaboration structure that allows for joint agendas, joint monitoring systems, joint progress reviews, regular communication, and the support of a coordinating caretaker can go a long way toward collective impact.[20] And it enhances both process quality and connectivity. But sometimes we can start really small—by attending to the pattern of interaction in our team—and find a way of playing together in a more synchronous way so that our collective impact grows.

Here are a few questions that help guide us toward *contextuality*:

- How do I keep up to date with trends and developments?
- How do we cultivate our attention to the pattern of interaction of our team?
- In what way do we ensure that our collaboration initiative is harvesting coordinated efforts for the best possible collective impact?

Mutual Support

Paulo Coelho writes in his novel *The Zahir* about the "favor bank": We make deposits by helping people with contacts that support their talent, pursuit, goal, or dream and without expecting anything in return.[21] By the time we need a favor, we may have banked enough to make some withdrawals. I never liked the comparison with a bank, which implies that helping others is a business built on earning interest. But the underlying principle is true; the world would have broken apart if people had not lived it out for thousands of years. We are here to support one another to grow, to develop, to thrive—or sometimes simply to survive.

Let's journey back to the orchestra. Mutual support is a mind-set. It is the awareness that music can create magic if we support one another in living our potential. It is not about being equal; it is about each person's, each stakeholder's, potential to contribute to the magic, to the impact. It is the realization that our contribution becomes successful if other people's contributions are delivered with high quality. Mutual support is serving us, the other, and the greater music. This is the magic of the orchestra in which we play. It increases tremendously the vitality of a system of actors, be it a team, an organization, or collaborating partner institutions. It is easy to tune in to this mind-set once we have experienced its impact. Life becomes easier, organizations thrive, collaboration efforts become more successful—and it is contagious.

Does it require a conductor like Simon Rattle to remind us of the importance of mutual support? It helps if we all develop the qualities of a Simon Rattle. That's why mutual support is also a technique—we can enact it more consciously if we see ourselves as connectors of people's potential and a greater music.

I started this book with a scene from a complex international collaboration initiative on sustainable coffee production. Over the course of three years this diverse group of actors had matured into playing music together by supporting one another. It was clear that the group's investment of time and resources would only be successful if each individual stakeholder was able to get the necessary institutional agreement and backing. Often this required support—industry members needed strong support from their associations, and some NGO boards required trust-building measures and reiteration of the larger purpose of the initiative. People began to offer one another help in convincing their institutions to stay in the process and travel the path together toward joint success. With mutual support we enhance one another's strengths, just as the Collective Leadership Compass works because the competencies mutually reinforce one another if you give them attention.

Here are a few questions that help guide us toward *mutual support*:

- If I've consciously paid in to the favor bank, what results have I observed over time?
- How do we as team cultivate mutual support, and what effect does it have?
- What would be three examples of team members strengthening one another's contribution in our collaboration initiative?

Contribution

Most people I know are not necessarily inspired by their achievements as much as by meaning. They genuinely want to serve. They want to have an impact. They want to make a difference. They are creative. Yet we are all human, and this means we get entangled in the traps of life that we have often unconsciously laid out ourselves. We are afraid of mistakes. We do not believe that our contribution counts. We doubt our expertise. We work tirelessly, heading toward burnout. Or we get hooked on success, become power-hungry, thrive on competition, and elevate ourselves above others. I am particularly fond of the quote from Steve Jobs: "Remembering you are going to die one day is the best way to avoid the trap of thinking you have something to lose. You are already naked. Follow your heart."[22]

The heart is probably the best guide to contribution. Passion is what creates energy, because it focuses attention. It organizes life, creates order in our path, and attracts people and opportunities. The amazing revelation is that we begin to dance to our own tune when we are in tune with a cause larger than ourselves. We gain clarity in how we can contribute, we have more energy in striving for excellence, we become more decisive in following our vision, and we are more willing to engage people in a future possibility. One of the musicians of the Berlin Philharmonic Orchestra captured this poignantly: "I think it is important that everybody keeps his personality . . . one notices if somebody is a little square-edged and angular, or oversensitive, but prepared to surrender to the music as a whole."[23] The magic of the sound emerges out of the friction of different personalities in a small space.

Diversity, then, is not a threat but an enormous wealth. Excellence becomes part of our willingness to serve. Then the music reaches into the hearts of people from every culture—the best payoff for our efforts. Contribution is a mind-set when we accept that it's why we're here. But it is also a technique. We can regularly ask the question: *How does what I know, do, or say contribute to a better immediate outcome, or to a better life on this planet?* On the individual level, mindfulness is an important route to clarifying our contribution—we need to discover our gifts. It is the individual contribution that counts and it is the developed competencies that create the magic in togetherness. Reconnecting with our dreams, our potential, and our intention to make a difference is paramount. It is a prerequisite for growing into our true potential. Can we transfer this to collaboration initiatives? Yes, because they would not come into existence without passionate people.

Most of the people I know who initiate impactful collaborations for sustainability are dreamers, yet they are also realists and leaders with excellent backstage diplomacy skills. They rarely become famous. They thrive on results and work tirelessly to bring people together for a larger goal. They are patiently and persistently establishing dialogue and collaborative change processes. Yet when collaboration initiatives get lost in administrative procedures, key performance indicator definition, or territorial fights for the right strategy—we can ask the same question: *How will what we do here best contribute to a better life on this planet?*

Here are a few questions that help guide us toward *mutual support*:

- What is my form of serving people and/or a larger goal?
- What is the larger context of our team's contribution?
- In what ways do we regularly reconnect with the purpose of our collaboration initiative?

Growing Impact

By attending to our human competencies in the six dimensions of the Collective Leadership Compass, we can enhance the likelihood of better co-creation. We can use the aspects in each dimension as signposts to illuminate our path. If they are consciously enacted jointly, the results are—in my experience—amazing. Outcomes become easier to achieve, people are more content, the impact grows. The vitality of a system of actors increases. This is a cornerstone for creating communities for change. A top manager from a multinational energy company once told me: "I really believe collective leadership can overcome all obstacles, when time and energy are devoted to positive collective intention on behalf of the whole and not on behalf of one's own ego. This makes a huge difference."

Yet we are human, and humans fail. A great idea from a visionary person can be lost because it seems to be too far ahead of where the world stands now and does not get the support it needs, or a team underperforms because passion for the goal has dried up. Our organization may be stuck in the old way of doing business and miss the window of opportunity for an innovation. The elaborate multi-stakeholder initiative addressing a pressing sustainability issue may be preoccupied with internal power fights while a second initiative—similar yet competitive—is being set up.

That's the real world we have to deal with. If we want to change the world, the first step is developing compassion for how people are. The second step is spotting the human competencies and building on their potential. And the third step is practicing doing things differently—perfecting our skills in being together differently. That is why we will find the Berlin Philharmonic Orchestra practicing before every concert. There is always something needing improvement. Hence, the Collective Leadership Compass is not a guarantee for perfection and harmony. It is a practice guide for navigating complex change and invigorating communities for collective action.

So how do you make the Compass work for you? I invite you to join the fellow travelers and their sustainability challenges. How will they make the Compass work for them? Will they find a path through the jungle of their complex collaboration efforts?

PART THREE

Making the Compass
Work for Us

People who lead collectively venture into the unknown. They take the road less traveled if it leads to innovation and allows them to test new approaches. They are visionaries who keep a sense of wholeness alive and connect with future possibilities. They craft consensual agreements among diverse perspectives with respect for difference. They inspire others to engage with an emotionally compelling goal. They are masters of relationship management and create a context of trust and continuity. They deal with conflicts and crises constructively and know that these are, in fact, often opportunities for innovation. And they follow through on agreed action.

All these qualities of collective leadership may sound exceptional, but we are all capable of evolving the traits we need to work toward a better future together. That evolution is often spurred on by leadership challenges in the outer world, and those challenges are always opportunities to grow—as individuals and as collectives.

The Collective Leadership Compass empowers individual leaders to unfold their potential to contribute to sustainability in collaboration; it enhances their self-efficacy. Groups of actors who aspire to achieve something together can also make the Compass work for them; it can improve the outcome of collaboration systems, be they networks, initiatives, partnerships, or other groupings. At each level of the Compass, there is an inward aspect—looking at how the individual develops—and an outward aspect looking at how a collective jointly enacts a new future in collaboration with others.

The Compass is a navigating tool, and at the same time it can be used as a form of checks and balances. It gives us a larger frame for evaluating whether the change approach we have chosen is getting us where we want to go and, most of all, whether it is improving co-creation through collective leadership. It helps us balance the six dimensions that we need for leading collectively and ensures that our human competencies become more present. The Compass emphasizes the pattern of human competencies in interaction that works best for our case. Remember, better co-creation is about increasing the impact for sustainability by getting things done faster, coming to better decisions, saving money, and being more content as we achieve results jointly. Table 3 table shows how we can make the Compass work for us at different levels.

We will journey into the pathways for all three levels and accompany our fellow travelers in mastering their challenges. There will be ample opportunities to review your own leadership journey, and the challenges you face in bringing sustainability forward.

Remember, too: Bringing about change—in ourselves, a group of actors, an organization, or a multi-actor collaboration system—is most often about setting free what is already there. The seeds for collective leadership are everywhere. We need to strengthen them and free their potential. Our work is about invigorating the human competencies that exist. The six dimensions function like centers of excellence that mutually support one another. When we—as individuals and as a collective—become strong in all dimensions we enhance the likelihood of better co-creation.

Table 3. Using the Three Levels of the Compass

Level	Application	Purpose
Strengthening individual leadership competency	Self-assessment, identification of development areas, personal development plans, coaching guide	Enhance individual holistic leadership capabilities and capacity to lead in conjunction with others; increase self-efficacy in sustainability leadership
Empowering collaborative action groups	Group assessment, identification of improvement areas, team reflection, definition of focus areas, action plans, team coaching guide, meeting planning	Enhance collaborative group/ team efficacy, refocus team on sustainability issues, increase awareness of the interface between hard and soft skills, improve impact of action plans
Building communities for change	Assessment and self-assessment of collaboration systems; joint action planning; planning of meetings, workshops, and collaboration events; monitoring quality of collaboration; progress reviews	Engage organization/department or cross-sector network for sustainability goals, improve collaboration results, strengthen collective action, increase collaborative impact

The Collective Leadership Compass can be used to find out who we are, where we stand, and how our journey came about on our way to better co-creation. It can also be used for planning our action and evaluating the results. This works best when we work through a set of three steps: observing, focusing, and enacting. These steps apply to all levels—individual leaders, groups, or a system of collaborating actors. These steps, each with three actions, create a repeating cycle.

Step One: Observing

Some people call this first step "diagnosing." That is fine, but humans have a tendency to be critical and judgmental, and most of us are trained to spot the gaps immediately and jump at the deficits. So I suggest that we take a slightly different approach. Observe what is already there. Spot the competencies in the six dimensions—even if they're tiny—that are already in place, in ourselves or within a collective.

That's why the first action in observing is important: *appreciating*. This is not a psychological trick; it could be the most important entry point for better co-creation. Remember that Peter noticed that collective intelligence was a hidden potential at DiverseAct even if it looked on the surface like territorial expertise coupled with silo mentality. With her strong listening skills Andrea identified collective intelligence as her personal strength and decided to take this as a starting point for her change endeavor at EnergyTech. Appreciating the competencies available may turn into the discovery of a hidden jewel or a leverage point for success.

The next action in observing is *assessing*. Here we look at the broader picture and assess our individual pattern of competencies—we can see this as our personal pattern—or that of our collective (team, organization, collaboration initiative). We look at the relational presence of the six dimensions and how we enact them. This can be done individually, in the form of a conversation, or through a more quantitative assessment.

The most important action is the third: *evaluating*. This is about making sense of information, interpreting our view in relation to our leadership challenge, the task at hand, or the larger goal we have set. It is about extracting insights. This can be done individually, but humans dwell in the house of language and talking it through with a peer can tap into collective intelligence as we make sense of the results. Evaluating is not about right or wrong; it's about laying the base for decision making and knowing how to improve—our leadership, a situation, or the collaboration. It's about learning to make better choices and seeing better results.

Step Two: Focusing

Have you ever experienced a fantastic strategy meeting that created an evaluation of strength and weaknesses—but in the end everybody left frustrated because the issues to be addressed became too overwhelming? The list of improvements needed was too long? Evaluating forms the base; focusing is what empowers us to act. If plans are overwhelming, our mind resists the change. Whether continuous improvement or radical change, the goals must be achievable. Focus is the route to success. It requires us to be specific and concrete, to be precise about time and measurements of success. It helps us walk in the jungle of complexity.

Focusing has three actions: strengthening the strengths, nurturing development areas, choosing the starting point for change. What does this mean? When we *strengthen our strength*, we give attention to our strength and make use of it. When we *nurture our development areas*, we spot what is missing or undervalued or simply not known, and we bring it in. When we *choose a starting point*, we empower ourselves to develop tangible next steps; that starting point can be our strength, our development areas, or a combination of a number of dimensions.

Step Three: Enacting Change

Most of our individual and joint actions are preceded by plans. When they are built on appreciative observation and focus, we are more likely to implement them with enthusiasm—a prerequisite for leading future possibilities. *Planning next steps* is important—short-term and long-term. We can do this weekly, monthly, quarterly, or once a year. Timing depends on the task ahead and on the structure of our collective. On my personal leadership journey I have benefited from short weekly planning sessions, quarterly target setting, and yearly goal creation. In complex collabora-

Table 4. Three Necessary Steps for Each Compass Level

Steps	Action
Observing	Appreciating Assessing Evaluating
Focusing	Strengthening strengths Nurturing development areas Choosing starting points
Enacting	Planning next steps Testing reality Watching the pattern

tion initiatives, planning with the Collective Leadership Compass can be combined with implementation reviews, steering committee meetings, or impact evaluation. We then need to *test reality* and check whether we achieve the impact we envisioned with our next step. This leads us to *watch the pattern* of the six dimensions and see how they interact. Reviewing progress takes us back to observing.

After a while this cycle, summarized in table 4, becomes second nature, but in the beginning it is helpful to consciously go through the three steps when we use the Compass as a lens through which we see the world, our actions, and our collaboration. With time we become more skillful in noticing what is missing and what can be enhanced. We develop ideas on how to strengthen certain dimensions and we notice how the dimensions support one another.

Chapter 8

Approaching Change and Strengthening Our Leadership

When we walk toward a common goal together with others, we change. So do the goals. They take on a different shape, grow bigger, and become more appropriate to what the future needs. Let's look at how our fellow travelers used the Compass and how it affected each of their journeys.

Using the Compass for Change

Peter, the new CEO of the Swiss NGO DiverseAct, knew that his organization had undergone a change management process a few years before he arrived—an attempt by the founder to professionalize the organization and introduce a more private-sector-oriented management style. It did not go well. The staff resisted the recommendations of the consultants brought in to help. Peter heard people laughing about how the change got blocked, as if they had defeated an enemy. He felt that there were a lot of untold stories, resentments, and injuries among the staff. Peter realized that these were now showing up as misgivings toward him, as if his background in the private sector was a threat to his staff. He decided to find ways to build trust with his senior managers one by one.

Since ENGAGEMENT and FUTURE POSSIBILITIES were his strong areas, he was familiar with various change management approaches, and one of his passions was reading books on leadership. That is also where he learned that change most often happened at the edge of chaos when times became turbulent or pressure increased. He wondered how he could get his staff to venture toward a certain degree of necessary chaos. He was confident in his engaging leadership approach, yet he wanted to use the

Compass to refine a few areas. Peter loved to start with the end in mind. He wanted DiverseAct to live its name fully—being aligned around the goal of protecting biodiversity and natural resource management, yet working toward the goal in collaboration with different actors and with respect for a diversity of approaches.

Andrea, the project manager at the sustainability department of the Germany-based corporation EnergyTech, had been exposed to a few change management tools while she was attending her leadership program for young professionals. What she liked most was change approaches that integrated people's dreams and their culture of working together and that addressed both behavioral change and the change of structures and procedures. But she had no idea how to implement any of this at her company. During a conversation with a colleague from the human resource department she heard that there were many change processes taking place in parallel. Recently HR had advocated for a more value-based leadership approach, as societal pressure was mounting. Andrea welcomed this new approach, which would support her agenda, but she felt that even if more emphasis was placed on humanity, wholeness—the future of energy and its relationship to people's empowerment—was still totally missing. And who was she to put this on the company's agenda? She knew this was not part of her job description, but she had a hidden warrior nature; the bigger the challenge, the more she felt drawn to start.

Mike, the CEO of a UK-based textile company, had been working with a US-based consultancy firm that focused on performance improvement and cost cutting, as TrendWear needed to maintain a profit margin in order to survive. A new balanced scorecard had been introduced a while before, but Mike was doubtful that this was all the right approach. Dealing with supply-chain sustainability challenges—especially the state of working conditions at their suppliers' factories in Southeast Asia—was cut off from the mainstream business focus, and mainly handled by the sustainability department. He made sure that the sustainability staff reported directly to him. They did their job well and were brilliant in saying all the right things in external communication—that TrendWear was on a path to improvement—but internally they had very little say. Profits were what counted. Mike decided to use the Collective Leadership Compass as both personal and professional challenge. He chose HUMANITY to be his development area because he sensed the issue was about people—the suppliers, the employees at TrendWear, his management team, and his own family as well.

Tina, the innovative social entrepreneur in South Africa, had never met a change management tool and did not like such approaches. She followed her heart and avoided anything too structured. Being spontaneous was a core philosophy for her. She did not see herself as a leader, but was interested in using the Collective Leadership Compass to help her build momentum and engage the hearts and minds of her fellow students. She identified FUTURE POSSIBILITIES as her development area and hoped to get some guidance from the Compass about how best to grow a mentoring movement.

Celine, the coordinator of the water committee in the Democratic Republic of Congo, had never used any change management tools in her engineering career. What she knew was that the consultants who regularly came into the country through different donor organizations often spoke about the need for institutional development. She agreed that public institutions were extremely weak in the DRC, but her gut feeling told her that it would take a long time to build institutions that had the efficiency and organizational culture of European public institutions. Rome was also not built in one day, she told herself. She was open to strengthening the institutions, yet the complicated processes that some of the consultants suggested failed to acknowledge the daily reality in Kinshasa. Skilled people changed jobs all the time, following the attractive offers of international organizations or the possibility of making extra money on the side. The stability and persistence needed to build world-class organizations were just not part of the current reality. Celine had recently attended a training on stakeholder collaboration, and she thought it was what she needed to improve the drinking water policy. She wanted to use the Compass to review her own skills in engaging stakeholders and to track the collaboration process she hoped to set up.

Nadeem, the coordinator of the multi-stakeholder initiative helping African farmers, was extremely knowledgeable in change management. He had not only attended various trainings—he loved learning—but also read many books. He facilitated leadership retreats for civil society and development organizations before he moved into his current position. He was familiar with the principles of large-group facilitation such as future search conferences, open space methodology, and appreciative inquiry—he had facilitated a number of such events.[1] He saw that people implemented what they had helped to create, and this became one of his most important mantras. That is why he favored change approaches that used collective intelligence and emergent change. The rigidity of the project plans he had to work with in his current position seemed to him bizarre. He knew how difficult it was for development projects involving small-scale farmers to plan a few years ahead. He also realized that neither the implementing agencies nor the private sector representatives were interested in the participatory approaches he favored—they jokingly called them "talk shops." He wanted to use the Collective Leadership Compass to look at the entire situation from a broader perspective and hoped the Compass would help him successfully navigate the differences in approaches to project implementation.

All of our fellow travelers took a slightly different approach to how they could make the Compass work for them, as we'll explore in chapters 9 and 10. But there were common denominators. First, they all needed to strengthen their own leadership capabilities. Then they needed to empower a small group of actors to enhance their contribution (chapter 11) and build a collaboration system into a community for change (chapter 12).

The Leadership Journey

I believe the time has come for all of us to commit to answering the question: *What is my contribution to a more sustainable world?* It will bring us back to our leadership quest. For many of us, redefining our leadership contribution is a road to freedom traveled slowly. We take one step at a time. Once our heart is committed and our intention is revived, we will find the means for our own maturation. When our inner field changes, we will notice changes in the outer field. Different things happen; we meet different people. Our driving force becomes the intention to serve rather than a need for recognition. We reconnect with our passion, nourished by compassion for the world and humankind; we hold our commitment with a feeling of freedom, now aware that choice and necessity are inseparable. Gradually, we cultivate reflection in action, knowing that the space inside us is not really separate from the outside world. It is a reminder that our leadership journey has been and always will be a quest.

While I was writing this chapter, I had the opportunity to meet the famous chimpanzee expert Jane Goodall at the University of Cape Town. In an inspiring speech that same evening, she touched the hearts and minds of people by telling her story patiently and persistently with admirable clarity and focus—a heartbreaking account of a young woman following her dream to learn about chimpanzees in Africa only to find out she needed to protect them and their habitat. She gradually realized that her passion for chimpanzees was part of a larger story: humankind's ability—or inability—to keep this planet a place of fascinating diversity and human kindness. That was when she started traveling the world, inspiring people to see the possibility of co-creating a better world—and she is still doing so at the age of eighty-one. She reminded us that it is possible for each of us to make a difference. That evening, in the reception area of the university, I saw a little booklet lying on the table. The cover said, *Life Is a Journey, Not a Destination.* It implies a promise: The longer the journey, the more we will understand the human mind and the human heart and the nature of co-creation. Jane Goodall certainly has seen this.

We are all on a leadership quest that involves our deeper values. It's important that we realign our action with these values and with the deep knowing they carry. We have all experienced such knowing—through other people, nature, books that resonated with our hearts, and movies that touched our souls. Nobody taught us. It did not reach us through the intellect. We knew it when we felt it. I have a quote that has accompanied me for more than ten years. I owe it to an admirable person and friend who had found his passion—playing the piano—and combined it with being a writer and change management consultant. Some of you may know Michael Jones, an author of beautifully insightful books on leadership.[2] This is the paragraph I carry with me:

> *Thus the question "must I lead?" is a perennial question that can never be settled once and for all time. Leading from our gifts is an art and, as with all of the art, is not something we choose, but a calling that also chooses us. In making this choice, we also become the ground upon which the forces of fear and contraction work against those of growth and expansion. In this fire our gifts gain the substance and the resilience to serve and also withstand the world.*[3]

Rereading these words helps me through crises and times of doubt, when failure lingers or when obstacles come my way. And my answer again and again is: Yes, I must lead. Leading—no matter if it is implementing an idea or serving as CEO of a multimillion-dollar enterprise—is about growing our potential to have a positive impact on the world. But, as the conductor of the Berlin Philharmonic Simon Rattle said, it is not about us. It is about how well we play the music together, so that the potential of the music lives and reaches the hearts of the audience.

Leading for sustainability is about growing life's potential—responsible supply-chain management, integrated water resource management, climate change adaptation, social justice, or attention to biodiversity. You name the challenges, the world is changing and so is what is expected of people in leadership roles. Before the Rio+20 conference in Brazil, the *Guardian* sustainable leadership hub asked members of the World Business Council for Sustainable Development's Future Leaders Team what they think is vital for a twenty-first-century leader.[4] The responses, shown in table 5, are

Table 5. WSBC Future Leaders on Vital 21st-Century Leadership Traits

Dimension	Vital Traits for 21st-Century Leaders
FUTURE POSSIBILITIES	"Decisiveness in ever changing environments with blurred boundaries," "have strong principles whilst being flexible and realistic," "have patience," "apply appropriate economic, moral and political incentives to actually incorporate sustainable development into our daily lives," "focus on facts and accurate details," "concrete and practical people who search for solutions."
ENGAGEMENT	"Ensure stakeholders' ownership," "collaborate and work together," "enjoy spending time with each other," "build awareness and mobilize commitment."
INNOVATION	"Foster innovation," "take risks and give the fruits to people," "be vigilant to the challenges and opportunities for innovation," "enjoy new and untraditional ideas," "recognize and provide innovative, sensitive, and meaningful sustainability possibilities," "deliver precision of end results."
HUMANITY	"Make issues deeply personal," "sincerity and fairness."
COLLECTIVE INTELLIGENCE	"Mediation skills to facilitate knowledge sharing," "working together with other farsighted leaders," "promote and drive common way of thinking and acting."
WHOLENESS	"Systems thinking to identify paradigms driving change," "vision rooted in community service and ethical behavior," "enthusiasm to create a better world," "define 'profit' in the context of what kind of impacts the company will have on the earth," "create a meaningful context."

varied but contain a common threat that aligns with the six dimensions of the Collective Leadership Compass.

What I have learned from the Future Leaders Team is that it's more important than ever that we "re-know what we already know," and that many people around the world already have the competencies that take us to better co-creation. We intuitively know the ingredients for leading collectively. We need to live them more consciously. As you find leadership development tools that speak to you, I encourage you to also heighten your attention to the pattern of co-creation, to the presence of the six dimensions and how they are emphasized or enhanced. Our work is to create a *pattern of human competencies in interaction* that works better for our common future. This attention to patterns will sharpen your skills to choose what is appropriate for your particular point of development. It will empower you to observe joint impact and the effect of human competencies that we hold and enact.

Observing, focusing, and enacting the six dimensions of collective leadership with our fellow travelers can inspire you to review your own pattern, define your action plans, and enhance the interaction patterns that lead to better co-creation.[5] Let's start by seeing how our six collective leaders began to use the compass in their work.

Chapter 9

Observing Our Pattern

Three of our fellow travelers decided that they would place strong emphasis on enhancing individual leadership competency before using the Compass to tackle their sustainability challenges. Tina decided to concentrate on her own leadership development, because she was reluctant to call herself a leader but was fascinated by the idea of seeing leadership as bringing about change without being others' superior. Nadeem realized that his strength—facilitation—was needed to help small-scale African farmers but was not sufficient to master the management challenges. He needed to build his competency in leading FUTURE POSSIBILITIES. Mike was inspired by the Compass because he saw the lack of concern for people in the supply chain—in particular their working conditions—mirrored in his own development area, HUMANITY. All three used the Compass to discover their individual pattern of the dimensions and relate the outcome to their leadership challenges at hand.

Tina: Dreaming a Better Future

Tina dreamed of a social change movement among university students all over South Africa to help educationally disadvantaged children improve their chances in life. When she had gathered friends and other students together after the panel discussion, she talked passionately about how important it had been for her to have her cousin as an "angel," persistently mentoring her to go back to school for her college degree. If only one in five students joined the movement, she explained, the difference would be extraordinary. Lives would be changed, opportunities would open up, and the confidence of having had support would stay with these children, so that they would do the same for others once they entered university. She noticed that her fellow students liked what she said, but she sensed that her dream was too big for some of them. She began to doubt herself and pondered whether to drop the bold dream, as she had done with so many other ideas, or commit to following her heart and the courage she had felt after the panel discussion.

When Tina thought about what her biggest challenge was, she realized that it was herself. Who was she to dream big? Wouldn't people ridicule her? Where would she get the support she needed? She reviewed her challenge by diving into the Collective Leadership Compass and identified HUMANITY and INNOVATION as her strengths.

As Tina was a visual person, she made herself a model of the Collective Leadership Compass on flip chart paper and put it on her wall. She wanted to have it present and be able to walk past it. When examining her personal pattern among the six dimensions, she did not distinguish between professional life and private life. As much as she would have loved to pinpoint FUTURE POSSIBILITIES as her strength, her intuition pointed to HUMANITY with a particular focus on *empathy*. It had always been easy for her to identify with weak people in society. Her capacity to identify with the disadvantaged remained her way of perceiving the world, and this gave her a strong urge to do something about people who were helpless or could not live up to their potential. She arranged all six dimensions of the Compass in the following order to describe her pattern: HUMANITY, INNOVATION, WHOLENESS, FUTURE POSSIBILITIES, ENGAGEMENT, COLLECTIVE INTELLIGENCE. She identified the first three as her strengths and the last three as her development areas and noted down a few insights for each dimension:

Humanity. I feel for the disadvantaged. People may call me a dreamer, but if this is what my heart is beating for, I'll stay with it.

Innovation. I am a risk taker. I can do what other people are afraid of. Great! Keep it up! Love to be spontaneous.

Future Possibilities. I am good at future orientation. I can inspire, but following through is not my favorite activity.

Wholeness. Supporting one another is my credo! I am also good at seeing the larger picture of an issue. Remember to choose and focus!

Engagement. Planning change systematically is totally new for me!

Collective Intelligence. Can't see the relevance at this moment. This must be a reason why I put it last.

Tina now looked at her development areas and used the aspects of the particular dimension for guidance to identify strengths even in her development areas. In FUTURE POSSIBILITIES she spotted *future orientation* as her strength—she was generally a positive person and would immediately look for solutions. In ENGAGEMENT it was *connectivity* that she immediately recognized as her strong point. She had many friends and it had always been a habit to connect people with others who could help or who were interested in similar subjects. She was a very active Facebook user. For COLLECTIVE INTELLIGENCE she could not make up her mind; she saw no particular strengths. What did she conclude from this exercise regarding her personal pattern? And what would this mean for her as an initiator of a thriving mentoring movement that could have an impact on hundreds of young people?

She had many daydreams but had not implemented any so far. Self-doubt had kept her from deciding to follow through on a dream. She also realized that she could only implement something if her heart was involved. Passion needed to be part of her journey. She knew she was a creative and free spirit that needed to design a life path in service of others, but not in an environment where she would have little chance to self-design. She realized that the panel discussion had not crossed her path by chance and the dream to help educationally disadvantaged children matched her own story. Was there a pathway that she should not decline, despite massive self-doubt?

She had three insights:

- The dream of mentoring educationally disadvantaged children came to her as a testing ground for her intention to contribute (WHOLENESS) to a better world. Her strong *empathy* (HUMANITY) got her to the dream; her ability to take risks (INNOVATION—*agility*) was a strong support. Her ability to connect (ENGAGEMENT—*connectivity*) was also supportive. She could build the first steps on her strengths.
- She would need to take conscious steps to exercise her development areas, which she identified as setting clear goals (FUTURE POSSIBILITIES—*future orientation*) and becoming better at focus and following through (FUTURE POSSIBILITIES—*decisiveness*). She needed to learn structured ENGAGEMENT (*process quality*).
- She needed to explore the gray area of COLLECTIVE INTELLIGENCE that she did not understand and find ways of playfully testing what it was all about.

Nadeem: Learning to Speak Different Languages

Six months into his new job of coordinating private sector partners, an international foundation, and four implementing partners in a multi-stakeholder initiative to improve the productivity and income of small-scale African farmers, Nadeem, who was known to be able to juggle many tasks, had one urgent desire—to reduce the complexity of the project. Operations took place in five countries—three French speaking, one English speaking, and one Portuguese speaking. He jokingly reported back to his family in India that he not only needed to become fluent in French and Portuguese in addition to his Hindi and English, but also needed to learn the language of the different stakeholders involved.

The private sector partners focused on facts and figures; they wanted to ensure quality supply from the small-scale farmers. The foundation was interested in showing the number of farmers that actually increased their income. The implementing agencies were busy telling Nadeem how difficult it was to recruit farmers for the project, as there were competing activities from other agencies. The government officials involved were concerned about how the project fit into their national development plans. And the farmers? Nadeem had no time for any visits to project sites and could not be in contact with any farmers. One chief who ran a farmers cooperative near the project office popped in once in a while to find out if he could get additional training courses for his cooperative members.

Nadeem had the feeling that everybody was working in parallel but not in synergy. He knew he needed to bring a new order to the collaboration structure, which was overly planned yet ineffective. He decided to take a day off and look at his personal leadership challenges first.

For Nadeem the conceptual background of the Collective Leadership Compass was more than familiar. He had come across the idea of co-creation long before he learned about the Compass, particularly in the context of the large-group facilitation. He was good at strengthening people's ability to find common ground and arrive at joint action plans. What drew him to the Compass was that he could use it as a tool to make the ingredients for collective leadership visible and discussable among the partners that he needed to coordinate.

Before he introduced the Compass to the group, he wanted to use his own leadership journey as a test and identify improvement areas. In his personal pattern he identified WHOLENESS, HUMANITY, and COLLECTIVE INTELLIGENCE as his strong areas and ENGAGEMENT, FUTURE POSSIBILI-TIES, and INNOVATION as his development areas. When he looked more closely into his development areas, he felt he was strong in the aspect *future orientation* in the dimension of FUTURE POSSIBILITIES. He had always set himself personal goals, but the new job required systematic project manage-ment. It seemed that was the aspect of *decisiveness* he had not yet mastered. Management just did not excite him very much. He noticed that he tended to think about the management tasks as side issues that took time away from his real passion—improving the life of farmers and inspiring people.

It was not until he got a very low-quality half-yearly report from one of the implementing agencies that he realized he needed to change his approach. Being firm and demanding improvement was the only choice. He increasingly felt overwhelmed. His position was sandwiched between the project managers from the four different implementing partners, who did not really cooperate with one another, and the donor agency and the co-funding private sector partners, who were only interested in results shown in figures. He reviewed the results from his first self-assessment of strengths and devel-opment areas. *Decisiveness* was one aspect to strengthen because he needed focus and follow-through. *Collective action* was another, because he wanted to build accountability and a sense of joint ownership for all the actors.

He noted three insights:

- He needed to use his strength in COLLECTIVE INTELLIGENCE (utilizing his facilitation skills and his ability to mediate among different inter-ests) to genuinely align all actors behind the common goal.
- He needed to change his thinking about the management issues—from annoying side issues to central to getting results (*decisiveness*).
- He wanted to find a way to bring *iterative learning* into this over-whelmingly complex project by putting learning structures in place that everybody would participate in.

Being used to taking a holistic view of himself and the challenges ahead, he decided to use his dialogue and facilitation skills (COLLECTIVE INTELLIGENCE—*dialogic quality*) to embark on an inquiry and engagement process with different stakeholders in the project. He termed the exercise "stakeholder interviews," a simple process that required no more than ten minutes' time from each of the interview partners. He chose ten people from the range of partners to represent the variety of stakeholders. He set up phone calls or meetings and asked a single question: From your point of view, what is the single most important move that you think will make this collaboration project a success? He noted down the answers in a table and evaluated them against the Collective Leadership Compass. The result was

Table 6. Feedback from Nadeem's Stakeholder Interviews Applied to the Six Dimensions

Dimension	Responses
FUTURE POSSIBILITIES	Turn the complicated project plan into five key performance indicators and let everybody commit to them as measurement of success (private sector). Keep track of quantitative results and impact (foundation). Revisit the goal and make it more qualitative—income figures are not enough to describe the improvement for farmers (implementing agency). Make sure that the project genuinely empowers farmers and avoids too much dependency on certain private sector companies (farmers cooperative).
ENGAGEMENT	Integrate the project into existing government and other institutional structures so that sustainability is ensured (government official). Create strong linkages between farmers and private sector companies (private sector). Don't just implement plans, ensure that people have a shared understanding of the goal and commit to it, not just to their particular milestones (implementing agency).
INNOVATION	Ensure a quality check for products so that the private sector can rely on the supply (private sector). Adjust implementation plans and integrate income generation beyond farming (implementing agency).
HUMANITY	Make the private sector understand how real small-scale farmers think, organize exposure trips (implementing agency).
COLLECTIVE INTELLIGENCE	Create a learning platform so that we can learn as we go, allow trial and error, follow the plan, but be open to changing it (private sector, implementing agency). Consult us more often (government official).
WHOLENESS	Create a joint approach for implementing agencies so that they can support one another (implementing agency). Do benchmarking of other similar projects and adopt best practices (foundation).

striking: On the one hand it showed the frightening disparity of opinions about how to run the project, and on the other it became clear that every stakeholder had a piece of truth that, together, hinted at the competencies in the Compass. Table 6 is how he evaluated the responses.

Nadeem was overwhelmed by how clearly the responses showed the differences in demands and expectations. No wonder he felt stretched. The responses were all valid suggestions for making the project a collaborative success, yet it was clear that each partner only saw one piece of the puzzle, influenced by the logic of that partner's own institution. Nadeem worried that some of the expectations were contradicting one another.

Mike: Getting to the Heart of the Issue

After Mike reviewed the Collective Leadership Compass, he defined FUTURE POSSIBILITIES as his strength and HUMANITY as his development area. The issue he needed to address was way beyond his comfort zone—people. He was bothered by the thought that HUMANITY was exactly what TrendWear needed. He did not talk with anybody about his thought. The question that nagged him was whether the lack of responsibility of TrendWear in the supply chain mirrored a culture within TrendWear where the focus was always on figures, not on people. This idea kept him awake several nights, yet there was no answer in sight and he felt stuck—something he hated. The demand from the board was unambiguously clear: Get the finances straight and don't mess with TrendWear's reputation. When he did the first Compass exercise on strength and development areas, he identified his personal-pattern sequence as follows:

Future Possibilities: People could rely on him delivering results; he was very single-minded and could focus brilliantly. That got him to where he was now. Goal setting was second nature to him.

Wholeness: He loved following trends and had a particular interest in future research, but there was another important point: He never delivered financial benefits only but believed that better business helped people—the customers as much as the staff. He always worked from a strong value of service. That's why he began to realize that sustainability was not a communications add-on, but essential to the future.

Innovation: His credo was excellence, yet he was also known for his spontaneity. If a different approach worked better, he was the first to jump on it. Privately he was always walking around with a notebook, because he needed to write down his ideas as they bubbled up.

Collective Intelligence: One thing he had always trained his staff to do was iterative learning. He conducted regular reviews, but he also admitted that they were not really dialogues. Because he was impatient, his tolerance for long discussions was close to zero. He opened up when people came to him individually with proposals, but was rather tough in meetings and did not allow people to waste time with long speeches. He loved informal conversation, which was why most of his ideas and business deals developed on the golf course.

Engagement: Being an innovator and decisive visionary, he expected his staff to be self-reliant. All he wanted to see was results; he did not bother with micromanagement. Admittedly he lost some good people, but he never thought about why.

Humanity: Mike considered himself a good person, honest and ethically firm. He once had a coach who wanted him to get more in touch with his feelings, but he perceived this as an artificial pressure on him and an unnecessary move. Yet he knew that when he focused on one thing, other aspects of his life tended to move entirely into the background. This had been the constant complaint of his family.

Mike loved facts and figures; the initial Compass exercise was not thorough enough for him. He wanted a more quantitative and objective assessment of the aspects for each dimension. That's why he chose the Collective Leadership Compass online questionnaire.[1] He compared his results with his first, more subjective, assessment of his strong and weak dimensions and noticed an astonishing variation. From the questionnaire results it became clear that in his development area—HUMANITY—he had one very strong aspect, *balance*. Not only did Mike take time to exercise regularly, he also knew that he operated at his best when he regularly arranged what he called "time out." He would spontaneously drive to the seaside for a day or two to simply relax and be by himself. This ability to ensure renewal had saved him from burnout. It was the time out that always brought his passion for his profession back. Could this be a hidden key to the challenges ahead of him?

....

Tina, Nadeem, and Mike chose different ways of using the Compass to observe and understand their personal pattern of competencies in interaction. They drew their conclusions in different ways, yet all worked in a mode of appreciative analysis. It gave them a chance to explore development areas while at the same time acknowledging strengths. All of them noticed that the challenge ahead turned out to be a next level of learning how to become more whole, more versatile in leading in the different dimensions. And yes, the assessment was also a test of their habitual ways of being. They saw a need to shift the pattern in order to master the leadership challenges ahead of them. How did they deal with finding the next steps?

Finding the Focus and Getting into Action

It's important to remember that finding our focus precedes action. Otherwise we become overwhelmed by to-do lists that are too long. We need to identify the entry points for shifting our pattern of competencies enough to address our collaborative leadership challenges. We can adjust our pattern—bit by bit—and see if we can find a pattern that works better. Overall, though, the goal is find a way to master our sustainability task, become better at leading co-creative change, and deliver against expectations—our own and those of others. If our pattern is more balanced, we are more likely to influence the pattern of a system of collaborative actors in a positive way. This empowers us to contribute a little more to changing the world and making it a better place.

My experience is that focus needs to be in relation to the task at hand. Human hearts and minds work best together if they are confronted with a concrete task, or if there is an urgent matter requiring attention. If there had not been an urgent challenge ahead, Tina would not have agreed that goal setting and focusing could take her forward, Nadeem would have continued avoiding operational management issues, and Mike would have continued to assume that he could deliver results in the same way he had in the past. Looking at the Compass is a way of acknowledging the status quo, while opening up to building strategies on strengths and also nurturing development areas. Let's see what our leaders chose to focus on and how they planned their next steps.

Tina: Taking a Dream into Reality

Tina's most difficult task was to say in one sentence what she saw as her current leadership challenge. As a creative innovator she loved entertaining ideas but rarely put them on paper or even thought about what the concrete challenges were in making them reality. She rephrased her current challenge several times until it finally read: *Building my own confidence in creating a university-student mentoring movement to help educationally disadvantaged children, and engaging a critical mass of mentors and supporters.*

To Tina, this challenge statement sounded uninspiring, but she decided it was good enough for finding her focus. How would her strong areas support this? She did not have problems taking risks, and ideas of how to grow such a movement bubbled up in her head. She began to take notes so that no idea would get lost. She also saw that her own story of dropping out of school but finding the way back—a personal history that she thought she needed to hide—suddenly became an asset because it was a lively illustration of what mentoring could achieve. That's why she decided to write down her story. For the first time in her life she realized that her own story could make a difference to others. Doing so was both encouraging and frightening. It was encouraging because the chance to implement a dream—one of *her* dreams—opened a pathway to actually do something meaningful and practical with her strong area of *empathy*. It was frightening because she sensed the obligation that would come with taking a dream into reality.

That's when she thought about how her development areas—FUTURE POSSIBILITIES, ENGAGEMENT, and COLLECTIVE INTELLIGENCE—would affect the challenges ahead. It was clear to her that she needed to increase her ability to set an achievable goal, take implementation steps, and have the *decisiveness* to follow through. Taking a dream into reality requires patience and persistence. When Tina considered how strengthening her development areas could actually help her, she immediately thought about two aspects. One belonged to COLLECTIVE INTELLIGENCE: Whom could she ask for recommendations on how to go about building such a movement? The second aspect belonged to ENGAGEMENT, more specifically to *collective action*: How could she use the experience of ten mentors as a testing ground to learn from? She wrote down the following as a result of her focusing exercise.

On strengthening her strengths:

- **Innovation/Humanity.** Take a risk, go for my dream, get going, it is okay to fail, but follow my heart.
- **Humanity (Mindfulness).** Writing down my story helps me understand how the mentoring process has an impact.

On nurturing her development areas:

- **Future Possibilities (Future Orientation).** Don't make goal setting too boring, visualize how a mentoring movement could look a year from now: Who would be involved? Who would benefit?
- **Engagement (Collective Action).** Get into action, gather fellow students again, invite them to a meeting on my dream via Facebook, get ten volunteers to test a mentoring role in the next three months.
- **Collective Intelligence (Iterative Learning).** Speak to people (including my professors, friends, relatives), ask for advice: What did they think about how I could build a movement? Ask them if they could refer me to others who would know. (Addition: Maybe also get ideas via Facebook.)

Tina now had her starting points clarified and her next steps decided. As part of her attempt to strengthen her *decisiveness* she translated the focus areas into a short written action plan (showing meetings and time frames) and set a period of three months for implementation, after which she would review the action plan.

Nadeem: Getting People to Speak a Common Language

When Nadeem pondered the results from the stakeholder interviews, he still felt overwhelmed by the task of aligning the almost contradictory expectations. With COLLECTIVE INTELLIGENCE being his strong dimension he had, as a facilitator, many times helped people find common ground, listened to different expectations, and reconciled conflicting interests. His dilemma was that he was no longer in a neutral facilitator role, but had accepted a management post with clear delivery expectations. It took him several rephrasing attempts to formulate his current leadership challenge. He finally settled on: *Expanding my management capacity to really lead this*

project to success and create a joint understanding and collective commit-
ment of all partners to execute this project with tangible benefits to farmers.

He made a note that "all partners" did not include only the implementing agencies, but all stakeholders—the foundation, the private sector
companies involved, the government partners, and also the farmers cooperatives. It was clear that in strengthening his strength he needed to use
his knowledge of large-group facilitation to get this fragmented system of
actors aligned and genuinely caring about a complementary approach and
high-quality delivery. The project had developed overall plans, as did each
implementing partner, but the challenge of five countries, three languages,
and a frighteningly wide range of important issues could not be tamed
by project plans and milestones alone. There was nothing wrong with the
project plans, yet they seemed to create a bureaucratic attitude. In addition,
the private sector partners did not bother to review the detailed planning
documents; they wanted short summarized PowerPoint presentations,
particularly when it came to reporting.

Nadeem had expected that everybody was as passionate as he was about
the farmers, but he learned that this was not the case. He detected a lack
of enthusiasm; even worse, he overheard some cynical remarks about the
impossibility of really helping small-scale African farmers. Some people
assumed that despite their efforts market trends would favor large-scale
and technology-intensive farming. For the private sector partners as well
as the foundation the solution was simple: It was about teaching farmers
business practices, helping them make technical advances, and getting
them financing. The agencies, however, frequently complained that the
speed of change expected was just not how development in rural areas in
Africa happened. Nadeem sensed a potential conflict building up.

With the Compass as a guide he wanted to create a culture of collective leadership among all stakeholders that included trust, commitment,
passion, and the willingness to deliver impact. The culture would be built
on iterative learning characterized by openness of all partners to adjust
plans and strategies as they learned from the first pilots. His insights
from evaluating the expectations of stakeholders was clear: In his next
leadership moves he needed to respond to the expectations by addressing
all aspects of the Compass. At the same time he needed to find a way of
helping each stakeholder step out of a narrow view of the challenge to see
the larger picture.

That's why he decided that the starting point would be COLLECTIVE INTELLIGENCE—getting people into a joint meeting—and WHOLENESS, so that everybody saw the larger picture and understood the differences in expectations. He set a date and invited everybody to a strategy review jointly prepared by the implementing agencies, whose representatives arrived a day earlier than others. The rest joined for an informal evening gathering, and the next day the whole group participated in a one-day exposure trip to farms. A one-day joint review meeting followed. Nadeem decided to take a holistic approach to his intervention plan and kept track of all the dimensions of the Compass by using a planning table, shown in table 7 below, deliberately starting with his development areas.

Table 7. Nadeem's Interventions for Each Dimension

Dimension	Interventions
INNOVATION	*Excellence.* For my personal learning: Benchmark two other projects with similarly complex challenges—how do they handle (1) measurements of success; (2) different stakeholder expectations.
ENGAGEMENT	*Process Quality.* Get a good facilitator for the strategy review (not me!), have him conduct interviews with all stakeholders before, prepare a road map for regular meetings to be agreed upon by all. *Collective Action.* Make sure people experience achieving a result jointly—could this be an agreement on key performance indicators?
FUTURE POSSIBILITIES	*Future Orientation.* Set a clear goal—in a year's time I want this project to score high on collective leadership in all dimensions. *Empowerment.* Have an in-depth conversation with each implementing agency about the feasibility of their plans and the synergy effects they see between agencies. Inquire into what they consider important for management, review functioning of management structure, and suggest improvements. *Decisiveness.* Be decisive on quality improvement of the reports, no compromises; withhold finances until the reports are okay. Get an expert in to get me up to speed on key performance indicators for a development project.
COLLECTIVE INTELLIGENCE	*Dialogic Quality.* Thoroughly pre-plan the strategy review with the external facilitator, make sure there is a good balance between listening and tangible results.
HUMANITY	*Empathy.* Make sure the strategy review has an informal side event; people really need to get to know one another as people. They need to reconnect with the purpose of the project.
WHOLENESS	*Contextuality.* Organize exposure trip to farmers particularly for private sector partners—they need to see the reality for farmers.

Two months later the strategy review had taken place. Preparations had some obstacles—two implementing agencies announced that they would not be able to attend. But Nadeem remembered his development areas (*decisiveness*) and insisted on attendance of all. The exposure trip was well received but the private sector partners did not understand why they should come earlier for an informal evening event. Again he insisted—in a friendly but firm way—and it paid off. People started the strategy review after sharing personal stories the evening before. They also spent a day on an exposure trip together that reminded them of the purpose of the project. The stories reduced the tension created by differences in expectations. Letting the external facilitator have pre-conversations with all participants turned out to be a brilliant move. Not only did it help Nadeem see the entire picture, but it also functioned as a complaint window—people could talk to the facilitator about what bothered them.

Overall Nadeem was pleased with the constructive atmosphere— entirely different from the report-back meetings he'd held earlier with the implementing agencies and the calls he'd had with the foundation and private sector partners. The exposure trip did the job: It brought reality back into the meeting room and enhanced the alignment around what the project was all about. But the most surprising result was that one of the private sector partners suggested rephrasing the complex project document into five catchy short objectives that everybody could remember and repeat in conversations with outsiders. The implementing agencies first laughed but then took up the idea—and actually liked it—as a basis for matching key performance indicators. They did not agree on key performance indicators at this meeting, but set up a small task force composed of private sector and implementing agency people that would suggest adequate, simple-to-measure indicators within two weeks of the meeting.

For the first time Nadeem felt relaxed. He considered the meeting a good start at how he wanted to run the project. He achieved a better alignment among the implementing agencies, and among them, the foundation, and the private sector. As a very accommodating person his biggest lesson was that having the courage to decide how to run the strategy was absolutely the right move. It was well accepted and he was seen as a leader. But one open question stayed with him: What was the role of the government representatives? Did they really take on this project as their own?

Mike: Reviving the Passion to Serve

It was a conversation over lunch that finally convinced Mike to tell his CFO to calculate the risk of *not* embarking on a sustainable supply-chain route for TrendWear. But he insisted the sustainability department be involved. He wanted the results on his desk three weeks before the management retreat that was to happen in six weeks' time. When he received an email the next day that the head of sustainability had met with the head of purchasing—the only woman at the top management level—he was pleased to see that the new dynamic had already borne fruit. The two department heads had suggested to the CFO that they conduct an internal study on the cost-cutting possibilities in TrendWear's supply-chain management while doing the risk assessment. This time the focus was not on increasing the margin—it was on how to hold the margin steady if TrendWear paid a higher price for their textile products to Asian suppliers.

The results of the study would be crucial: Would a price increase at the supplier level affect TrendWear's shop prices in Europe, or was there a chance to avoid the retail price rise and preserve the margin by increasing productivity and logistics efficiency? Mike knew that preserving the margin would be a prerequisite for asking the suppliers to increase wages to their workers, invest in building safety, ensure occupational health and safety, and undergo management training—essentially an audit that could qualify them as fair suppliers. He also knew the Fair Trade terms would mean reducing the number of strategic suppliers and building more long-term relationships with them.

Mike felt in a good mood when his fifteen-year-old daughter came to stay with him over the weekend (which happened only every two months). He was prepared for trouble, as he knew his daughter had been oppositional lately, but he did not expect a straightforward attack. They spend the weekend arguing. She had seen a documentary about garment factories in Bangladesh and explained to him that she had decided to tell all her friends to not buy from TrendWear anymore, because who wanted to be seen with clothes that had been produced under horrible working conditions? Mike was not only furious, but really down.

His daughter, like him, was upfront and straight. She wanted to know if he had any evidence that TrendWear's textile products were produced under fair labor conditions—with full traceability of all accessories. He loved challenges, but this was tough. Late that evening he went back to the Collective Leadership Compass and without any hesitation wrote down his leadership challenge in one sentence: *Turning TrendWear into a brand that my daughter will happily recommend to her friends while ensuring top financial performance and a yearly staff survey that shows a high identification with the company.* He wrote an email to his daughter saying that she should give him some time; he would get her the evidence. He grumbled to himself that he had never thought a daughter would become more painstaking than a board. Before the weekend he had felt he was on a good track, but now he realized the urgency of the matter even more.

His financial instincts had told him already what the study would show: that without a price increase for consumers, TrendWear would not be able to pay higher prices to suppliers. Yet higher consumer prices would impact their market position and severely endanger the company's financial performance. Mike decided to get the data and focus on next achievable steps—relying on his strength: FUTURE POSSIBILITIES. But he was an innovator and solution finder, so ideas were already popping up; he jotted some of them down in his notebook. He would ask the sustainability department to find out whether TrendWear should join the Fair Labor Association. He wanted pros and cons, and a decision-making proposal. Regarding consumer prices, he only saw two options. One was to link the price increase with turning TrendWear into a sustainability brand, a close-to-impossible task in the short term and the current market environment. The other was to collaborate with competitors who would informally agree on a price increase across the industry—a move that would be very suspicious to the antitrust authorities and equally impossible in the short term.

Mike noticed his warrior nature: The harder it was to identify immediate solutions or make quick decisions, the more driven he became. He decided to take a step-by-step approach, calm himself down, and look at the Compass. How would he plan his actions for the coming weeks by strengthening his strength and nurturing (he battled with this term) his development areas? Mike's mind loved questions. That's why he phrased some thoughts into questions when outlining his intervention strategy, shown in table 8.

Mike had never worked with a written-up personal action plan; he always had his priorities in his mind. But he printed the write-up of the six dimensions and put it on his desk as a reminder—just in case he started

Table 8. Mike's Intervention Strategy

Dimension	Interventions (6-Week Time Frame)
FUTURE POSSIBILITIES	Don't embark on a new vision/mission statement for TrendWear, but check how far we can integrate sustainability into the existing; wait for the risk report from CFO, then discuss with him how we can integrate sustainability issues into our controlling system.
WHOLENESS	I personally need to understand more about the system's dynamic in the "race to the bottom" for supplier prices, also need to check what informal information I can get on how other companies deal with the issue. Get the sustainability department involved—create a task force.
INNOVATION	Task the head of purchasing to find expertise, someone who knows about responsible supply-chain management in depth. Get the expert to give a presentation at management retreat.
COLLECTIVE INTELLIGENCE	Need to install a culture of iterative learning at top management level. How can I get all of us to work with the Compass? Just noticed that I never cared much about who would facilitate the retreat. Talk to human resources and get a top facilitator.
ENGAGEMENT	Whether it's my strength or not—we need a serious cultural change at TrendWear. I need to engage the top management in my vision of TrendWear as sustainability brand. Who could help me with that?
HUMANITY	Three different thoughts: **Empathy.** Staff of 5,000 at TrendWear. Do they care about responsible products? What do I know about what they think? **Balance.** My strong point in the development area. Here is a courageous thought: Can we reinvent measurement and include all dimensions of the Compass into our balanced scorecard? How would this include sustainability issues? Keep this thought in the background; don't act now. Evaluate results from risk assessment and margin study first; see under future possibilities. **Mindfulness.** I think my life would be easier if we jointly worked with the Collective Leadership Compass at the top management level. Get everybody to do the online assessment and reserve 1½ hours for reflection and discussion.

to become the quick solution finder and troubleshooter again. He actually started enjoying the adventure, and invited his daughter to join him for a weekend trip to the seaside before the management retreat. It would be good to see her more often anyway, he thought. The human resource department was totally surprised when Mike approached them personally insisting that he needed a top facilitator for the retreat who was familiar with the Collective Leadership Compass, and that he would directly get involved in preparing the management retreat. Would his top team be open to working with the Compass?

Chapter 10

Empowering Action Groups

The fact that we make the future together seems so self-evident that we almost forget about it. Have you ever read case studies about successful collaboration initiatives? Those I read typically don't talk about the people involved. The story seems to take place as if human beings were not around. It is all about institutions, tools and instruments, agreements, plans, and measurable results. None of those pieces is unimportant, but the most important one is the people. What they do and don't do, how they think and feel, how they work together, how they communicate with one another. Is this so self-evident that it disappears from view? It's about time that we make the collaboration among people more conscious, more fruitful, and easier to achieve. We also need to make it more predictable and more successful in an understandable way. So to quote Margaret Mead again, how does a "small group of thoughtful committed citizens" form, and how does that group "change the world" together?

Collaboration for sustainability requires well-functioning groups of people who lead collectively—be they management teams, project teams, core groups, committees, partnership teams, task forces, working groups, or a leaders network. They exist within one organization, or across organizations. They can be composed as cross-sector groups—with representatives from civil society, public sector, and private sector. They may have a hierarchy, or may not. People in these groups have differences in power, experience, education, and culture. They may have language barriers. This is all part of our sustainability endeavor. Luckily, we are diverse, and this is the key prerequisite for success in collaborative sustainability initiatives. For all these different groups, can we find common features that make them successful?

These are the ten features that I have observed in well-functioning teams in collaboration initiatives:

1. There was an *urgent case for change* and it was clear to everybody.
2. People were dedicated to and *emotionally engaged with a goal,* even if they differed in *how* to bring about the change.
3. Whether hierarchy existed within the group or not, the atmosphere was *non-hierarchical.*
4. People were prepared to take on *diverse leadership roles,* from engagement to advocacy, from pushing through plans to tediously monitoring implementation, from backstage diplomacy to facilitation and brokering—whatever worked best.
5. People learned to *understand one another's languages,* to be open to differences in institutional cultures, organizational procedures, communication experiences, and personalities.
6. People were willing to *hold the change process* collectively, carry the goal forward, and step in for one another—through phases of success as much as through phases of conflicts, doubts, mistrust, or failure.
7. There was an attitude of *openness to learning* that everybody shared.
8. People were willing to *embrace the complexity* of the task and move forward step by step.
9. *Value contribution* was more important than ego gratification.
10. The collaboration goal was seen in a *larger context* of contributing to sustainability.

If these ten features are present, success is almost guaranteed. The group has become a good container for change—a home from which the change initiative can grow into the world, gradually building a larger community for change. Paying attention to the six dimensions of the Collective Leadership Compass helps build good containers.[1] If this is not the job of only one individual, but is seen as a collective task, then everybody becomes a guardian of the quality of interaction. Each member of the committed group will feel responsible to create a pattern of human competencies in interaction that works.

The same steps we reviewed for enhancing our leadership competency can help us work with collaborating groups of people. It is important to *observe* the existing pattern of dimensions and appreciate what is present, assess what is missing, and evaluate the situation collectively. *Focusing* builds on the strength of the group, shifts the development areas, and discovers a starting point for better co-creation. This leads to more consciously *enacting* the dimensions of the Collective Leadership Compass. We integrate the dimensions into action plans, test them in the real world, observe how the pattern changes, and review the results.

Observing the Pattern of Collaboration

Let's take a look at how two of our fellow travelers started building good containers for change.

Mike's intention was to align his top management team behind a profound change at TrendWear that would lead to responsible supply-chain management.

Celine had an even bigger challenge: She needed to find out who, within her water committee or outside of it, would really be committed to improving the water situation in the DRC.

Mike: Confronting Reality

Mike decided to start the change at TrendWear by changing the culture of interaction within the top team. It was clear that the change he envisioned would feel to the top managers like something he'd simply decided and then required them to enact in the rest of the company. They were used to fixing problems, shifting procedures or workflows, and setting up new targets. But having risen in the company based on their ability to tackle clear-boundaried assignments alone, they would face a new challenge in making things happen jointly.

How could Mike expect TrendWear to change unless the top management team learned to understand the challenge and work together in a different way? Mike knew it would not be easy, but this had been one of his major insights from the Collective Leadership Compass. If he wanted to change how TrendWear operated in the supply chain, he needed to first change how TrendWear operated within. And the top team was a good starting point. He invited the top managers to a day-and-a-half management retreat and announced (1) that he wanted everybody to stay overnight, and (2) that he would inform them about preparatory work to be completed (in addition to the short reports on current status and key performance indicators that everybody prepared anyway).

He felt well on track when the external facilitator phoned for a preparatory call. After a short check-in, the facilitator raised the question of desired outcomes. "Let's say this retreat goes really well, everybody is happy. Can you summarize in three bullet points what will be different after the event—one for results, one for relationships, one for process?" Mike immediately said: "Number one is: Everybody supports my agenda for change." He struggled with clarifying the two others, but the facilitator insisted on an answer. "We acknowledge our complementary competencies to master the challenge," he eventually added as the second. The third was: "The team is prepared to venture into a learning journey with action and joint reflection."

To Mike's surprise the facilitator suggested that he work toward these goals right away—almost six weeks before the retreat. She asked to have a preparatory call with each top manager to get a sense of where they stood. She also recommended that Mike have bilateral meetings beforehand with each top manager. Before he could begin to argue that, with the current travel schedule, this would not work out, she reminded him that this was where he could plant the seeds for success and make the most of the day and a half. "Get into relationship building, talk about your vision for TrendWear, let them contribute. Humanity counts," she reminded him. She also asked him to do the online team assessment of the Collective Leadership Compass and invited him to let each manager fill in the individual assessment and send her the results.[2] It was too early to let everybody do the team assessment, she advised; this would best be done just before the retreat. They set up a call to evaluate the results of his own team assessment and his colleagues' individual assessments and pre-plan the retreat. Mike loved her decisiveness, yet he had to chew on the results from the team assessment (his perspective) for a while. Table 9 shows how he described the team.

The most interesting part of Mike's preparation was the bilateral meetings he had, some of them over the phone to Asia. Where he could, though, he carefully chose the environment for the meeting—a lunch in town, a late-afternoon walk, or a meeting in his office. For the first time, he enjoyed thinking what would best fit the person he wanted to meet. He just asked questions and listened. He learned from the facilitator that the ratio should be about two to one in favor of asking questions and listening over talking. He realized the meetings enhanced his competency for COLLECTIVE INTELLI-GENCE—*dialogic quality*. In a trusting atmosphere the managers opened up to real conversations. Even though Mike always started more formally by asking

Table 9. Mike's Initial Team Assessment

Dimension	Comments
FUTURE POSSIBILITIES (75%)	Generally, the performance of the top team is task-oriented and people deliver according to targets. I know I can rely on them. But what future possibilities are we not seeing as a team? Has our strongly territorial and competitive culture become an impediment?
ENGAGEMENT (77%)	I feel people are engaged, but the internal collaboration could improve. Delivering results is TrendWear's culture and I want to keep it like that, but do we see our efforts as joint success? Are we really acting as a team?
INNOVATION (60%)	That's too low for what lies ahead of us. Instead of risk taking we have a culture of risk management. That's necessary, but what can I do to get the passion for change revived? There are some unknown territories that we need to venture into!
HUMANITY (33%)	I admit, as a team we hardly know about one another's personal lives— or is it only me who does not know? Awareness of how we interact is close to zero, I suppose.
COLLECTIVE INTELLIGENCE (32%)	Shocking results and time to change. Can we learn to think together and build on our different strengths? I thought iterative learning was well set up, but it obviously needs improvement. Will make a note to suggest a procedure.
WHOLENESS (17%)	Shocking result, can hardly believe that, but to me the reason is clear: We might be good at knowing trends and market developments, but possibly narrow it down to what is immediately relevant for business. Mutual support is not our culture (we tend to be all lonesome fixers). And contribution to sustainability? That's what this journey is about, I guess we are at the beginning.

them what future trends they saw as critical for TrendWear, the conversation went on to what each manager's passion was, and how their families coped or did not cope with the workload. Only toward the end of each meeting did he explain his vision—turning TrendWear into a company his daughter would readily recommend to her friends. This often produced laughter. He asked the managers to take this question with them: *Could you think what steps will take us there—and have them ready for the management retreat?*

Celine: Identifying a Core Group for Change

The fragmentation of water governance structures in the DRC was a major obstacle for Celine. There was no single water ministry, a situation she knew from other countries, but it meant responsibilities were distributed among a number of different institutions with little incentive for cooperation. Five distinct ministries shared responsibility for different aspects of water management, making her work in the water coordinating committee difficult. The two main players were the Planning Ministry, responsible for the new drinking water policy, and the Ministry of Water Supply and Energy. Three other ministries—the Ministry for Environment, for Rural Development, and for Public Health—had influence on the supply system of drinking water. In addition, public service provisions would only have an impact if they were taken from the national center to the regional and local level for implementation.

The new DRC constitution mandated that each provincial government provide drinking water for its inhabitants. Engaging the important players would mean constantly involving new stakeholders in the process. The priority was on creating harmonization mechanisms between the national and provincial levels, but implementation on the national level also required better coordination and alignment of efforts.

When Celine started to talk with different stakeholders in Kinshasa and two provinces about what they thought the route to success would be for creating safe and reliable drinking water in the DRC, one feature was frighteningly obvious: Every person discounted and belittled the approach of other institutions, often making a cynical remark about the impossibility of the task. In colonial times the Congo had a well-functioning water authority, but that had disintegrated. Attempts to privatize and sell it to foreign companies had failed. Progress in drinking water supply was almost entirely in the hands of various development organizations that did not cooperate smoothly. Celine realized that her task as head of the coordinating committee for water issues required her to do a lot of work—but she had no power. In addition, people complained that her committee was not functioning well.

Her diagnosis was clear: All the right structures were in place, but the fact that the responsibility for water was distributed among five ministries made coordinated implementation difficult. Yet Celine thought it was not impossible. With good communication structures in place it could work, but three important factors were missing: (1) actors aligned behind the new policy for drinking water, (2) coordinated implementation of the policy among civil society, private sector, and the development agencies, and (3) a shared understanding that success could only be achieved jointly.

When she reviewed the Collective Leadership Compass for herself, she clearly identified that her strength would support her strategic effort to change the situation; goal setting and *decisiveness* were second nature to her. When she had started to talk to different stakeholders, she wanted to get a true overview of existing activities and approaches—showing her love for WHOLENESS—*contextuality*. The real challenge was to align the different actors behind coordinated implementation of the drinking water policy. She knew that structured ENGAGEMENT and harvesting COLLECTIVE INTELLIGENCE were needed, but those were her development areas.

When she conducted her stakeholder interviews, she asked engaging questions—those that inspired people to think, tune into a better future, see things from a different perspective—rather than asking content questions. She got better with every conversation she had. Her inquiry style paid off—people stayed connected with her, offering more ideas in follow-up emails after the interviews, and she felt that her entire exercise was already part of improving relationships. But how could she convince the public sector to be open to collaborating with civil society and the private sector? How could she get the competitive development agencies to align behind her strategy?

What she had taken from the stakeholder engagement course was simple, yet not easy to achieve. The essential tools were in her development areas—COLLECTIVE INTELLIGENCE and ENGAGEMENT. She defined her leadership challenge in the following sentence: *Building a committed cross-sector group that jointly leads the establishment of a cross-sector dialogue platform for the implementation of the drinking water policy.*

Table 10 shows the plan she came up with.

Celine set herself a period of two months to get a core group together that would support her approach. Her focus point was to design an engagement strategy. As a first step, she convinced her colleague on the committee that this would be the sole route to success. They did a stakeholder mapping together, looking at all actors active in the water sector in the DRC. Because this was overwhelming, they did a deeper analysis by evaluating interest and influence. The first people to target would be those with high interest in really delivering around the drinking water policy and the power to act—even if they currently worked in competition. The result was shocking—they concluded that only two of the responsible ministries were really interested in implementing the drinking water policy. The other three had too many other issues to address. The committee needed to find a way of raising their interest. Two NGOs were actually doing good work on the ground, yet were not very influential; could the committee bring

Table 10. Celine's Plan for Building a Committed Group

Dimension	Insight and steps
ENGAGEMENT	**Insight.** Although formal structures are in place they are not strong enough to deliver water infrastructure. Reality is that most of the actual delivery is done by development agencies. This is not sustainable! There is a lack of ownership on the public side. Important to appreciate: All actors are actually somehow connected—there is already an invisible network. Can we make it more explicit and build on it? **Steps.** I need to find a group of committed actors beyond the public sector and beyond the water committee (including private sector, civil society, and development agencies). I actually have brilliant informal networks that I could revive. Need to be clear on the strategy.
COLLECTIVE INTELLIGENCE	**Insight.** The different ministries do not really talk with each other; despite our committee's work the approaches to water management are fragmented. Iterative learning is nearly absent. Everybody is driving his or her own agenda. The potential of private sector contributions is not tapped at all. On the plus side: Could we create a potential out of the fact that there are many different strategies to water management? **Steps.** My ideal is to set up a dialogue platform that comes together on a regular basis discussing implementation and reviewing progress (this needs to include all relevant actors!).
WHOLENESS	**Insight.** I wonder if any of the actors has an overview of who is doing what in water in the DRC—I certainly don't have it. **Steps.** Get the complete picture. Map stakeholders including an analysis of their interest and their influence.
HUMANITY	**Insight.** I need to make an inner shift here. This is not only about professionally managing my task; it is about reviving the passion for water in the people I speak to. **Steps.** When I talk to people, get them out of their cynical mode by asking them to give me at least one example where drinking water implementation actually worked!
FUTURE POSSIBILITIES	**Insight.** My goal is clear, I want to see the drinking water policy implemented and see how people benefit, both in Kinshasa and in at least two provinces for a start. On the plus side: There are lots of project plans in place from different actors—is there a way of building on them and aligning them into one road map? Also: I know there are people who are not cynical about our country, but thinking in future possibilities, how can I find them? **Steps.** Not sure yet.
INNOVATION	**Insight.** What we need to do is overcome territorial boundaries. The real innovation here is not about technology; it is about getting people to talk with one another in a fruitful way that leads to better implementation. **Steps.** I need to convince five influential people who will support me in this approach.

them on board so that that they would have more power? And would the public sector actors be interested in talking with NGOs?

The next task was even more difficult: assessing the people inside the institutions. Who would be the change makers in the institutions they had identified? This is where Celine's networks paid off as well as the conversations she'd had with different actors. In the triangle of interest, influence, and potential change makers, she identified seven people to approach as an initial core group. What would be the best strategy to engage them?

Finding the Entry Point for Better Co-Creation

Finding the entry point for better co-creation in team collaboration happens once we have identified the current pattern (this can include a stakeholder analysis, and context and conflict mapping) and decided which of the dimensions to focus on when taking action. This does not mean we are neglecting other dimensions of the Compass; it means we take steps to rebalance interaction. Most often this means that we focus on what we need to bring in, because a certain dimension is missing or undervalued. But it can also mean that we first strengthen what we have identified as strong in the pattern of a team.

Mike wanted to build on the strengths of his top team—delivery of results, accountability, and commitment to success. He wanted to gradually enhance all other dimensions—bringing in HUMANITY by seeing the people behind the tasks, improving the way they communicated with one another, and encouraging open exchange of challenges rather than only demanding success reports (COLLECTIVE INTELLIGENCE). His intention was to get people to see the relevance of sustainability trends for TrendWear (WHOLENESS) and to inspire them to join him on an adventurous journey in changing TrendWear into a more responsible company (INNOVATION—*agility*/WHOLENESS—*contribution*).

Celine's action focus was on what was missing: structured ENGAGEMENT and getting as many actors as possible to see the entire picture. Her first step was to engage a core group for joint water action and gradually build a dialogue platform that could function as a network of committed actors to support coordinated implementation, best practice reviews, *iterative learning*, and *mutual support*.

Mike: Rallying a Team for a More Responsible Future

A few weeks before the management retreat Mike met the facilitator in person. They had one hour to talk about (1) the summary results from the individual assessments, (2) Mike's assessment of the team, and (3) the content and structure of the retreat. The facilitator explained to him that—not surprisingly—across all members, the team had a strong bias in FUTURE POSSIBILITIES. Analyzing in more detail, she found that in the strong dimension of FUTURE POSSIBILITIES, *empowerment* was weak, which hinted at a non-collaborative culture, while in the weak dimension of HUMANITY, *empathy* was relatively strong. "I think we should go for a team assessment by all now," she advised, "and discuss the results. This is the conversation we need to have, and it will increase your chances to build the new strategy on the premise of collective leadership."

Mike was curious. Would the team assessment results resemble his assessment or be entirely different? He agreed to set aside an hour and a half during the retreat for reflection on the Compass—almost a revolution, he thought, as this team had never done such a thing. The facilitator reminded Mike that he needed to set the frame for his intention to change the company right at the beginning, and because *empowerment* was so weak across the team, he needed to step in and be empowering, inspiring the team, telling his story, and relating why the goal of transforming TrendWear was so close to his heart.

This was far beyond Mike's comfort zone, and he agreed only half-heartedly. His suggestion was to bring these soft issues back to hard facts and remodel TrendWear's balanced scorecard so that it would resemble elements of the Collective Leadership Compass. The facilitator responded that this would be a great idea, but he should be patient. She was sure that the moment COLLECTIVE INTELLIGENCE found its way into the team interaction, somebody else would suggest this—that would create much more ownership. Table 11 outlines their plan for the retreat.

Mike was ambivalent before the retreat, with no idea if it would work. He had never given so much attention to the details of a meeting procedure. What happened? People arrived in a skeptical mood, but the dinner and drinks helped them loosen up and get more private conversations going. Mike had overheard the occasional joking remark about the retreat and the individual and team assessment in particular.

Table 11. The TrendWear Retreat Plan

Dimension (Aspects)	Intervention Points to Ensure Enhanced Team Collaboration
HUMANITY (*empathy*)	Let people arrive the evening before for a joint dinner, then design a short session as a "check-in" where people can drop their mental luggage by talking about what are the most pressing issues at the moment.
FUTURE POSSIBILITIES (*future orientation/ empowerment*)	Clear framing by Mike: What is different and why? What is his intention and why is it so important to him? What is the challenge ahead?
WHOLENESS	Data presentation on risk assessment of non-sustainable supply-chain management and discussion; urgency of action. Presentation of results from study on profit margins. Would it be affected if TrendWear paid higher prices to suppliers? Seeing the broader picture: Can we turn risk management into making a better contribution?
INNOVATION / COLLECTIVE INTELLIGENCE	Thinking the impossible: Can we turn TrendWear into a socially and environmentally responsible company? How could this increase our success? Open dialogue.
INNOVATION (*excellence*) / FUTURE POSSIBILITIES (*decisiveness*)	Presentation by expert—key elements of sustainable supply-chain management, discussion of implementation possibilities for TrendWear, strategic conclusions.
HUMANITY (*mindfulness*)	If this is the route to take, how can we get there by leading collectively? What can we keep? What needs to change? Review of team assessment.
HUMANITY (*empathy*)	What do we know about how our staff think about our future? How can we engage staff into the new vision?
ENGAGEMENT (*process quality, collective action*)	Next steps planning, allocation of responsibilities, agreement on cornerstones for staff engagement, agreement on date for next meeting, summary of results.
HUMANITY (*empathy, mindfulness*)	Open reflection on results and process of retreat.

The atmosphere shifted after his introductory remarks. At first, it was only the head of purchasing (the only woman in the room) that stepped in to say that she was glad to get the support she had always wished for. For the first time she openly admitted that the issue of supplier working conditions had been bothering her and that there must be a solution, although the results from the study clearly showed that if TrendWear stayed in the current price range the margin would be endangered. A lively debate started between the head of sustainability, the CFO, and the head of purchasing— all supporting a hypothesis that there must be a solution even if it meant finding an industry-wide approach. The head of purchasing insisted that TrendWear should first do its internal homework. Action steps were listed.

When the discussion on the results from the team assessment around the Collective Leadership Compass started, it was clear that this was an unusual conversation. People stayed reserved until the head of sustainability openly admitted that he was relieved to be given permission to be human at work, to consider more than facts and figures, and to actually consciously integrate soft and hard aspects into planning results. Two other managers announced they would use the Compass in their departments.

The most surprising result was that the head of marketing suddenly suggested they should summarize the new strategy in something easily understandable and emotionally engaging. Even though addressing supplier working conditions seemed difficult to change, in the end wouldn't they want people who bought clothes at TrendWear to know that the company supported decent living conditions in Asia? "At TrendWear we align our success with our contribution to fairness" was the motto he suggested for internal communication on the envisioned change process. Mike was pleased (and not surprised) when the CFO suggested that they needed to rewrite the balanced scorecard so that it would capture the new strategy.

Mike cherished the atmosphere of fun and the sense of a new beginning. The list of agreed next steps was long, but he felt that each of the top team members would shoulder the bundle and walk the path jointly. He smiled when he thought about how to report back on this first milestone to his daughter. And the board? With an aligned top team he was sure that he would get them behind the new strategy, even though facts and figures would count in the end.

Celine: Getting People to Meet in a Collaborative Space

Celine had a definite plan. She wanted to set up the cross-sector core group for coordinated water management within two months, and see a dialogue platform-launching meeting within at most five or six months. This time schedule tested her patience, but she had learned that simply inviting people to a platform would not create the ENGAGEMENT in terms of commitment and ownership that she needed to make it a success. She needed to build it step by step and ensure that as many dimensions of the Collective Leadership Compass as possible would be taken into account.

In order to ensure *process quality* (ENGAGEMENT), she defined her action plan by three typical ENGAGEMENT steps and related them to the Compass, as shown in table 12.[3]

What happened? Celine decided to focus on the national level first. Getting different actors to join a core group was not an easy task. The misgivings toward any new approach were strong; some people had given up on improvement ideas. But she managed to get six out of the seven potential players to agree to joining a first meeting, to which she also invited the deputy minister of water supply and energy (a friend of a friend of hers,

Table 12. Celine's Action Plan for Engagement

Step	Action Points	Dimension (Aspect)
Creating resonance	Personal contact/meeting with potential members of core groups. Ensure appreciative, inspiring conversations about water situation. Find common ground for change; open up possibilities. Invite them to join a core group, ask them who else needs to support this.	FUTURE POSSIBILITIES (*empowerment*) COLLECTIVE INTELLIGENCE (*dialogic quality*) INNOVATION (*agility*) ENGAGEMENT (*connectivity*)
Understanding the context	Contract a study on who is who in water management in the DRC; get support from donor agency. Identify best practice example on water platforms from other countries. Complement this with conversations among key stakeholders; focus on possibilities. Explore openness of public sector decision makers to involving civil society and private sector into platform.	WHOLENESS (*contextuality*) INNOVATION (*excellence*) FUTURE POSSIBILITIES (*future orientation*) COLLECTIVE INTELLIGENCE (*diversity*)
Building a container for change	Invite interested actors to an initial core group meeting. Ideal outcome: jointly agreed process plan for establishment of dialogue platform. Ensure good environment, invite for lunch or dinner (get donor to sponsor). Ensure presence of high-level public sector people to show commitment for the dialogue platform. Carefully plan the agenda: Ensure people can meet as people, appreciate current activities, bring in results from context study and best practice benchmarking, jointly work on process road map and structure for dialogue platform.	ENGAGEMENT (*collective action*) HUMANITY (*mindfulness*) FUTURE POSSIBILITIES (*decisiveness*) HUMANITY (*empathy*) ENGAGEMENT (*collective action*) FUTURE POSSIBILITIES (*decisiveness*)

and an easygoing person). She had a bold objective: to get the group to agree on a road map for a dialogue platform.

Without the strong advocacy of the deputy minister, it probably would not have worked. Not all responsible ministries were present, and Celine knew she would face an additional engagement phase after the core group meeting, relying on a number of bilateral meetings lining up. But this first meeting went well. People started thinking about who else needed to get involved and how they could convince other actors to come on board. For the first time, Celine had the feeling that there was a spirit of possibilities in the room, a fraction of the dream she had for the DRC. If only people were able to set free the potentials of collaboration.

Once the atmosphere of the meeting became constructive (thanks to the outgoing personality and status of the deputy minister), they had an open discussion about the results from Celine's contracted context analysis. The analysis showed many implementation gaps, but also hinted at existing best practice examples. The conclusion had not been surprising. Several things were needed: better-enacted coordination, better integration of national and provincial plans, and, of course, strengthening the institutional environment. Most important, the study supported her gut feeling that aligning stakeholders was crucial because any steps toward success could only be reached through complementary actions.

For the first time, she felt it was easy to talk about next steps: a road map and a possible structure for the dialogue platform. Conflicts came up when it came to who should be invited. Not everybody wanted the private sector involved because of fear they would take advantage of the platform for their own businesses. When Celine saw that this was too hot an issue, she stepped back and suggested that this could be decided at a later stage. Once the platform was up and running the role of the private sector could be decided.

She was pleased with the results; creating the core group first and getting them to adopt her proposal for the dialogue platform had paid off. What really counted was that they had joined her in preparing the platform launch. Each of them would get their networks and constituencies involved, and they decided to meet regularly to properly prepare the launching event. Celine and her colleague went for a drink together to celebrate a successful adventure. But both knew that the bigger challenge was still ahead of them. Would the different stakeholders successfully engage in the launching of the bigger dialogue platform?

Chapter 11

Building Communities of Change Makers

For change to take root in institutions, companies, and networks, we need more than committed teams. We need people in various organizations or at various places who lead collectively toward a goal. These are the people who become the force for change in their departments, their organizations, their ministries, their countries. They engage people for sustainability standards in supply-chain management, create action networks around biodiversity, build social enterprises to address pressing societal issues, drive social cohesion, establish good governance mechanisms, campaign against dumping chemical waste in Africa, foster climate change adaptation for an entire region, implement sustainability strategies in companies, design fossil-free energy concepts, or offer socially disadvantaged people a new perspective.

When I interviewed thirty-two global collaboration practitioners from the private sector, the public sector, and civil society, I discovered that, in all successful examples, it was the joint capacity of leaders to become catalysts for collective responsibility that made the difference.[1] Personal passion was crucial, but did not automatically translate into more fruitful collective action unless people succeeded in building such communities of collaborative change makers. They applied three distinctive strategies across cultures, projects, topics, positions, and types of organizations:

1. Fostering trust-based co-creation.
2. Modeling evolutionary change processes.
3. Invigorating collaborative networks.

These strategies are in their essence engagement strategies for outcome-oriented stakeholder collaboration.

Fostering Trust-Based Co-Creation

Respect for difference seems to be the most crucial element in dealing with the challenge of multi-actor settings. Appreciating the dignity of another person or acknowledging a different worldview or an opposing opinion without necessarily agreeing fosters trust and unleashes a dynamic of contribution. In high-quality collaboration processes people open up, bringing in not only their expertise but also their connection to other experts. They start leveraging support. The value of taking things forward outweighs skepticism, criticism, and doubt. However, differences need to be explored and acknowledged before any investment in finding common ground, the better solution, or the breakthrough innovation. The intelligence that develops does not rest only on individual brilliance, but on a process of construction that requests diverse input. Yet if the goal of a change endeavor is not inspiring, people withhold their contribution. A common cause creates the feeling of being part of something larger, a community, a force for change. Sharing ideas, building on one another's competency, and moving things forward jointly opens gateways to innovation. Rethinking the way we do things is possible when trust has emerged.

The entry point for the trust-based co-creation strategy is humanity: mindfulness of difference and dynamics, balance between task and human encounter, empathy for the story that exists behind each person. Humanity values collective intelligence (dialogic quality of conversations and diversity of perspectives). Both dimensions enhance innovation (with people becoming more creative in a trustful environment) and wholeness (the willingness to engage and contribute increases). It becomes easier to move into future possibilities together and move the engagement toward collective action.

These are good practices in enhancing trust-based co-creation:

- Ensuring that people can listen to one another's differences in a structured way—to different points of view, approaches to solve a problem, or interpretations of a situation—acknowledging the inputs of all people involved.
- Helping people see the limiting effect of judgment and creating an atmosphere of building on one another's ideas, being transparent about disagreements but focusing on commonalities.

- Identifying the common cause and jointly clarifying the common goal, acknowledging if people differ in how to reach it.
- Attending to relationship building and backstage diplomacy when conflicts occur.
- Working on something tangible together, creating experiences of joint achievements, even if small.
- Seeing people not only as representatives of a group, an institution, or a party, but as human beings with all their strengths, shortcomings, and desire to make a difference.

Modeling Evolutionary Change Processes

Successful change initiatives build on step-by-step engagement. Plans are important; rigidity is not. The role of a caretaker is crucial—a person or group who carries the change process farther, regularly attends to engagement, and keeps the communication flowing. Combining flexibility and openness to adjustments with commitment and reliability seems to be the key to success. No engagement can be maintained without a larger and emotionally charged vision for change with which all actors identify.

Another aspect of successful initiatives is that they break down the vision into pathways that people can travel in their own area of expertise or responsibility. Engagement and commitment can only be maintained if people see tangible results. Contributing to an impact keeps people going.

The entry point for the modeling-evolutionary-change strategy is engagement and in particular process quality. Initiators take to heart the need to build very reliable change processes that start small and grow gradually. They often begin with a small group and create a good container before they include many more stakeholders. The members of the initial group become ambassadors for the change and empower and inspire others to join. This brings energy into a system of actors and invigorates future orientation—people begin to see future possibilities that may have been dormant before. With that, it becomes easier to deal with differences and diversity in opinion and create a culture of iterative learning.

These are typical good practices in modeling the evolutionary change processes:

- Invest time sensing the need, testing the urgency, and building resonance with a change endeavor early in the process.
- Start small and engage a group of relevant people (already representing the differences), building engagement and inclusivity step by step.
- Diagnose the situation jointly and integrate diverse perspectives into future planning.
- Invest in trust and relationship building in the beginning.
- Ensure that sufficient knowledge and expertise are available or built.
- Follow up on agreed actions, but maintain a dialogic approach.
- Maintain confidentiality, if needed, and avoid the media at an early stage.
- Keep the larger vision visible, but break it down into achievable action points and celebrate results accomplished.
- Create a culture of iterative learning, reviewing progress jointly.

Invigorating Collaborative Networks

Networks are the backbone of change toward sustainability: The impact of changed mind-sets, behavior, and actions stretches out along their connections. Networks can be formalized or not. The purpose may be different, but how they contribute to change is similar. Initiators are often catalyst for the change to come, but not all actions are planned or determined by them. People are not members of only one network, so the multitude of connectivity is complex and has a stabilizing impact. In water sector networks, people meet from a variety of countries—even those that may be in conflict.

The goal is to gather people who would not normally come together, creating access to different worldviews and easing mutual understanding. Collaborative networks often turn into personal networks that last. Despite the fact that we have built societies with competition at the forefront, people are touched when they experience how symbiotic we must be in the evolutionary process. Helping one another move forward may at times be a calculated choice, but most often it contributes to a deeper emotional satisfaction. Once people start supporting, support grows and collective impact is possible.

Networks often come with rules and structures; some of them may be covert, others overt. But the rules and structures are important—they help people stay in a collaborative field and navigate between seemingly irreconcilable positions. If rules and structures come in too early, they have a deteriorating or demotivating effect. People may accept them, but they prevent engagement and contribution. Overly formal structures seem to drain energy. Overly loose structures cause a group of actors to disperse, and the energy for change gets lost. Getting the balance right among formal agreements, plans, rules of participation, and unstructured human encounter is paramount.

The entry point for the invigorating-networks strategy is a mix between connectivity in engagement and mutual support in wholeness. The mix builds on the human desire for living in communities where people are supportive of one another. It addresses the sense of belonging that we all have. The dimension of humanity is strongly enhanced through networking, as it always includes a professional and personal component. In functioning networks people identify both with the issue or content and with the espoused values of the network—how to live, how to act, how to do things professionally, or how to bring about change. This can range from exchanging best practice examples to actually implementing change together. Networks thrive on impact. They become strong over time, if encounter and exchange are combined with implementation that members can experience or that can be demonstrated. It is the collective action element of engagement that ensures the long-term success of networks.

These are good practices in invigorating collaborative networks:

- Use opportunities for cross-sector, interdisciplinary, cross-cultural connections, joining issue-related or thematic networks.
- Understand and use social media networks.
- Get complementary expertise together.
- Ensure that implementation results are fed back into the network.
- Use opportunities for joint projects among members of a network.
- Invite experts from an entirely different discipline to contribute their views.
- Build personal relationships beyond professional boundaries.
- Attend to the emotional component of sustainability and the desire to make a difference.
- Grow rules and structures gradually in line with the progress of an initiative.
- Live the values of support and contribution; it is contagious.

Chapter 12

Getting into Collaborative Action

The three strategies outlined in the previous chapter are distinct, yet it is the combination of them that strengthens sustainability initiatives. How can the Collective Leadership Compass help enact these successful strategies more consciously? Even when we want to build communities of collaborative change makers with the help of the compass, we can follow the cycle of observe, focus, enact.

It's important to first *observe* what we can build on, appreciate the competencies that are already well enacted, and fully understand the context we are operating in. Who is doing what in the field? Are there similar activities? What is the state of the matter? To answer these questions, we need to understand the current patterns of interaction as they relate to the dimensions of the Collective Leadership Compass. If many people are involved in a change process—within one organization or a large group of stakeholders—not everybody may be familiar with the Compass. Online assessments are an option, if people are prepared to join in. It may be beneficial, especially for organizations, to conduct an assessment before and after a change process.

Whether we build trust-based co-creation, design a step-by-step engagement process, or invigorate a network of actors—we need to *focus*. This entails working with the strengths that are there, and transparently identifying the development areas of a whole system of actors. It is crucial to carefully choose our entry point and build our intervention steps gradually with regular reviews.

This leads to *enacting* a more balanced pattern of competencies. Even for large systems of change it is possible to build an intervention plan on action steps allocated to the six dimensions. This leads us to looking at the experiences of our fellow travelers.

Two of our fellow travelers wanted to *build communities for change within their organizations*. Peter could do this from the comfortable position of being the CEO of the international NGO DiverseAct that fought for protecting biodiversity. Andrea had no power at all, being a project manager in the sustainability department at EnergyTech, but she had the willingness to take the risk of initiating a course correction of this old, heavy, yet extremely powerful company.

Two others needed to *bring different institutions into a collaboration.* Celine wanted to achieve this by creating a national stakeholder dialogue platform on the implementation of the drinking water policy in the Democratic Republic of Congo. Nadeem's goal was to deliver an impact for small-scale African farmers that resulted in increased income for them. For that he needed an aligned effort among the foundation, the private sector partners, the implementing agencies, and the governments of five different countries.

The last two intended to *create a network of actors* that would have a better impact on sustainability. Three months after she wrote down her first action plan Tina had achieved a lot. She had the vice chancellor of her university behind her dream, and ten students were prepared to actually implement the first round of mentoring. She started to dream big—this was only the beginning of a networked mentoring movement that could potentially spread throughout South Africa. Mike was an achiever. Six months after the legendary management retreat, change had taken root at TrendWear. But he realized that his initial thought was right—a profound change of the supply-chain practices would only take place if companies collaborated across the textile industry. His new goal was clear—getting the major companies to talk, find a joint strategy, and move into networked action.

Peter: Invigorating the Drive for Impact on Biodiversity

When Peter noticed the culture of debate, judgment, and opposition among the 250 employees of DiverseAct and the misgiving toward him because he came from the private sector, he decided to find a mentor. At his age, the title *mentor* seemed wrong, so he decided to use the term *thinking partner.* He thought that there must be other people who had made a career change from the private sector to the top level of an NGO, and he wanted advice that would complement his management experiences. He found a real partner, and while Peter received advice on NGO cultures, he offered advice on engagement strategies and goal alignment. The two became sparring partners, doing an organizational collaboration diagnosis with the Collective Leadership Compass and designing a change strategy for DiverseAct.

The first step was for Peter to have one-on-one conversations with all heads of departments and short meetings with some people they recommended to him. Some of these were official meetings, others simply lunch appointments. After each conversation, Peter noted down important points, allocating the issues to the six dimensions. He wanted to know two things from people: (1) how they saw DiverseAct operating at the moment in relation to what was needed in the future, and (2) what three things they could learn from biodiversity that might help this effort. The purpose of the first question was to get a basis for the assessment around the six dimensions of the Collective Leadership Compass. The second question was intended to trigger their out-of-the-box thinking and give Peter ideas for his engagement strategy.

The three biodiversity aspects mentioned most were that biodiversity (1) increases plant production, (2) increases yield stability in certain environments, and (3) increases resilience toward diseases and soil demineralization. Peter translated this into management terminology: increased productivity, long-term financial stability, organizational resilience and agility. He was pleased; this was exactly what DiverseAct needed as an organization. This is how he phrased his leadership challenge: *Turning DiverseAct into an organization with higher efficiency, better effectiveness and impact, as well as strong resilience in the face of competition for funding to finance the mission.* He had agreed with his challenge partner that they would design an engagement strategy based on the strong areas they found in the assessment. Their results are shown in table 13.

Based on the assessment, Peter's first step was to engage a core group of people to become ambassadors for the change. Because he had experienced the strong skepticism and a critical attitude toward him among his top management team, he continued trust-building measures (such as regular conversations and joint funder visits), but he sensed that he needed to involve more people into the core group to speed up the change. He invited the human resource team to a meeting and explained his idea. Peter wanted to design an appreciative process that would build on the hidden strengths of the organization, which he had identified as *empowerment* (self-reliance and self-initiative), *collective action* (drive for project implementation), *excellence* and *contextuality* (top-level expertise, brilliant

Table 13. The DiverseAct Engagement Strategy

Dimension	Aspects	Comment
FUTURE POSSIBILITIES (35%)	*future orientation* (27%)	Complaint mode, skepticism toward the future, people busy with internal issues, glass-half-empty mode, lack of clarity on goals.
	empowerment (62%)	High self-reliance and initiative on action in projects.
	decisiveness (16%)	Low rate of follow-up, low accountability (decisions are not always implemented).
ENGAGEMENT (39%)	*process quality* (20%)	Mix between strong administrative procedures and stepping over rules, inefficient meetings, lack of clarity of envisioned change process.
	connectivity (58%)	Discrepancy between low internal collaboration structures (everybody pursuing their own goals in territories) and brilliant internal informal network (if you want to get a project going you know who to connect with).
	collective action (39%)	Somehow things get done at DiverseAct, but more because of individuals driving their projects. (This is both a weakness and a strength: While there is no collective ownership, there is individual ownership.)
INNOVATION (66%)	*creativity* (63 %)	Despite many administrative procedures, people seem to find ways to go around rules and get things done; wealth of ideas for new projects.
	excellence (86%)	Strong emphasis on knowledge and being up to date, real experts working here, amazing wealth of experience.
	agility (48%)	There seems to be an underlying rule of how we do things here at DiverseAct that should not change, yet people are extremely courageous in setting up projects and acquiring funding.

overview of the global context), *empathy* (for the issue of biodiversity and the people in the countries where DiverseAct implemented projects), and COLLECTIVE INTELLIGENCE—the debate culture (not really *dialogic quality*, but at least a culture of lively exchange). He also made the goals clear: better efficiency, higher measurable impact, financial resilience. He stated his assumption that this would require diversification of funding options, more cooperation with the private sector, and possibly even an investment into other income areas like teaching or consulting to the private sector on biodiversity strategies.

Dimension	Aspects	Comment
HUMANITY (47%)	*mindfulness* (38%)	Everybody is busy with content, little awareness of interaction patterns.
	balance (27%)	There is a tendency to be busy being busy, people work overtime but inefficiently, too many meetings.
	empathy (77%)	Toward external: strong empathy with projects and target groups; toward internal: extremely judgmental culture.
COLLECTIVE INTELLIGENCE (52%)	*dialogic quality* (57%)	Debate and exchanging opposing views is a habit, meetings take far too long and are inefficient (no closure of results, no follow-up), yet there is a lot of informal communication that actually seems to lead to new projects.
	diversity (44%)	Despite the culture of debate and the espoused diversity there seems to be a fear of getting diversity in; most staff is European, projects are mainly designed at headquarters.
	iterative learning (54%)	There is no structure in place for this, it just happens by default, but it does happen!
WHOLENESS (57%)	*contextuality* (85%)	Top! People know the world context on biodiversity, some of the best experts work for DiverseAct.
	mutual support (41%)	Very little along official lines, but somehow there; needs to be harvested.
	contribution (46%)	Great clarity on what we want to see, little willingness to improve our contribution.

What happened? The human resource team listened attentively, asked a few questions, and suggested that they would think about it and propose a way forward within a week based on the Collective Leadership Compass. Peter was amazed, because the resulting proposal exceeded his expectations—a process design that was beyond Peter's comfort zone but was convincing. They explained that in the culture of DiverseAct, consensus was important and it would lead to ownership, yet they had also seen over the years that people had become more and more territorial.

As a first step they suggested an "Open Space" conference with about a hundred staff—taking up Peter's topic of what DiverseAct could learn as an organization from biodiversity.[1] In the run-up to the conference they would do an online questionnaire on what DiverseAct should not change (what was going well) and what people saw as challenges for the future. They reckoned that the planned two days would result in concrete change initiatives that staff felt they owned. Peter's task would be to get his vision across—emotionally and authentically. They recommended he give a speech that touched on why he had made a career change.

Following the conference, they would create a cross-departmental task team to align the conference results and turn them into a maximum of three change areas—each with a catchy title and an easy-to-remember tagline. They would cross-check the results with the participants of the conference and then, in alignment with the top management, suggest priority areas for (1) what needed to be consolidated, (2) where they needed to become better, and (3) where they wanted to venture into new areas, identifying potential prototypes—issues where change could be implemented fast. Peter felt he was an expert in engagement, yet the participatory approach the human resource team suggested was way beyond what he felt comfortable with. He feared that his management team would feel sidelined and overpowered, but he decided that he would take a chance. The suggested process made sense to him.

One year later, not only had the conference taken place but the change process had taken root. The road had been bumpy at times as Peter's management was split into two factions, one that really loved the change process and one that blocked wherever they could. He needed to deal with the consequences and he replaced two people. Most of the staff began to be excited about the new direction, and more people came up with ideas on how to partner with the private sector.

Two years later they had introduced a balanced scorecard inspired by the Collective Leadership Compass, and the staff survey was done with the Compass. People really identified with the idea of leading collectively. Two partnership agreements with private sector companies had been signed, and they had created a department that would bring DiverseAct's expertise into educational programs. Peter could look back at a successful change of career, and even if his salary level would never match what he earned in the private sector, he had the feeling of contributing to a mission in the world that really made sense to him.

Andrea: Shifting the Course of a Vessel

In the beginning Andrea felt overwhelmed when she thought about the size of change she wanted at EnergyTech. She was aware of her weak role as a project manager in the sustainability department. Who was she to initiate profound change? Despite her self-doubt, she had an idea how to start and needed the support of her superior. Because Andrea's strength was COLLECTIVE INTELLIGENCE and in particular *dialogic quality*, she asked for a lunch appointment with her superior. She wanted to know (1) more about the history (why the company decided to create a sustainability department) and (2) what he thought the current challenges of the department were. She simply asked interested questions. It turned out that he had led the department for more than ten years. In its early days, it was called the environmental department—a small team of three people in a company with twelve thousand employees with a crystal-clear point of view: Sustainability would become the topic of the future, and they had no doubt about the business case for it.

But getting sustainability on the agenda in a company like theirs (a well-established electricity market and no serious pressure to change) was a steep mountain to climb. The vague concept of sustainability needed to be broken down into tangible and measurable targets related to the core business, hence every sustainability manager needed to learn about the business priorities of all other departments. Only recently the public criticism toward EnergyTech had increased. More and more individual clients left for companies that could assure electricity from renewable energy sources. When Andrea asked what the stumbling block was, he said: "People do not talk with one another at management level. It's all about figures and results delivery. No space to think. But when I meet some of them on the golf course they are quite discontent. Some of them say jokingly they would not tell people at parties where they work, because EnergyTech is under so much public criticism."

Andrea paused, but instead of asking him why he thought he had made so little progress, she simply asked: "What if we do not talk about sustainability, but reach them where they are—by only talking about business?" This short lunch conversation developed into a series of further conversations that involved the entire sustainability team. The team formed an idea that started with engaging the board. They would convince the board that they needed information on how top managers saw the future of EnergyTech, then conduct about sixty interviews across all departments asking managers two simple questions: (1) What trends are most relevant for your current area of responsibility? (2) In view of good future business, what do you think EnergyTech needs to improve?

After compiling the results, they would get at least 60 percent of the top-two-level managers into a half-day workshop to jointly draw conclusions and develop recommendations to the board. Every manager would receive a summary of results beforehand. Andrea did not share the Collective Leadership Compass with her team at EnergyTech. She wanted to continue to use it with the support of her peer group from the Young Professional Leadership Program and see success before she bothered colleagues with a new tool. She discussed with her peers that the approach the sustainability team chose would address most of the dimensions of the Compass:

- Acknowledge the roles and responsibilities of managers by asking for their expertise (INNOVATION—*excellence*) through questions that tapped into their *creativity* and their sense of FUTURE POSSIBILITIES.
- Build on the current culture of doing business—competitive, but focused on delivery (*future orientation/decisiveness*).
- Play into WHOLENESS (*contextuality*) by asking about trends.
- Enhance COLLECTIVE INTELLIGENCE by having both personal interviews and the workshop (*dialogic quality*), and by interviewing managers across all departments (*diversity*).
- Build HUMANITY by simply and directly asking for their opinions, giving them room to talk and be listened to.
- Recognize the need for reliable processes (ENGAGEMENT—*process quality*) by waiting for the go ahead by the board, informing everybody about the purpose, making the time frame clear, and outlining what would happen with the results and the recommendations to the board.

Andrea's boss shared an assumption with her that managers who talked about the future would talk about sustainability issues. She was stunned about how right he was—there was not one manager who was not aware of the dilemma between sustainability and business priorities. Most saw the need to reconcile the two. At the workshop, they debated intensely about ways to get there and extracted ten action areas where the company needed to improve. The sixty top managers agreed that these would go as recommendations to the board. Eight of ten action areas were related to sustainability issues such as investment into renewable energies, getting into stakeholder dialogues with consumers, and tackling issues around working conditions in the mines of EnergyTech's supply chain for coal.

Andrea could not believe that it had all started with a lunch conversation, nor could her peers from the leadership program. She was allowed to assist when her superior presented the results at the board meeting. The board changed three of the recommendations, but the rest remained. The sustainability department was galvanized; it was the first time they had action areas to track. That's when Andrea's homework started; it made her think of future possibilities and the importance of goal setting, focus, and measurements. Her task was to get indicators clear for all ten action areas, in consultation with some of the line managers. They decided to keep the indicators simple, using a traffic light—green for okay, yellow for on the way, red for not started.

The result that they brought back into the next board meeting was embarrassing—so many red lights! The sustainability department was then tasked with taking a company-wide approach to improving the traffic light results within a year. The board added a clear top-down decision that every line manager had to cooperate. One year later the ten action areas were published in the company's sustainability report. When they celebrated their success in the sustainability department, Andrea finally introduced the Collective Leadership Compass to the team.

Nadeem: Turning Complexity into Impact

After the two-day strategy review meeting with all cross-sector partners, Nadeem sat down to evaluate where he stood and how to proceed. He did a quick check with the Compass and saw improved relationships among people (HUMANITY) and better engagement of all actors. He also thought they'd made headway in seeing the big picture (WHOLENESS); even the private sector representatives that only operated in some of the countries acknowledged the complexity of the project. He was content with these first steps in harvesting collective intelligence and considered the task force on key performance indicators a reasonable sign of progress. But the real fruits of collective intelligence—a culture of dialogue (*dialogic quality*), making use of complementary competency (*diversity*), and *iterative learning*—were still far in the future. He wanted to make sure that the good energy of the strategy review did not simply evaporate in the day-to-day activities of the different stakeholders. So he suggested at the end of the meeting that the partners meet twice a year and have a regular exchange of information in between.

Everybody agreed, so Nadeem started thinking about how to implement this in a way that would meet his quality expectations. So far, he thought, not much was happening around innovation, yet this was an extremely important contributor to success. The project plan entailed detailed activities, but were they all leading to success? How could he ensure cross-agency learning and also integrate the private sector into the learning strategy? The latter was not as easy because, even though the private sector was expecting a lot out of the project, its members were very hesitant to give any detailed information to the project about their activities, markets, and supply-chain strategies. Yet how could the project learn as a whole without this information? And wasn't there a need to actually work much more closely with the private sector supply chains?

Nadeem was also not happy with the level of engagement of government partners. Their expectation was that all operations should be aligned with government priorities, yet their willingness to give time to the project was very low. He did not know if this was because of real time scarcity, lack of interest, or skepticism toward the project. In his personal evaluation of the situation he looked at key improvements and key challenges. Table 14 shows how he summarized his thoughts.

Six months later Nadeem sent out invitations to an extended strategy review. Four weeks prior to the meeting he asked all participants to answer the Collective Leadership Compass online questionnaire on the collaboration among all involved actors. The results were encouraging with WHOLE-NESS at 60 percent (clarity of contribution and understanding of the larger context being high) and FUTURE POSSIBILITIES at 65 percent (with *future orientation* high, *empowerment* medium, and *decisiveness* slightly lower, despite the agreed-upon key performance indicators). HUMANITY scored 45 percent (*balance* was very low as everybody was totally overworked). ENGAGEMENT scored only 38 percent (across all aspects), so he took this as

Table 14. Nadeem's Assessment

Dimension (Aspects)	Key Improvements
FUTURE POSSIBILITIES (*future orientation, decisiveness*)	People have much more clarity on the goals. The definition of five short goals and respective key performance indicators is a step forward.
HUMANITY (*empathy, mindfulness*)	People know one another better, it is easier to pick up the phone and simply ask for advice or find out what is happening, etc.
WHOLENESS (*contextuality, contribution*)	The exposure trip did the job—people now feel much closer to what this project is about, and they see its complexity and challenges.
COLLECTIVE INTELLIGENCE (*iterative learning*)	The fact that people agreed to regular joint strategy reviews is a step in the right direction. It eases my management task.
ENGAGEMENT (*collective action*)	We need to find a strategy to engage governments or—better—to first understand under which circumstances they would engage and join forces with us. It may be different from government to government. (Note: Plan engagement trips.)
FUTURE POSSIBILITIES (*decisiveness*)	The five goals and the key performance indicators must develop into a guiding structure that everybody in the project (top to bottom) understands, uses, and can report on. (Note: Make sure that the key performance indicators really reflect the project's complexity and challenges, and that they are easily understandable to everyone. Once finalized, communicate them regularly, and make them part of reporting and management meetings.)
INNOVATION (*creativity, agility, excellence*)	We haven't even started to think about innovation, yet I am convinced we need innovative approaches to get to results faster. We need to not only exchange what works and what doesn't, but also bring in expert knowledge and new ideas to get to maximum effectiveness. (Note: Combine the next strategy review with an innovation and learning event, make sure more stakeholders from the field are involved, get best practices from other projects to present, have working groups on innovative ideas.)

top priority for his action plan and decided to find out in preparatory calls what the problem was. COLLECTIVE INTELLIGENCE scored 44 percent (across all aspects—he expected this to improve even more after the meeting).

The lowest was INNOVATION at 22 percent (with *excellence* being higher, but *creativity* very low). So Nadeem decided to extend the strategy review by one day to include an innovation and learning session where people would present innovative ideas and discuss them with regard to their usefulness for the project. During the following strategy review, this session led to a thorough discussion on the effectiveness of the training strategies for small-scale farmers. One outcome was a change in strategy: Rather than training large numbers of farmers, they decided to look much more closely into the existing and potential value chains of the partnering private sector companies. They analyzed the value-chain conditions, looked at the involved actors, and decided to reshape the project plan to take a more holistic approach. The aim was to invigorate a whole system of actors around specific value chains that included private sector, government agencies, NGOs, community organizations, and farmers cooperatives.

As they attracted an international IT company to partner with the project, the empowerment of the farmers cooperative was supported by a simple mobile-phone-operated software that created the possibility of better transparency and traceability of products in the value chain, and also allowed farmers to easily access market information. The private sector had been ambivalent about this, as it made their operations much more transparent, but they finally saw the benefits of the more reliable sourcing it would create. Nadeem was happy—this was exactly the direction he wanted to see.

Apart from the innovative result, the entire collaboration culture seemed to shift. The involved implementing agencies became much more engaged and willing to share their lessons. With respect to engaging the government sector more, Nadeem had learned a lot from his consulting and engagement trips. He had to reduce his expectations, as many of the involved government officials were simply too busy navigating the many parallel projects operating in their country, but he felt successful because three countries suggested that their extension services engage with the project, particularly around the value-chain approach.

Looking back after one year of coordinating this project, Nadeem was proud that he had turned his development areas in management into his strengths. All the reports he received from the implementing agencies were up to standard, and they enthusiastically implemented exciting, innovative activities that had not been part of the original plan. The key performance indicators served their purpose as a steering tool for overall success. The meeting structures had worked out: Not only were people happy with the results, but they enjoyed the time together. Nadeem was invited by the funding foundation to give a talk about the project in the United States. They wanted to use it as a best practice example, not because of his management capabilities or the innovative learning structure, but because the key performance indicators showed amazing results. More than one hundred thousand farmers had been trained and about 60 percent of them were part of the value-chain approach, which had already resulted in considerably higher earnings after one harvest. That's why he decided to integrate the Collective Leadership Compass into his presentation.

Celine: Building a Dialogue Platform for Better Water

When Celine started out with her ambitious plan to improve the water situation in the Democratic Republic of Congo (DRC), she did so in the context of weak and fragmented institutions with inherent conflicts, distributed water governance structures, mistrust, disconnect among stakeholders, and lack of concerted action for change. The core group she had built gave her hope. Their second meeting took place in a more relaxed atmosphere and, to her surprise, everybody except the deputy minister of water supply and energy had turned up. The deputy minister had sent a representative from his ministry whom he had briefed personally. Celine realized that the deputy minister wanted this to succeed, and that boosted her courage. She discussed with the core group who needed to be invited to the launch of the stakeholder platform, and then she repeated the stakeholder analysis with all core group members.

The result was similar to the earlier analysis she'd made with her colleagues, yet with important variations. One representative from a donor organization was closely working with the Ministry of Public Health, which had been classified as a powerful stakeholder that should be interested in change, but was not due to the lack of commitment by the responsible department head. The donor organization representative suggested he could approach the ministry at a high level and present the idea of the stakeholder dialogue platform.

After the analysis everybody also agreed on the importance of getting NGOs on board, since some of them had very innovative approaches to creating a committed network of actors. They were thriving on community-based approaches in which people created small water councils, ensuring a high level of ownership for the improvement of water issues, particularly among women. The core group finally listed fifty-four people to invite to the launching of the platform and agreed to test their resonance and willingness to participate in their networks and constituencies. The result was unexpected—more than eighty expressed interest in joining.

Celine was happy that she had taken the step-by-step approach to engagement. Six weeks before the launch, she sat down with her colleague to plan it using the Compass. They first made a rough assessment of the new situation and agreed that some dimensions of the Compass had improved. FUTURE POSSIBILITIES were more prominent on the horizon because of the support of the core group. Its members were sufficiently ENGAGED. INNOVATION was not yet on the agenda, but the idea to bring best practice examples to the launch of the water platform had been mentioned. COLLECTIVE INTELLIGENCE had already improved slightly. HUMANITY had improved—at least in the core group—as people saw one another's willingness to make a difference as well as the struggles everybody went through. They planned the details of the platform launch with the Compass to make sure the event addressed all six dimensions and also used the stakeholder ENGAGEMENT methodology Celine had been exposed to in a training on stakeholder collaboration; this Dialogic Change Model showed four phases of successful stakeholder engagement.[2]

They were happy with their first phase, which focused on building sufficient trust among key actors and establishing a stable core group for joint action. Their next challenge was to make the second phase successful—formalizing the stakeholder platform, creating a base for further cooperation, agreeing on objectives, collectively planning next steps, and co-designing the structure of the platform. Table 15 shows their rough plan for a successful phase 2.

What happened? The run-up to the launch of the platform was not without obstacles. People started questioning the approach, and the donor agency with which Celine discussed funding waited on the approval until the last minute. Finally the event took place. Of the eighty invited stakeholders, seventy-four arrived. The participants had lively discussions on governance approaches most effective at implementing drinking water policies. The group listed really good examples of how to involve local communities. People had expected a rather stiff and formal meeting, but Celine went out of her way to find a facilitator who would create a warm atmosphere in which people would get to know one another, tell their stories on water issues, and work in small groups.

Table 15. Phase 2 for the DRC Water Initiative

Dimension (Aspects)	Stakeholder Engagement Steps	Action Points
FUTURE POSSIBILITIES (*empowerment, future orientation*)	Clarifying common goals and resources	Have additional preparatory conversations with more actors to understand their expectations toward the platform; use this to tune even more people in to future possibilities. Evaluate the conversations and assess what could be suggested as a common goal of the platform.
HUMANITY (*empathy*)		Choose an event format that allows people to connect with one another (meet people as people). Create space for informal conversations.
COLLECTIVE INTELLIGENCE (*dialogic quality*)		Have a session during the event on jointly diagnosing the current situation. Bring in the results from our context analysis study, but ensure that people can define their own reality.
ENGAGEMENT (*collective action*)		Create workshop sessions on specific issues with jointly achieved results; report back to plenary.
INNOVATION (*excellence*)	Planning the future together	Bring in best practice examples from other countries (but do not overwhelm people). Then bring in examples from the DRC where water supply really worked. Ensure that these examples are balanced—slightly more public sector, but also NGOs and donor organization or private sector examples. Make sure the future is visible! People must have a "yes we can" feeling!
ENGAGEMENT (*collective action*)		Create workshop sessions on specific issues with jointly achieved results. Consolidate the water topics the platform will be working on in the coming year. Show with practical examples how exchange and collaboration will lead to better water delivery.
ENGAGEMENT (*process quality*)	Consolidating agreements and establishing structures	Prepare a road map for the purpose and process of the water platform, but allow working group formats to discuss it so that we achieve a joint result (even if this result is different from our plan).
WHOLENESS (*contribution*)		Get a high-level sponsor in for the keynote to show the bigger picture and support for the establishment of the platform (ideally the deputy minister of water supply and energy and the secretary of state from the Ministry of Planning).

One year later the platform was operational and had produced three cross-sector projects that integrated different approaches and increased impact through joint delivery. Alongside the structural and technical intervention in water infrastructure, the creation of the water platform led to a number of results that Celine had only dreamed of. Better coordination impacted better maintenance of existing and newly installed technological infrastructure for drinking water in Kinshasa. It also improved the communication among the different ministries, and for the first time there was a better coordination between NGOs and the foreign donor organizations.

The stakeholder platform created on the national level was repeated at two provincial levels because both governors had been part of the launch of the national platform. In an interview on Congolese TV, Celine said that she had learned a lot in a short time—particularly that even institutional weakness throughout a sector could be alleviated by a dialogic and collaborative approach. She emphasized that it strengthened joint vision, better planning, and cross-sector execution of activities. For her this was an example that could take the DRC into the future.

Tina: Creating the "Live Your Potential" Movement

Tina evaluated her action plan after three months and was pleased. It wasn't so bad to work with a plan, after all. In her room she had a wall reserved for what she now called *her* project. There was the goal visualized—a map of South Africa's universities. Her university had a blue flag, which meant mentoring had started. She had also pinned the flip chart with the Collective Leadership Compass to the wall. In between was a chaotic arrangement of handwritten notes. To her, it felt as if she could look at the future reality every day. This gave her the courage to continue dreaming. She wanted to create a movement of people who lived by example, showing how a society of the future could function on the basis of mutual support.

For the follow-on meeting with the group of students she invited somebody who was experienced in mentoring, and the idea paid off. It turned out that some of the other students had also experienced being mentored. This resulted in a lively discussion about approaches and success factors, until one of her friends suggested they stop discussing and get into action by asking who would actually be prepared to join a pilot group. All ten students were in. They agreed on a short preparatory afternoon workshop with the experienced mentor and created a Facebook group to share experiences and encourage one another.

Tina had made a note on her board under INNOVATION: "Having the courage to venture into the unknown and go beyond my comfort zone is crucial to success." She did what she feared most—asking people for advice. Her method was simple: she asked for five minutes of time from somebody, explained in one sentence why a mentoring movement could make a difference, and then asked: "What do you think must I do to make this a success?" She called these "stakeholder interviews."

The results were amazing. Although some people ridiculed her, the majority gave her extremely helpful advice. Ideas included: Get your idea to spread via Twitter, report on it, create a blog with your story and with your project, get experienced mentors to coach the mentors, work together with schools, get people from the corporate world involved, create a social enterprise, and convince the vice chancellor to support the project. The latter was the biggest hurdle; how would she get an appointment? Having practiced asking for advice, she simply asked her psychology professor, who turned out to have a good connection with the vice chancellor. She got an appointment.

One year later the group had grown to fifty mentors, and eighty young people had already benefited from the movement. The vice chancellor had made it an official project at his university and gave as much support as he could—from distributing information to making contact with schools and private sector companies. For Tina, it had not been an easy task to find the right size for a core group to carry the project forward. In the beginning everyone was welcome, but then the group became too big and it was nearly impossible to make decisions. She realized that organizational structures could actually make sense, and that their purpose was to ease communication and action. That's when she began to think big—she discussed with the core group the idea of starting a nonprofit organization that could look for funding and grow the movement.

For the first time in her life Tina decided to set herself yearly goals. She had finished her bachelor's degree and, instead of looking for employment, she wanted to become a social entrepreneur and found an organization that lived the values she stood for—empowering disadvantaged young people to live their potential. On Facebook she posted that she was looking for a

Table 16. Tina's Action Items for the Six Dimensions

Dimension	Aspects	Action
FUTURE POSSIBILITIES	*future orientation*	Think big, think even bigger, set my yearly goals, make them concise, and follow up my action steps quarterly, monthly, and weekly. Keep my vision board on the wall and develop it further.
	empowerment	Set up a blog, start with my personal stories, make it a story-based site that can inspire people about the difference that mentoring makes.
	decisiveness	Focus on my project, give it all the attention it needs. Discuss monitoring tools in the core group; how can we show impact?
ENGAGEMENT	*process quality*	Discuss with the core group a possible organizational structure; get advice about which form of social enterprise. Make a step-by-step plan to set up a social enterprise.
	connectivity	Get somebody to volunteer to be the social media community manager; I can't do everything by myself. I will focus on connecting with a network of sponsors. Start with those with whom I'm already connected, asking them who else I need to involve. Get information packages ready, make it story-based—show the impact of the first mentoring, get people to give me testimonials.
	collective action	If I want to succeed with my dream, I need a structure that works; as a matter of fact I need funding, people full-time working for the movement, and a clear allocation of responsibilities. What will be my role—will I become the boss? Not sure if I want this, and what do I need to learn?
INNOVATION	*creativity*	I don't want my passion and creative urge to dry up because of all these management issues! Have fun in the core group! Could we use a design thinking process to develop our social enterprise?[3]
	excellence	Improve the preparation of the mentors—establish a proper training. Try to get funding for this. I want to ensure that we deliver quality—I agree with the core group on quality standards in mentoring. Important idea: Make the Collective Leadership Compass part of the mentoring process; teach people how to work with it.
	agility	I have read somewhere that the bigger the ambition, the more obstacles will come my way, as if the universe is testing me. Keep reminding myself that crises are opportunities in disguise. With every obstacle, ask myself: What is the opportunity to learn here?

Dimension	Aspects	Action
Humanity	*mindfulness*	This whole issue of creating an organizational structure is a steep learning curve for me. I do have my resistance. Stay aware of how I feel, particularly when the management issues drain me.
	balance	I am on the way to becoming a workaholic; I must make sure to have time-outs.
	empathy	Regularly refocus on what my passion is—helping educationally disadvantaged young people. Be a mentor for at least two young people myself. Get the mentees together so that they can share their experience and learn from one another.
Collective intelligence	*dialogic quality*	Pay attention to the way we interact. I notice how conflicts are increasing in the core group as we move toward becoming more professional. Make an effort to introduce dialogic practices into our meetings (pay attention to voice, listen, respect, suspend judgment).[4]
	diversity	Following on from the above, we have a culture of debate in the core group. I am afraid people will start fighting; I also notice more opposition toward me as the initiator. Can I learn to see this as a normal process? Can I learn to deal constructively with opposition? Find somebody to help me. Could I find somebody who has built a social enterprise?
	iterative learning	I hate structures and enjoy things to be spontaneous, but I need to consolidate our learning structures; I will seek to find an agreement with the core group about how we learn—what meeting structures, forms of evaluation, organization and management, also allocation of responsibilities will help us.
Wholeness	*contextuality*	I must admit we have not been paying much attention to what else is happening in the area of mentoring and educationally disadvantaged young people. It is time that we find out and connect. I need to get one of my core group members to take on this task and give us feedback so that we can decide in the core group which other activities are relevant for us and where we should connect.
	mutual support	The entire idea is about mutual support, but here is a good point—how can we get the mentees to give back? Let me bring this into the core group
	contribution	It is all about our impact. Here is an idea: I will convince my professor to allocate a couple of students to a research project so that we accompany a number of mentees throughout their process. We may even consider a quantitative evaluation of the mentoring process.

name that everybody could easily understand, but particularly the disadvantaged young people. The response was tremendous, and she took it as a glimpse into the future. The mentoring movement had obviously spotted a solution to a problem that many people saw—they could identify with her project's way of alleviating a societal problem. The Facebook question also led to media contacting her. Most important, she got a phone call from a foundation that was interested in potentially supporting the project.

Tina took the many positive responses as an indication that it was time to reveal how she used the Collective Leadership Compass for evaluating and planning. Looking at her project, she concluded that she had worked very much in tune with her own style, putting her strength in HUMANITY into the forefront and maintaining her strength in INNOVATION by watching her creative space while being courageous and venturing into the unknown. She had also used COLLECTIVE INTELLIGENCE with her stakeholder advice interviews and was good at ENGAGING potential mentors and supporters. The mentoring movement built on people's desire to make a contribution (WHOLENESS) to society. Tina herself had improved in decisiveness and *future orientation* (FUTURE POSSIBILITIES). All the dimensions were addressed, but she had the feeling that she was at a threshold to a new level and needed to look at how to enhance the dimensions in view of the growth of the movement. She felt that the movement could disappear as quickly as it had grown if she did not give it a more solid home. She remembered the advice on founding a social enterprise. Table 16 describes how she reestablished her action items according to the six dimensions and adjusted her plan.

After another year, Tina had established a nonprofit social enterprise with six full-time staff members. They had received a small institutional grant from the government, and the vice chancellor of her university had been very helpful in getting it. A foundation had stepped in with funding for specific projects—the mentoring of girls, the focus on specific geographic areas, and close cooperation with the private sector. Following the recommendations she received on Facebook the movement had adopted the name LYP, standing for "Live Your Potential."

The road to becoming more structured and professional had not been easy for Tina. Not everybody in the core group supported the big dream and the necessity it implied of setting up a professional organization. The fights had been tremendous, and Tina had been accused of taking advantage of the volunteer work that group members had been doing. But she had organized a mentor for herself—somebody who could help her through ups and downs of setting up an organization and all the pain that occurs when one loses people who do not identify with the new strategy. She had remembered her mantra that crises are opportunities in disguise and remained open to learning. She did not exclude anybody in the core group from becoming part of the social enterprise, but in the end two people left and three new people joined.

Four years later, LYP operated at five South African universities. They had established a board of patrons with high-level people from government, private sector, and civil society. More than five hundred students had joined the movement throughout the country, and more than a thousand young people had received mentoring support. Tina had brought her dream into reality and lived her own potential.

Mike: From Competition to Cooperation

Six months after the legendary management retreat, sustainable supply-chain management was no longer a side issue at TrendWear. It had become part of the company's incentive systems and performance appraisals. Beyond looking at the social issues in the supply chain, they had also started measuring environmental issues, particularly carbon and water footprints. They integrated sustainability and compliance issues into the company's risk management procedures and operated with customized balanced scorecards that included sustainability. Mike felt the internal motto—"At TrendWear we align our success with our contribution to fairness"—had made a difference to many of the employees. People had begun to identify more with the company.

He had never thought that such a thing would have become so important to him. It had not been easy to get the board on board, but they gave him a grace period to achieve financial success. What pleased Mike most was the change in culture in the management team. He'd never paid attention to such issues before, but he noticed that his top staff helped one another out, communicated more across the different departments, and had formed cross-departmental task forces to tackle the hot spots in sustainability management.

The focus was responsible supply-chain management with particular emphasis on Asia, but it was already clear that this was only the start. A future task force was calculating TrendWear's path to becoming a sustainable textile company. They were busy working out what this would mean on the operational level and had suggested to Mike a twenty-year plan. He chewed on this for a while, as he only had a contract for a few years, but it made absolute sense to him. One thing became clear to him: Once they started to really take sustainability issues seriously, it began to affect almost all aspects of business. It was like reinventing the company. As a visionary, he could see revolutionary action on the horizon, such as zero environmental impact, total elimination of waste, and 100 percent reliance on renewables. He knew he could not push much more, but his ambition became to show what is possible and to turn sustainability into a business advantage.

The future task force was busy looking into the chances for TrendWear to increase their price range slightly, but to brand as a sustainable company once the basics were in place. He knew this would take years, but he also noticed that his managers and staff were galvanized around the prospect of TrendWear becoming a sustainable company. When he conducted a "six-months-after" team assessment with the Collective Leadership Compass, it showed significant improvements in WHOLENESS (from 17 to 45 percent), mainly due to *mutual support* and *contribution*. Staff saw their operations become part of a pathway to sustainability. HUMANITY had increased from 33 to 51 percent due to higher awareness of how they interacted and a better understanding of one another's challenges. COLLECTIVE INTELLIGENCE moved up slightly, from 32 to 39 percent, showing an increase in finding solutions jointly. Mike noted that *iterative learning* required further improvement and started thinking about what practices and procedures would help. INNOVATION was slightly improved (from 60 to 65 percent), while ENGAGEMENT and FUTURE POSSIBILITIES had remained almost the same (both around 77 percent). The sustainability department had turned into a real coordinator of knowledge and was reporting to him on a weekly basis.

What bothered Mike was his realization that even with the best of all intentions, TrendWear could not master the challenges of wages and working conditions in the supply chain by itself. For most of the strategic suppliers in Asia, TrendWear was only one of many clients, and their influence on changing working conditions, pay, or building safety was not strong enough. TrendWear had joined the Ethical Trading Initiative in the UK, but even this seemed to be insufficient.[5] As the sustainability department reported directly to him, he tasked them to give him an accurate account of existing industry-wide or cross-sector initiatives and a recommendation on which to join. He was amazed that they had used the Compass to diagnose the collaboration situation in the textile industry. See table 17 for the short version of his diagnosis.

Table 17. The Collaboration Diagnosis for the Textile Industry

Dimension	Status Assessment
FUTURE POSSIBILITIES (high)	Not only at TrendWear, but across the European textile industry (and partly also US companies) the issue of wages, working conditions, and building safety at Asian suppliers (particularly Bangladesh) had moved to top priority on the agenda. The trend was clear; no company could ignore these issues any longer.
ENGAGEMENT (medium)	Many partly parallel multi-stakeholder initiatives (strongly driven by European companies and mostly country-based) existed; an overall initiative was missing. Approaches were still fragmented, with sometimes questionable impact. Competition among initiatives resulted in some factories in Bangladesh being approached by more than one initiative.
INNOVATION (low)	Everybody had by now understood that the auditing of suppliers in Asia alone was not sufficient; shifting into capacity building and management training was paramount. Many companies had begun to cooperate with NGOs, yet innovation was missing: Nobody really looked at the supply chain as a whole.
HUMANITY (medium)	Astonishingly, the joint initiatives among companies, several European governments, and companies had led to all pursuing the same goal—a sustainable supply chain and decent working conditions—by easing communication between companies and NGOs. This led to collaboration projects on the ground.
COLLECTIVE INTELLIGENCE (medium)	Cooperation and exchange took place among different initiatives, mainly at conferences, but joint learning was insufficient; reinventing the wheel was a common feature. Many parallel activities to improve the situation of workers took place in parallel in Bangladesh, with about one-third of the factories actually receiving double support. The involvement of the Asian countries' governments was low.
WHOLENESS (low)	Overall the collective moves to address the supply-chain challenges jointly were seen as positive, but they were still fragmented. What was missing was a sector-wide approach that called for joint responsibility of buyer companies like TrendWear and collaboration with governments and NGOs.

As a conclusion, the head of sustainability recommended to Mike:

- TrendWear should invest in screening other initiatives beyond the UK and do a brief benchmark of innovative approaches. (The Dutch seemed to be front-runners in sustainable supply-chain management.)
- TrendWear should adopt an approach to its supply-chain management that would place emphasis on dialogue with suppliers and engage textile associations in Asian countries.
- TrendWear should start partnering with NGOs to achieve tangible results in selected supplier companies, particularly in Bangladesh— and do this jointly with other buying companies.
- TrendWear should not develop its own standard, but use the sustainability standards that were already available.

Mike gave the go-ahead to all recommendations, but something bothered him. Nobody talked about the issue of price, yet he knew from their internal study on margin that part of the solution had to be a price increase for consumers; not all costs of better buildings, working conditions, and safety could be passed on to the suppliers or solved by teaching better management. That's why he made a commitment to create an informal network—he needed to get in touch with some of the CEOs of other influential companies. It was about time, he thought, that they moved from competition to what he called "co-opetition" and then maybe to cooperation. He looked forward to spending a week on a seaside vacation with his daughter. He was sure that the question would come up about how far he'd gotten in ensuring she could recommend TrendWear to her friends, and he was confident he'd have an answer.

PART FOUR

Scaling Up Collaboration for a Better Future

Now that we have seen how our fellow travelers used the Compass to master their collaboration challenges, it's time to take an even broader perspective. If we do not want cross-sector and cross-institutional collaboration to be a temporary fashion that people discard as too messy and complicated, we need to learn from our collective practices. We have a call to action—sustainability—and we have a call to learn collectively, to get even better at working together. Building competencies for a better future is an exciting proposition. Now we need to identify scaling-up strategies for collective leadership.

At the beginning of 2012 Charles Leadbeater, a leading authority on innovation and creativity, wrote in a *Guardian* article: "Most of us are born helpful and generous, co-operation is written into who we are."[1] He cites scientific evidence that collaboration has been more beneficial, overall, than competition in human evolution. Our global collaboration journey is nothing new to humankind, but it has become more urgent that we understand and strengthen the human competencies we have. "It is only through co-operation that we create more effective solutions to complex challenges," says Leadbeater.[2]

Biologists emphasize in living systems theory that our fatal illusion of independence has given us a distorted view of reality and our place in ecosystems. The lack of awareness of the planet functioning as a whole (including humanity) has created the notion of scarcity and the need for competition. Elisabeth Sahtouris and James Lovelock remind us of the obvious in their book *Earthdance*: "The social view of individual people pitted against one another in . . . struggles makes little more sense as an ideal than the notion that our bodies' cells are competing with one another to survive in hostile bodies. It is simply no longer useful or productive to see ourselves as forced to compete with one another to survive in a hostile society surrounded by hostile nature."[3]

But what does this mean for our day-to-day business reality?

As we have seen in the previous chapters, if we want to build our competency for the future, we need to enhance our skills in leading collectively. It is useful to learn how to empower committed groups of citizens and how to build communities of change makers by designing collaboration processes with the six dimensions of the Collective Leadership Compass in mind. But how do we scale up these processes? What approaches do we need to practice in training for collaboration? Since practice leads to success over time, we must train our collaboration muscles and gradually rewire our brains to both notice collaboration opportunities and harvest their potential. As always, we will have the tendency to fall back into old habits—competing while we pretend to collaborate. Yet the urgency of sustainability helps shift our perception. How do we harvest the treasure of collective leadership on a large scale? How do we scale up collaborative impact?

There are uncounted testing grounds for better co-creation. Large companies such as Unilever, Nestlé, Coca-Cola, and Mondelēz have made stakeholder collaboration part of core business strategies. Many smaller companies are engaged in dialogue and cooperation projects as well. Industry-wide initiatives join up with NGOs and governments for better impact, be it in the Ethical Trading Initiative, the Global Seafood Sustainability Initiative, or the ACCORD, a legally binding independent agreement by more than 150 industry partners to ensure safe factories in Bangladesh.[4] These are just three examples of the many cross-sector initiatives aimed at solving pressing sustainability issues. Many governments are keen to apply a structured stakeholder collaboration methodology to secure water resources, improve the education system, find lasting solutions to public health challenges, or harvest chances for better economic development. Yet it is the quality of structured dialogue, cross-sector collaboration, and negotiated solutions that will determine whether we can take humankind into a better future. That is why I would like to invite you to look at different approaches to stakeholder collaboration through the lens of the Collective Leadership Compass.

We will look at:

- **Stakeholder dialogue** is a methodology increasingly used to find solutions to complex sustainability challenges.
- **Cross-sector partnering** aims to enhance the impact of sustainability projects and create shared value.
- **Sustainability leadership** empowers leaders to build sustainable futures.
- **Networks for change** is a way of ensuring knowledge sharing and aligned implementation across institutions and countries.
- **Innovation as collective design** harvests solution finding for simple and complex problems.

Chapter 13

Improving Stakeholder Dialogue

Companies, public sector institutions, and civil society increasingly use stakeholder dialogues as a methodology for structured exchange among people who have an interest in a course of development, an issue, or a decision. These include people who advocate for a cause, who have power or influence, who may become key players in project implementation, or who are affected by an issue.[1] Dialogue allows the integration of different perspectives, standpoints, and interests. Such guided and structured conversations improve planning and decision making, solve problems, and contribute to finding innovative solutions. They help design or implement joint interventions for change. Stakeholder dialogue is a vital stepping-stone in achieving common goals, and is therefore often embedded in a short- or long-term societal or global change process. It can lead to practical outcomes that could not be achieved otherwise and that can more easily be implemented because all those involved experience a higher degree of ownership.

In that way, dialogue becomes a bridge between the individual's capacity to tune in to sustainable action and the collective's negotiated solutions for the future. Dialogue complements and improves democracy; even in non-democratic societies stakeholder dialogues are used as a first step to ensure collective input into road maps for the future. Structured dialogues complement corporate or public procedures, reduce or prevent conflicts, and build confidence between sometimes adverse interest groups. They also cultivate innovation, inventiveness, and pragmatism, as well as enhancing people's ability to implement initiatives jointly.

Stakeholder dialogues can be onetime consultation events or can be conducted on a regular base to ensure the integration of different perspectives into long-term strategy or policy development as well as planning. If we look at the methodology of stakeholder dialogue through the lens of the Collective Leadership Compass, the entry points of such an approach to shifting a system of actors into better co-creation are the dimensions of COLLECTIVE INTELLIGENCE and ENGAGEMENT. Whoever has implemented or experienced a stakeholder dialogue knows that success hinges on the *dialogic quality* of the exchange, on good preparation, and on the investment in trust building. Well prepared and conducted, the process thrives on ENGAGEMENT and COLLECTIVE INTELLIGENCE, but also contributes to improving relationships (HUMANITY), helps people to see the larger picture (WHOLENESS), opens up new pathways for change (FUTURE POSSIBILITIES), and brings in ideas for new approaches to solutions (INNOVATION). It is a perfect opportunity for better co-creation.

If the process is not run well, stakeholder dialogue can lead to mistrust ("this is greenwashing"), fatigue ("all talk no action"), and participants feeling exploited ("we never knew what they did with our input"). Engaging stakeholders authentically is an art that can be learned. There are a lot of resources available that support this truth.[2]

For companies, discovering the needs and benefits of dialogue with stakeholders can be a painful experience. Anticipating the potential in stakeholder dialogues and following a step-by-step guide can lead to successful shared value creation. Visionary companies are tapping into these trends and understand the interdependence between societal and company performance on the global scale. However, for many companies the nagging question remains: Is there a formula to make stakeholder dialogues a fruitful experience, rather than opening Pandora's box? There can be misunderstandings and pitfalls in stakeholder dialogues, and we need to filter out what works and what does not. Let's look at two examples that worked—one from the corporate world and one from the public sector.

Breakthrough Dialogues in the Corporate World: The Tchibo Example

One of the many private sector firms pioneering stakeholder dialogues as part of its business strategy is the German company Tchibo, a medium-sized company retailing coffee, textiles, and other consumer goods.[3] About ten years ago Tchibo realized that it had to take its role in the working conditions of its coffee and textile suppliers more seriously. In 2005 the Clean

Clothes Campaign—an NGO advocating for better working conditions of workers in the textile industry—accused the company of sourcing from suppliers in Asia that had unbearable employee working conditions.

The crisis was, in conjunction with a reorganization of its strategy and board structure, a stepping-stone for profound change at Tchibo. The corporate social responsibility department—at that time a part-time manager—grew extensively and was mandated to proactively lead the change. Internally, staff raised awareness of the benefits of responsible supply-chain management, built knowledge on sustainable sourcing, and integrated sustainability measurements into incentive systems and controlling targets. Within a few years sustainability issues moved from being a necessary add-on to an integrated part of the company's business strategy with ambitious targets.

It was a continuous learning process that opened up new pathways for change. Tchibo engaged with the Common Code for the Coffee Community as a mainstream sustainability standard and then added certification standards such as Fair Trade, UTZ Certified, and Rainforest Alliance in the premium assortments.[4]

The textile division had to cope with different challenges. As a comparatively small company, Tchibo did not have much leverage over the working conditions of its Asian suppliers, which had many other buyers as clients. Tchibo joined industry-wide initiatives such as the Ethical Trading Initiative in the UK and the Round Table for Social Standards in Germany.[5] Yet it was an innovative dialogue approach of a collaboration pilot project with German Development Cooperation that shifted its relationship with suppliers.[6] The project objective was twofold: improving the working conditions in the factories through dialogue between management and workers, and helping the company's purchasing officers better understand the conditions in the factories of their Asian suppliers and engage on that with the public sector and civil society. It was an unusual approach for a company to place HUMANITY (relationship building), COLLECTIVE INTELLIGENCE (dialogue), and ENGAGEMENT in the forefront of their activities. What did they learn from all their stakeholder engagement?

For Nanda Bergstein, head of vendor relations and sustainability non-food, stakeholder dialogue was an opportunity to learn how the company could further improve sustainability issues and which internal processes needed to be put in place. Exchange with stakeholders brought in new perspectives and added to the internal expertise. "There is a clear trend towards more stakeholder dialogues among companies. Everybody wants to engage stakeholders. Yet, I believe it is important to ensure quality and thoroughness in the way we do this. There must be a tangible impact, a profound meaning. Otherwise stakeholders feel misused. Everybody needs to benefit from the dialogue." This was the lesson they transferred to their supplier factories—that dialogue could lead to better management.

She continues: "Today I see Stakeholder Dialogues as a way of bringing about substantial change. At the beginning we tended to impose social standards on our supplier, but over the years we have learned that such an approach only has limited success. That is why we took a dialogue approach that created a space for both workers and management of the factories to converse about basic human rights and subsequently working conditions. We went a step further and empowered them to adopt problem analysis and change skills, supported and mediated by local trainers. The process triggers breakthroughs—once trust begins to take root, and the companies start changing, the conditions began to improve, the productivity increased—and the factories actually began to do better."[7]

In 2010 teams from eight Asian factories—composed of management and workers—presented the results of their breakthrough changes to a stakeholder forum in Berlin. Over the years Tchibo managers had learned to use stakeholder dialogue as an approach to their own change and that of their supplier factories. They realized that high-quality stakeholder dialogue requires a new set of skills and staff to engage with the world beyond. Stepping into the shoes of others required practice. Today Tchibo has rolled out the approach to 320 factories worldwide in nine countries.

Many companies lack a clear strategy in stakeholder engagement and do not consider it to be part of day-to-day operations of the core business.[8] They delegate it to communications departments, underutilizing its tremendous potential or even risking damage to their reputations. Many companies also suffer from a lack of focus when engaging stakeholders, failing to define when and why and for what they want to engage. A CSR manager from a large international bank recently told me: "I do not know where to start—we have so many stakeholders!" A large retailer organized a stakeholder dialogue with 150 guests, only to end up with a long list of recommendations from external stakeholders—of which only a fraction could be implemented by the line management. Stakeholders are often involved inappropriately, without focus and without adequate processes.

But there is an increasing tendency for companies to do what good governments already do—become better organizations by engaging their stakeholders.[9] Coca-Cola, for example, is practicing this by taking a collective action approach to rising water challenges, Nestlé is wrestling to find a more sustainable cocoa value chain, and Mondelēz supports African cashew and cocoa farmers.[10] Stakeholder dialogue can create shared value if strategically embedded as part of the way a company does business. It creates impact, both for the company and for stakeholders, when it has the following characteristics:

- It's issue-based with a clear focus (*contextuality/mutual support—* WHOLENESS).
- It's based on knowledge about the diversity of stakeholders (COLLEC- TIVE INTELLIGENCE) and a thorough understanding of their concerns (HUMANITY).
- It's implemented proactively instead of reactively (FUTURE POSSIBILITIES).
- It's learning-oriented (COLLECTIVE INTELLIGENCE—*dialogic quality/ iterative learning*) and geared toward tangible issue-based results (ENGAGEMENT—*collective action*).
- It creates measures of a company's internal targets (FUTURE POSSIBILITIES—*decisiveness*).
- It's based on a thorough methodology (ENGAGEMENT—*process quality*).

Depending on the issue, a company needs to define whether stakeholder engagement is consultative (the final decision on how to move on lies with the company) or cooperative (the company is prepared to take joint action together with stakeholders). Issue-based dialogue often starts with consultation and then develops into cooperation projects. Companies need to distinguish company-specific stakeholder engagement ("we engage with 'our' stakeholder") from sector-wide stakeholder engagement ("in order to have an impact on an issue we join a stakeholder initiative—for sustainable coffee, living wages in Asia, African cashew processing—and this benefits the issue *and* our core business").

When does it make sense for companies to engage in stakeholder dialogue? Good reasons include:

- **Risk management.** "If we don't do it, we can't operate." For example, consider companies in high-conflict environments such as mining or gas field and oil explorations.
- **Sustainability compliance management.** "If we don't do it, we won't be successful." This could be applied to sustainable coffee sourcing or responsible supply-chain management.
- **Market development.** "If we do it, we can access new markets." This often applies to companies that have adopted a base-of-the-pyramid approach—engaging in serving poor people who tend to get ignored by large companies.[11]
- **Innovation.** "If we do it, we'll be up to speed with our products." Although in practice there are few examples of this, the networked company Premium Cola is one.
- **Strategy.** "If we want to grow, we have to do it and it will not only save us money but make us better." Again, there are very few companies engaging for strategic purposes. Tchibo as a smaller company is an example; Paul Polman's Sustainable Living Plan at Unilever is another one. High-quality stakeholder engagement can serve the world and business and is an exciting scaling up strategy for collective leadership.[12]

Dialogue Toward a Nation's Performance Target: Rwanda Case Study

In 2014 Rwanda celebrated twenty years of post-genocide recovery and reconstruction in a stabilized political, social, and economic environment. The country has ambitions to transform itself into a private-sector-led middle-income country with a healthy, educated, and prosperous population by 2020.[13] This requires extraordinary commitment to reform, and the result has been high rates of economic growth in recent years. The World Bank's *Doing Business Report 2014* mentions Rwanda as one of the countries with considerable improvements and ranks it thirty-second in its international comparison of business environments.[14] But challenges remain. The Rwandan economy has been dominated by a public-sector-run business environment, and it has not yet been possible to take full advantage of the improved business environment, particularly for small and medium-sized enterprises.

Productivity of the private sector is a cornerstone for creating employment opportunities and improving the employability of the overwhelmingly young population. One of the challenges has been the barrier to the efficient functioning of local businesses. In October 2012 the Rwandan government launched a new national Public Private Dialogue mechanism—a structured stakeholder dialogue platform established to address issues impeding small and medium-sized businesses. The dialogue has been implemented across sectors and on thematic issues at both the district and the national level. The aim is to engage the public and private sector in dialogue to identify and resolve business-related issues at the local and national level. The decision to establish the dialogue mechanism was made at the highest level with impetus from the National Leadership Retreat (a gathering of three hundred top executive, legislative, judiciary, and private sector national leaders). The process created a sense of urgency, as performance targets for all relevant government agencies were based on such high-level resolutions and progress was measured annually.

The practical implementation of the dialogue mechanism presented challenges because it was public-sector-led. Dialogue leaders expected that the business community would welcome and embrace the initiative. David Rugamba Muhizi, the head of the Strategy and Competitiveness Division at the Rwanda Development Board, highlights the biggest challenge: engagement of the private sector into the future possibilities that would emerge from the dialogue. "It is very important to forge a common understanding around the objective of such [a dialogue] mechanism," says Muhizi. "Building a collective vision and purpose and of course at the same time creating a win–win situation."[15]

In the beginning the private sector, particularly smaller businesses, did not quite understand the purpose of the dialogue. They saw it as a means of getting things from government without doing their own adjustment in ways of operating, accountability, and transparency. David remembers that implementing the dialogue mechanisms at the provincial level required iterative learning. "It is part of the [growing] collective action. You need to understand both parties. Government and private sector need to have a collective future that is designed, commonly understood, [with a] shared vision and shared action."[16]

Building understanding of the other stakeholders' constraints and roles became the cornerstone of success. Humanity and empathy were essential to

stepping into the shoes of the other to jointly solve the problem of misalign-
ment and to find resources for small and medium enterprises to participate
effectively in the Rwandan economy. What led to a successful outcome
despite the original challenge of a low private sector sense of process ownership? It was the combination of conscious approaches to a clear and transparent process, genuine stakeholder engagement, and iterative learning:

- Because a public–private dialogue initiated by the government required
  clear administrative procedures, the secretariat set up a process plan
  showing how the dialogue mechanism would be enacted in the provinces. The immediate lesson was that the private–public collective
  action envisioned required slowing down the process and ensuring its
  quality by first building relationships. Pushing the private sector into
  dialogue did not work (ENGAGEMENT—*process quality*).
- The investment in relationship building with the private sector paid off.
  Through bilateral conversations with selected entrepreneurs, listening
  to the situation from the other point of view changed the impression
  that the private sector was not interested in dialogue. Gradually, the
  secretariat of the public–private dialogue mechanisms conveyed the
  bigger goal—contributing to the country's future economic performance (HUMANITY—*mindfulness, empathy*).
- The secretariat learned quickly that keeping the big picture alive was as
  important as building the trust that the view of the private sector was
  increasingly important to shaping policies and laws. Convincing the
  private sector to become part of a larger vision was essential to success
  (WHOLENESS—*mutual support*).
- David recalls: "In fact we were trying to shape that vision of collective
  action [and] . . . a future that was full of possibilities, trying to show
  them that it's very important for this country's policies and laws to . . .
  take into consideration the private sector"[17] (FUTURE POSSIBILITIES—
  future orientation).
- Yet the next challenge arose when the secretariat discovered that not
  all public representatives in the provinces would approach the dialogue
  with a genuine openness to contributions. Not only did the private
  sector need to get engaged, but the provincial authorities needed to more
  deeply understand the potential of a dialogic approach and begin to see
  themselves as partners of the private sector (INNOVATION—*agility*).

The perseverance and focus on continuous engagement yielded results. The secretariat knew that both the private and public sectors would stay engaged when they saw results. It required strong and committed leadership at the national and provincial levels to ensure that the results would benefit both the public and the private sectors. With the public–private dialogue mechanism established, Rwanda can now move to the next stage—addressing issues that lie below the surface of an improved business environment such as integrating more vulnerable groups into the local economy and promoting women's economic empowerment.

Chapter 14

Cultivating Effective Cross-Sector Partnering

Partnering for development among the public sector, private sector, and civil society is a growing approach to mastering the challenges of sustainable development. Almost every major international future-oriented event, whether the Rio+20 world summit, the High Level Panel Report on the Post-2015 Development Agenda, or the UN's Sustainable Development Goals process, has emphasized that only cross-sector partnering will be able to deliver on both business and development goals. This is based on the assumption that cross-sector approaches are a better way to make use of resources and complementary expertise, and they enhance joint learning for development.

Cross-sector partnering takes into account that there is a neglected intersection between the performance of companies and the functioning of society. It supports an approach of shared value creation—creating economic value in conjunction with social value.[1] Partnering requires patience and persistence but, when managed well, can build stability and enhance the innovation we need to address global challenges.

If we look at cross-sector partnering through the lens of the Collective Leadership Compass, it is clear that the entry point is ENGAGEMENT; partnerships are all about *collective action* on the ground and tangible results. Partnering plays into INNOVATION, as it often results in pioneering products or approaches. Any attempt to initiate, implement, or facilitate such partnering processes is an intervention into a fragile and often controversial system of actors, requiring careful attention to the quality of relationships and interaction among stakeholders. Partnering fails when the partners underestimate how important it is to understand the larger context (WHOLENESS—*contextuality*) of the issue, the target group, and the partnering organizations. Efforts falter if partners do not pay attention to trust building or do not develop an understanding for different organizational cultures (HUMANITY—*empathy*). Implemented well, partnering is a stepping-stone for driving FUTURE POSSIBILITIES and INNOVATION.

My experience is that well-functioning cross-sector partnering leads to deeper commitment to sustainability, engagement of new actors, or scaling up of activities. This can take place in the form of development partnerships or public–private partnerships.

Development partnerships are broad joint initiatives to push an agenda for change or to jointly implement very focused development projects around a particular issue or for a particular target group. Partnering is both in the interest of the common good and in the interest of the partners. It addresses a particular development issue and includes social, economic, and environmental aspects. The degree of contractually binding relationships varies; initiatives often require that the different partners fulfill agreed-upon rules of participation. Implementation-oriented initiatives or partnership projects have binding contracts with specified deliverables for each partner.

Public–private partnerships take place when the public sector alone does not have the resources to provide the public infrastructure required for the maintenance or development of stable societies. Many examples can be found in the transport, health, and educational arenas. These partnerships entail various degrees of private sector involvement and do not always take sustainability issues into account.[2] Public–private partnerships in infrastructure require a thorough legal framework and are normally accompanied by detailed contracts that regulate delivery and revenue generation.

Both forms of cross-sector partnering—public–private partnerships and development partnerships—can use the approach of stakeholder dialogue as a means to strengthen the implementation capacity and ensure that stakeholders affected and involved are appropriately engaged. Both need nothing more urgently than competencies in collective leadership. Why? Because attending to the different dimensions of collective leadership eases complexity and helps project delivery. Let's look at some examples.

Creating a Spirit of Possibilities: Public–Private Partnerships for Infrastructure in Southern Africa

Throughout the southern African region, the demand for roads, bridges, railways, information and communication technology, water supply, sanitation, and energy is growing rapidly. Private investment in infrastructure has been on the rise in recent years, and public–private partnerships are increasingly being considered an important vehicle to close the infrastructure gap. However, since the onset of the financial crisis in 2007, African infrastructure development has faced a major challenge in leveraging private sector and foreign direct investment. This is mainly due to insufficient policy frameworks, an inadequate skills base in administrative apparatuses, and a lack of public–private dialogue that not only raises the awareness of possibilities for partnering but also takes both concerns and expertise of various stakeholders into account.

In 2013 the first ever public–private dialogue on the potential of partnering took place in Johannesburg, South Africa, and engaged 160 cross-sector participants—an astonishing testament to the interest in moving forward on the issues in the region. The dialogue was co-hosted by the Southern African Development Corporation Public Private Partnership Network (SADC3P), a public-sector-driven regional platform to enhance capacity for public–private partnerships, and the New Partnership for Africa's Development Business Foundation (NEPAD), a continent-wide business-driven initiative in support of infrastructure development.[3] The co-hosting alone sent a clear message to the public saying, *We can tap into future possibilities if we join forces.*

Despite the high number of participants, the event was extremely practical. Seven potential public–private partnership projects had been chosen for presentation and discussion. The public sector highlighted their prospects and challenges. A panel of experts for real-time advice discussed the obstacles and potentials, and came up with forward-looking recommendations to get the projects accepted for financing by banks and read for implementation. Everybody listened, and the event was an enormous learning opportunity that generated an atmosphere of future possibilities and collective action.

Said Kogan Pillay, the head of the SADC3P network, "Infrastructure projects are key developmental advancements and if we work together we can contribute to changing the world, one step at a time."[4] Lynette Chen, the executive director of the NEPAD Business Foundation, added with confidence: "This forum will . . . [be] a platform to move forward with the presented projects to tackle them collectively."[5] Why did this forum make a difference? It had been designed with the Collective Leadership Compass in mind and the core question: How do the co-hosts need to implement the dialogue forum so that they achieve a maximum of willingness for collective leadership within a day and a half? These were the key ingredients:

- A clear focus on prospective concrete projects with high potential (FUTURE POSSIBILITIES—*decisiveness*).
- Thorough pre-engagement of all key actors—project owners and advisory panelists (ENGAGEMENT—*process quality/connectivity*).
- A dialogic setting that allowed maximum participation (COLLECTIVE INTELLIGENCE—*dialogic quality/diversity*).
- High-level and reputable advisory panels (INNOVATION—*excellence*).
- A strongly led preparatory cross-institutional core group that worked with weekly teleconferences and established a culture of *collective action* (ENGAGEMENT).
- Project representation across countries in southern Africa so that everybody could construct the larger picture (WHOLENESS—*contextuality*).
- A FeedForward style of advising; panelists were asked to turn every remark into a forward-looking recommendation (WHOLENESS—*mutual support* and FUTURE POSSIBILITIES—*future orientation*).
- A meeting setting (round tables) and space for interaction; time to get to know one another at the beginning as well as for coffee and lunch breaks (HUMANITY—*mindfulness/empathy*).
- A joint dialogue on lessons at the end (COLLECTIVE INTELLIGENCE—*iterative learning*).

It was the head of infrastructure from a large South African bank who summarized one important lesson: "Get people around a table at an early stage—financial, legal, technical and political advisors, and experts—and talk through prospects and challenges. This alone would contribute to de-risking the projects."

Partnering Across Sectors to Strengthen Small-Scale Farmers: The African Cashew Initiative

Funded by the Bill & Melinda Gates Foundation, the German Federal Ministry of Economic Cooperation and Development, and private sector partners, the African Cashew Initiative is a cross-sector partnership to increase the competitiveness of cashew producers and thus reduce poverty in Benin, Burkina Faso, Ivory Coast, Ghana, and Mozambique. When the partnership started in 2010, approximately 40 percent of all cashews produced globally came from small-scale African farmers in rural areas who struggled to earn $100 US per year from cashew production. GIZ, Germany's largest development agency, played a lead role as implementing agency, delivering the objectives together with three other international implementing partners: the African Cashew Alliance, FairMatch Support, and Technoserve.[6] Further stakeholders were farmers cooperatives, traders, local processors, and a number of large global private sector companies (Olam, Kraft Foods, Intersnack, and SAP), which all contributed to the project and allocated resources.

The partnership took an innovative approach targeting the entire cashew value chain. It taught farmers better entrepreneurial practices and farming techniques. It advised African cashew-processing companies on business and technology issues and worked on increasing access to credit. The initiative focused on the creation of additional income for small-scale farmers, the creation of new jobs in the processing industry, improvements in cashew nut quality and increased yields at the level of production, and the expansion of improved cashew processing on medium and large scales. In addition, the partnership aimed at improving market linkages along the value chain, promoting the African cashew on the world market and improving the framework conditions for investments and business activities in the selected cashew value chains.

Over time the roles of national governments and civil society as well as the role of the initiative's private sector partners gained importance. It became increasingly clear that tapping into the entrepreneurial, innovative, and managerial capacities of businesses of all sizes could help scale up the delivery targets of the initiative. The challenges were manifold and most of them not visible to the public. The complexity of the project required sophisticated coordination of partner activities and managing different stakeholder expectations. The project management needed to navigate between very different organizational cultures and subsequent demands on milestone delivery and reporting.

One of the key challenges was creating alignment in implementation and a collective commitment to fast strategic learning. Ultimately, the African Cashew Initiative succeeded by inspiring and empowering all stakeholders to take the support offered and develop it further into a long-lasting economic development of the sector. This required strong management with a coherent implementation strategy that all implementing and funding actors could identify with. However, it also required tailor-made strategies for each country to adequately cultivate a sense of ownership for the initiative's goals on the ground.

Ulrich Sabel-Koschella, one of the masterminds behind getting the private sector companies into partnering for the African Cashew Initiative, reflects on the challenges: "Today, large scale development projects are not as simple as in the past. We need to deal with many partners from very different organizational background that do not always speak a similar language—and yet, they need to lead collectively and work together in an efficient way. This requires that we get to know each other much better and that we adjust to each other's needs. In a complex project like this it is important that all stakeholders have a say and that they can bring their perspective to bear and feel listened to. This is what leads to ownership and joint delivery. The more complex the implementation environment is the more crucial is the identification with jointly agreed goals and strategies. Only this leads to the delivery commitment we need. Paying attention to this is of utmost importance."[7]

What worked in this complex initiative?

- Considerable effort was put into bringing all partners into a space that everybody could identify with: the goals were clear, but the steps to reach them needed to be aligned to ensure that partners did not implement actions in an uncoordinated way (ENGAGEMENT—*process quality/connectivity/collective action*).
- The ENGAGEMENT only worked because it was accompanied by a thorough understanding of perspectives, worldviews, and capacities. With a sufficient level of empathy, the initiative handled the next hurdle well (HUMANITY—*empathy*).
- Several meetings were needed to integrate the expectations from the private sector; they demanded more facts and figures, clarity on milestone achievements, and measurable results (FUTURE POSSIBILITIES—*decisiveness/future orientation*).
- The private sector also needed to understand more about the complex reality on the ground (WHOLENESS—*contextuality*).

- Establishing learning structures opened up the opportunity for discovering new approaches and for the focus on activities that would generate easier results (COLLECTIVE INTELLIGENCE—*iterative learning* and INNOVATION—*creativity*).

Partnering for the Needs of Nature and People: Toward an Alignment of Actors in Lao Forestry Management

Degradation and fragmentation of forests in Laos has accelerated over the past decade, with negative repercussions for communities, biodiversity, and the climate. Weak governance permits an opaque and corrupt forestry sector, meaning that local communities remain entrenched in poverty. The agricultural and forestry sectors account for approximately 33 percent of the country's GNP while employing 75 percent of the workforce.[8] Export of illegal timber, however, is at least five times the sanctioned volume, with unprocessed wood sold mostly to Thailand, Vietnam, and China. Processed wood products are then sold to other countries, especially to Japan, the United States, and the European Union (EU). In parallel with increased deforestation in Laos (after Myanmar, the most forest-dense country in Southeast Asia), international demand for wood that is sustainably produced, legally harvested, and traceable to its source has also increased.

The EU's Forest Law Enforcement, Governance and Trade Action Plan of 2003 invites major wood-producing countries in the tropics, such as Laos, to enter into bilateral Voluntary Partnership Agreements for trade in verifiable, legally produced wood. Such bilateral agreements can help Laos continue to access the international market while channeling more revenues into state budget and community pockets. For that to happen, the definition of what is legal timber production in Laos must be developed in a participatory and transparent manner involving all forestry stakeholders there.

Due to the country's political history there is a lack of experience with participatory processes, especially among government agencies, businesses, and nonprofit associations. Given that the economic stakes are so high, the forestry sector is politically sensitive, highlighting power imbalances between provincial governments and the central government, as well as antagonism between the government and nonprofit associations.

The forestry business sector has a few players that carry considerable influence. Results-oriented and trust-based cooperation in such complex, politically sensitive multi-stakeholder settings requires skills in dialogue and collaboration.

Despite differences in interest, most stakeholders recognize the importance of cooperating for more sustainable forestry management. Yet while the roles of some key players from the public and private sector are well defined, others—such as those from civil society, local communities, and unorganized private sectors—are still emerging and trying to understand how best to contribute. Finding common ground, structuring communication and decision-making processes, as well as designing processes that encourage commitment and ownership become a challenge in an environment that is often hierarchical. Stakeholder engagement across sectors was new for most in Laos. Cross-sector understanding needed to be built.

Sometimes it is the first jointly achieved result that encourages actors to stay on board for a long collaboration journey requiring robust commitment from stakeholders and strong political will. In June 2014, a group of representative Lao stakeholders came together in what was designed as a mix between exposure to stakeholder collaboration skills and joint strategy workshop. The complex system of stakeholders was present in the room with representatives from three ministries, the wood-processing and furniture industries, the public sector, and Lao civil society. All stakeholders experienced the effect of co-creative planning. They also took ownership of a proven methodology to prioritize their engagement strategies and plan the their voluntary partnership process. It was exactly this experience of partnering that laid the groundwork for a structured collaboration process among all actors of the timber value chain. The shift happening in the workshops was a glimpse into how collaboration for more sustainable forestry could work in the future.

Here is how using the Compass achieved tangible results:

- It was the process of not only sketching a shared vision for forestry management in Laos, but also actually drawing a picture that created palpable resonance. After selected stakeholders from the groups presented the jointly consolidated vision, it was adopted as a guiding document for the planning process to come (FUTURE POSSIBILITIES—*future orientation/decisiveness*).

- From there the group took a deep dive into looking at the bigger picture as they jointly created a network actor map that helped them to define engagement strategies (WHOLENESS—*contextuality*).
- They learned about the delicate balance among administrative procedures, planning processes, and the *dialogic quality* of the engagement of all relevant stakeholders (COLLECTIVE INTELLIGENCE).
- This enabled them to move toward engaging relevant stakeholders, thoroughly planning the further process together (*process quality*) and prioritizing *collective action* steps (ENGAGEMENT).
- The result was an agreed process map for the coming months. On the final day the group presented the sustainable forestry vision and plan to high-level actors (FUTURE POSSIBILITIES—*future orientation/decisiveness*).
- For that they chose a vivid picture drawn by participants—they presented a bus analogy as an artwork representing the cohesion that had been created among the stakeholders as well as the clarity in direction. The moment had come to see if everyone was "on the bus." And they were! Everyone chose to sign their name to one person in the bus, including the high-level actors in the driver's seat (HUMANITY).

Chapter 15

Invigorating
Sustainability Leadership

In 2001 I co-facilitated a sought-after international leadership development program for multinational companies—reserved for high-potential leaders on the rise to top-level posts and on the list of the must-do trainings. What struck me years later was the impact of the program: About half the participants left their companies within a period of three years! Why? What had happened? Did we wake up deep desires that led to different career choices? Did the program alienate leaders from the dominant culture of their company?

These unanswered questions have accompanied me ever since. I talked to a number of the participants years later and discovered that there was a connection between their career turn and our leadership program. The training worked with a mix of a dialogic approach, reflection techniques, and personal development methods as well as systemic change management—all skills needed in the large companies the participants worked for. Participants reported that their work benefited, but the training also pushed them to ask important questions. *What is important? Why am I here? For whom am I doing this?* The leadership development program opened them to new territory within themselves and initiated greater awareness of their true responsibility in the world. Great impact, but not the impact I had been hired to produce.

I realized that there was a missing piece in the program. We stirred up questions of meaning, but we did not show opportunities to get these questions answered. Wanting to make a difference for a better world is probably the most widely suppressed desire in organizations and among senior leaders. Beneath the surface of many high-performing top executives is a vague disappointment with the competitiveness of the corporate world, and an unexpressed deep desire to create more meaning, more connectedness, and more relatedness.

A senior manager from a multinational company told me, "What I feel is that every person actually has a core that wants to serve . . . and it is more about uncovering it, because this gets silenced, cut off, nobody is asking for it, nobody is rewarding it in the company. You almost have to do it against all odds." I believe that, deep in their heart, leaders want to improve the lives of others. If they only knew how, they would contribute to a better world.

The times of paralysis are over. There is a larger goal everybody can tap into. Sustainability leadership is on the agenda, yet many are afraid to make a move that pushes the comfort zone. Today, ten years farther along in our global discussion on sustainability, the answer is there: If we want to learn to lead better, we can place our leadership in the context of sustainability. Sustainability is a leadership task. It creates meaning. It creates a better world. Can we afford to delink leadership development and sustainability? Is it even possible to separate the *how* of leadership from the *what for* and *where to*?

Let's approach this from another angle. If we read a few annual business strategy reports from large international corporations, we find a collection of the following mandates:

- We need to build on connectivity and collaborate fast and efficiently to be able to adapt to volatile markets.
- We need to innovate effectively across countries in a complex ever-changing business environment, understand different cultural contexts, and make the most out of our diverse workforce.
- We need to think globally and find quick solutions to local challenges, making sure that the learning is distributed fast across the entire company.

These business challenges are similar to sustainability challenges. We should integrate those things that belong together—leadership development and sustainability issues. Such integration would move our planet in the right direction and retain high-caliber employees who are searching for meaning in their work environment. It would also encourage more leaders to do the work that needs to be done—changing organizations toward sustainable business action. Embedding the Collective Leadership Compass into leadership development programs is a viable option. How could this be done? Here are three possibilities:

1. Review existing intra-organizational or cross-institutional leadership programs for alignment with the Compass. Do they systematically address all dimensions? Do the espoused leadership values take the dimensions into account? Adjust programs and values when necessary to incorporate all dimensions, even if you don't want to explicitly work with the Compass.
2. Look for external leadership development programs that particularly address issues of collaboration, dialogue, and innovation. Evaluate the ways in which they address all six dimensions of the Collective Leadership Compass or address dimensions complementary to your already existing leadership development approaches.
3. Make the Compass the basis of your leadership program designs. Take the Compass as an overall orientation and ensure that leaders or aspiring leaders know which special program enhances competencies in which dimension. For example, project management and time management would fit with FUTURE POSSIBILITIES; communication skills with ENGAGEMENT; and so on. If you design a modular development program, ensure that it addresses all dimensions systematically. Empower leaders to apply the Compass in their day-to-day operations. Customize the content behind each dimension and aspect to your organizational needs.

If companies want to retain executives who desire meaning and recruit the Generation Y employees who demand meaning, they need to look into shifting their cultural paradigm toward career development that integrates flatland-delivered performance around facts and figures with wonderland—the inner well-being and contribution to something larger. The future of human resource development will be tested against its contribution to more sustainable action in the world. It requires parallel development of candidates' inner resourcefulness, reflection, and mindfulness with manifestation in the outer world as leadership for better co-creation. Future-oriented, high-quality leadership programs need to at least have these ingredients:

- **Future Possibilities.** The programs show that the global trends affecting business and governments are all related to sustainability. They inspire an attitude of sustainability as the only choice—and a great business opportunity! And they back this up with facts and figures.
- **Humanity.** They make the inner search for meaning and impact a topic one can talk about openly with fellow leaders, and acknowledge that inner maturation is vital for sustainability leadership.
- **Collective Intelligence.** They teach leaders the art of dialogue and equip them with practical skills in collaborating with stakeholders whose interests are different. They integrate a collaborative practice project with external stakeholders into the program.
- **Innovation.** They encourage leaders to step into the unknown, foster inventiveness, and train problem solving beyond the company's boundaries. They take leaders into examples and exposures that show how negotiated solutions are efficient problem-solving techniques.
- **Engagement.** They create a network of leaders who become ambassadors for changing the company, the organization, and the world. They teach the art of inspirational engaging—from groups of committed citizens to communities for change.
- **Wholeness.** They illustrate with exercises and practice examples how mutual support rather than competition helps individuals perform better, lets the company or organization thrive, and delivers more value for the global society.

Let's look at two examples of leadership development programs that take the dimensions of the Collective Leadership Compass into account.

Changing the World One Step at a Time: The Young Leaders for Sustainability Program

All over the world, young people are eager to contribute to a positive future and are looking for ways to be active. They represent a great potential for societal progress and sustainable development. They need support to channel their energy into a positive way of leading and driving change. How can young professionals meet the challenges of uncertainty, complexity, and sustainability that impact our organizational environment with real consequences? By learning to turn the challenges into opportunities with a unique set of skills to build on connectivity and collaborate with stakeholders, to adapt to volatile markets, to innovate effectively across countries in a complex environment, and to understand different cultural contexts and make the most out of a diverse workforce. Thinking globally and finding quick solutions to local challenges ensure that the learning is distributed rapidly across entire organizations or networks.

The professional qualification program Young Leaders for Sustainability (YLS) offered by the Collective Leadership Institute has a unique approach to meet these urgent needs through equipping young professionals with the skills to navigate complex change in ever-changing environments.[1] They learn the art of collaboration and at the same time start building a network of change agents across business, government, and civil society. While applying the dimensions of the Collective Leadership Compass, participants are supported to step into the unknown, go beyond their comfort zone, and create new opportunities out of sustainability challenges.

The methods conveyed in the program demonstrate practically how COLLECTIVE INTELLIGENCE works in fast and efficient problem solving. Participants learn the art of engaging with stakeholders as a cornerstone for successful collaboration while turning the real challenges they are facing in their professional environment into FUTURE POSSIBILITIES. They experience that innovation is not something allocated to specific people but a competency leaders must both harvest in themselves and foster in others. They notice that it is the human-to-human connection that makes the world a better place. The connection between contributing to a larger purpose (WHOLENESS) and taking care of one another (HUMANITY) becomes second nature to them. They build essential skills for agility including seeing change as inevitable and finding ways to partner with it.

The key principle of the leadership program is that the participants go through the four modules with a specific and real project that they advance in the course of the program. For example, an NGO participant worked on a project to increase representation of minorities on management boards in Berlin.[2] The YLS program supported her in building her stakeholder engagement campaign and creating a road map to establishing an online jobs platform boosting diversity. Other participants have set up structures for measuring their companies' carbon footprints, successfully advocated for youth engagement in global biodiversity negotiations, helped forge intergovernmental agreements to save the argali sheep in Central Asia, and contributed to establishing an innovative corporate responsibility strategy in a large software company.

As they go through the four modules, they deepen their understanding of how to enact all six dimensions of the Collective Leadership Compass. They are equipped with tools and approaches that help them manage change in a complex environment of differing stakeholders. As Cornelia Richter, board member of GIZ and member of the advisory council of the YLS Program, summarizes it: "In a globalized world challenges must be tackled jointly. Shaping positive societal change and cooperating with different stakeholders are therefore core competencies for young leaders. YLS develops exactly these skills."[3]

Seeing the Larger Picture:
The "One Planet Leaders" Business Education

In the business world, leaders are still expected to be heroic individuals and often feel isolated at the top. But increasingly complex business environments, uncertainty of markets, and an interdependency of challenges require new approaches to leadership development. Business leaders hold an enormous potential to contribute to the sustainability of our world if they shift their mind-sets. Often managers do not yet grasp the connection between their professional task and sustainability. Values need to be addressed and successful stories told to inspire change. The path ahead requires the anchoring of sustainability at the core of business organizations and integrating sustainability skills building into the career journey of business leaders.

The business education program of "One Planet Leaders" co-designed and co-facilitated by the World Wide Fund for Nature (WWF) addresses this by inspiring leaders to drive change in collaboration and build businesses so that they create more value for people and the planet. The program uses interdisciplinary content and draws on expertise from the WWF as well as educational institutions such as Exeter University in the United Kingdom and the University of Cape Town.[4]

It focuses on collective intelligence, collaboration, and engagement, inspiring business leaders to open up new and future possibilities for themselves and their companies. The underlying principle is taking a whole-person approach to leadership development, to expand the mind, touch the heart, and inspire action.[5] The program takes the dimension of wholeness into account by exposing participants to current and future sustainability challenges viewed from economic, social, and environmental perspectives. This is balanced by diving deeper into humanity by reflecting on one's own relationship with nature. By bringing in examples from companies leading the sustainability field and an exposure to practical instruments for sustainability leadership, the program encourages both innovation and collective action.[6]

Carolina Möller, responsible for conceptualizing One Planet Leaders, emphasizes the shift in insight that leaders experience in the program. It strongly builds a sense of possibility in the how and what of sustainability engagement.[7] Personal values and authentic motivation to change play a clear role in participants' success in the program. But it also conveys practical tools for addressing sustainability challenges in the companies participants work in. To support them as they tackle their challenges, best practices are conveyed through stories to connect participants to the human and emotional side of sustainability leadership. Möller sees the emotional engagement as a driver that can transform the way businesses, markets, and even whole societies operate.

Chapter 16

Building Networks for Change

Change comes about fastest in a web of relationships. This isn't just the lesson of social media, or social movements; it's also a lesson from nature. Decentralized networks with internal feedback loops that give every part of the network timely access to relevant information are not only able to easily adapt to change, but can also generate change. Engaging in networks cannot be considered simply a "nice-to-have" activity, but must become part of the overall strategy for change toward sustainability.

Collaborative efforts are most robust in such a web of relationships when diverse actors come together around a common cause. Networks, whether they are place-based or virtual, draw together individuals with a passion for change through a compelling purpose. Examples abound. A network in Potsdam, Germany, is protesting against factory farms; the Swim Across America network raises funds for childhood cancer research in the United States; a committed multi-sector network is focused on making the timber supply chain transparent and sustainable in the Democratic Republic of Laos; and the International Union for Conservation of Nature convenes virtual global networks specialized in key aspects of biodiversity conservation.

In his book *Blessed Unrest* (2007), Paul Hawken points to the countless non-governmental and community organizations that, in his assessment, constitute the "environmental and social justice movement."[1] In his groundbreaking research on eighty networks, Steve Waddell provides a helpful framework that shows how addressing complex social and environmental issues already takes place as networked action. He coined the term *Global Action Networks* for multi-stakeholder networks that span beyond geographic and institutional boundaries in their attempt to effect systemic change.[2]

A core strength of such networks is their emotional appeal to environmental sustainability or social justice. When a compelling and specific purpose is grounded in concrete and strategic opportunities for action, people passionate about the cause are eager to join, never again having to feel alone in their work. A well-organized network creates a feeling of unity and inspires contribution from its members. Active members and use of social media can lead to visibility and tangible results. Networks are not about command and control, but about connectivity and creativity. They extend beyond conventional structures and boundaries, linking like-minded people in distant corners of the world.

Empowering Citizens Through Networked Action

Avaaz (which means "voice" in many languages of the Middle East, Eastern Europe, and Central Asia) is a global movement of some forty million people describing itself as a "Campaign Network" that influences political decisions through citizen voices. Based on their local knowledge of issues, members are empowered to start their own petitions, collecting support from individuals around the world. Strength in numbers has meant that Avaaz members have been able to win victories for the Maasai in Tanzania, for bees in Europe, for textile workers in Bangladesh—and the list goes on.[3] Avaaz trusts its members to put forward informed and compelling petitions and then creates a space for the collective intelligence of its membership to emerge. It is a movement that understands that systems transformation requires relevant and accurate information to get to the right people at the right time. In this case, this means citizens first and then politicians.

The network in support of the global climate change movement, called 350.org, is active in 188 countries.[4] Young indigenous climate activists, those who often have the strongest emotional commitment to a sustainable planet for future generations, drive the movement. While climate negotiations move slowly at the international level, networks in local communities, cities, universities, think tanks, social enterprises, and businesses are taking mitigation and adaptation into their own hands.

Networked action is not new. The abolition movement in the United States, for example, succeeded in making slavery illegal in the nineteenth century. While this hard-won victory should be celebrated, there are new networks that address modern-day slavery that sells women, men, and children for sex and labor. After the drug trade, human trafficking matches arms dealing as the largest criminal industry in the world, making approximately $150 billion each year. Organizations like Not For Sale have taken up the banner, raising awareness, building global networks, working with survivors of trafficking, and ultimately seeking to abolish slavery for a second time.[5]

Beyond information, robust networks tell stories that celebrate successes to keep momentum high. Just as negative headlines generally beget more of the same, sharing positive news helps people envision a better world and inspires them to contribute. Social change networks are purpose-oriented and dynamic, ebbing and flowing based on the perceived urgency of their cause. By identifying systems that need to be transformed, networks challenge the status quo, seeking to create a better future.

A Network of Organizations for Pro-Poor Land Governance Globally: The International Land Coalition

In many countries access to land is an increasingly conflict-prone issue, particularly when land is the basis for securing the livelihoods of a large part of a country's population. The distribution of land is a difficult and complex issue, often determined by the country's history, short-term economic interest, and power imbalances. Poor people are less likely to secure and maintain access to land. Hence approaches to land policy development, land rights, and tenure reform processes strongly impact attempts to reduce poverty.

A more equitable distribution of land would enhance chances for the poor to benefit from and contribute to economic growth, to participate more fairly in the increase of agricultural productivity, and to take charge of their own development. Beyond that, adequate land policy strategies contribute to sustainable natural resources management, without which agrarian livelihoods would not be viable. Equitable access, securing tenure rights—especially for women—and good governance in land administration are continuous challenges to be addressed at the national level, yet influenced by global developments.[6]

What emerged as an idea from a conference on poverty and human rights in 1995 developed into the International Land Coalition (ILC) in 2003. Today the ILC has become a network with 152 organizations from fifty-six countries, all of them concerned with promoting access to land for rural, often poor people through capacity building, dialogue, and advocacy. Climate change and the global food and financial crises have brought about even greater challenges as land has become more and more commoditized. It can be expected that disputes over resources will increase, which in turn will make it even more difficult for poor people to secure or gain access to land. Thus the work of the ILC strengthens the discourse by supporting governments, development agencies, social movements, civil society organizations, and the private sector to respond to land challenges.

One of the key challenges for the ILC in creating tangible impact was finding the right level and intensity of engagement around land-related issues. While the global ENGAGEMENT of organizations was key to strengthening their local action, regional platforms created a more accessible identity for different stakeholders to join and define *collective action* steps for their specific, regional challenges. The ILC adds further value by also taking a broader perspective (WHOLENESS), raising the issue of land and land access to the global level. This helps actors within a country to identify with a larger global movement while addressing land issues in their particular country.

The connection to a global identity was a cornerstone in getting more governments on board to change or adjust their policies toward securing access to land for the poor. Meanwhile, the strategy of the ILC has broadened the approach to generating COLLECTIVE INTELLIGENCE by ensuring the participation of a diversity of stakeholders. Not only government and civil society, but also the private sector (initially seen as adversaries) are committed to developing and implementing pro-poor land policies through national platforms. It has become clear that *iterative learning* is at the core of the coalition's success. Over time, the ILC built more explicit structures for learning and strategy adjustment, such as peer-based learning and mentoring, ensuring a robust and sustainable global network.[7]

Chapter 17

Turning Innovation into Collective Design

Joseph Schumpeter introduced the term *innovation* decades ago as a critical component of economic development and a competitive advantage for enterprises in their process of sustained growth.[1] But the term is now used just as much in the social sciences in the context of creativity and renewal, the development of new insights and pathways to social change. More recently the term *social innovation* has emerged to describe new ways to overcome social inadequacies and help address societal challenges (through products, services, or organizations). The creative process behind innovation is as important as the process of prototyping a new idea in reality and testing its relevance, applicability, and resonance. Innovation is the driving force sustaining the growth of organizations and the development of societies. It is at the core of the human evolutionary process.

At the point where innovation turns into collective design and integrates collaboration and input from various stakeholders, it moves from isolated improvement or brilliant invention into a service to humankind based on collective intelligence. Dr. Bettina von Stamm, founder of the Innovation Leadership Forum, says that "innovation doesn't happen out of the blue. It is an evolving process that requires learning, challenging existing knowledge, and understanding something new. Ultimately, innovation leads to change and to creating new wisdom."[2]

This process does not happen in isolation; it is built on encounters, conversations, exchange of ideas, and inquiry. In that way it happens through a combination of factors that come together.[3] Making this individual and collective process more conscious is a cornerstone in creating a sustainable future.[4] The new idea is often a result and manifestation of a set of interactions between people deliberately structured into a process generating innovation.[5] It places humanity and connectivity at the center—recognizing that people have ideas, inspire one another, and then digest the information and experience. Insights gained lead to creative designs in a mix between individual creativity and collective input.

As von Stamm puts it: "Creating an innovative organization requires a people-centered approach; after all, it is people who come up with ideas and transform them into innovations, not processes. It is impossible to command innovation, you have to inspire people to want to contribute."[6] It is the emotional connectedness between people around the issue to address that brings about new ideas.

Creating a New Way of Working Together: The Collective Design of Premium Cola

Can we redefine what a company means through collective design? Uwe Luebbermann founded Premium Cola, a small but highly innovative German beverage company. He has often been asked why he decided to create a business model based on consensus democracy among all partners, from suppliers to end consumer. His answer was that he loved to prove that one can overturn traditional theories of business administration suggesting that a private sector company thrives on hierarchy and top-down decision-making structures. The twelve-year history of Premium Cola has shown that it is possible to build a people-centered company based on innovation, humanity, and engagement that benefits from collective intelligence, future possibilities, and wholeness. Looking back at the beginnings, Uwe Luebbermann ponders: "From the perspective of the normal way of doing business, Premium Cola must be doing it all wrong: No logo on the label, no advertising, no sponsoring, no freeware, no bikini girls, no contracts, no boss who decides everything on his own."

Indeed, for the twelve years that Premium Cola has been on the market, Uwe's experience was that 99 percent of the people he collaborated with stepped up to the challenge of advancing the endeavor if treated as equal partners (HUMANITY). In a company where most decisions are made collectively—by all involved—the process may at times be slow, but has proved to be superior and more sustainable than the traditional way of doing business (COLLECTIVE INTELLIGENCE).

Premium Cola started as a small collective and was deliberately designed to function that way while constantly generating INNOVATION. The company quickly grew into a medium-sized firm that sells six different beverage brands, carried in 220 cities to more than ten thousand end consumers with 1,650 commercial partners. In 2013 Premium Cola moved one million bottles (FUTURE POSSIBILITIES). Yet there is no office, no salaries, and no actual boss in the traditional sense. People who want to work with (not "for") Premium Cola can choose how much time they would want to contribute (WHOLENESS). Everything is decided collectively (ENGAGEMENT). There are no employees because everybody works as an entrepreneur or a contractor. There is no factory because the partners who produce beverages are part of the decision-making networks (as are the logistics partners). There is no office because everybody works remotely, connects through the Internet, and makes the joint decisions by email and conference calls.

At Premium Cola there is no distinction between internal and external; everybody is part of a network that ensures the high-quality beverages reach the consumers. The creativity and connectivity are both extremely strong as everybody feels ownership for the collective endeavor and has the drive to improve it. Focus is on "proper" branding by operating ethically and environmentally responsibly in a highly competitive business environment. This includes the fact that Premium Cola is only sold in outlets whose ethical stance matches with that of the brand.

Continuous attention to humanity was the cornerstone of success. Maintaining good and reliable human relationships reduced risks, enhanced agility in pressure situations, and made the company more stable. The founder's role is not that of a boss; he is the organizer of a network maintaining connectivity and ensuring iterative learning. This way of working together is experienced as fruitful and fulfilling for the entire business chain, from suppliers to outlets. As Uwe states: "When it comes to making decisions, one should involve all parties—including, for instance, the truck drivers. Ask about their needs, appreciate their opinions, let them contribute their expertise, and take as much as possible of it into account."[7] The return on the invested engagement has been invigorating; everyone started contributing valuable information, improving the project, and actively thinking along the same lines.

Uwe's mission is to show that business and ethics are not opposed, but can work together in a day-to-day experience. This is why he has started to think beyond beverages. He sees the networked "company" as a collaboration system organized around an innovative operational core, rooted in social, economic, and environmental responsibility; the outcome is the product of the original collective design constantly improved through collective intelligence. The resources of the people involved are highly valued. He is dedicated to making this innovative form of doing business available to many more people in ways that encourage them to think about mental boundaries and collectively designing economic enterprises that deliver both products and human fulfillment.

Co-Designing Bold Steps Toward Sustainability: The Example of a Sustainable Textile Alliance

If the sustainability challenge feels too complex, one can either give up or take a bold step toward involving a wide range of stakeholders in the actual innovative co-design of a change process. When the newly appointed minister of development cooperation in Germany announced in the spring of 2014 that he wanted his new suit to be produced in a sustainable way, most people tended to ignore the remark. The challenges of sustainable supply-chain management in Asia were well recognized, and most companies felt they were on a good path toward improving their supplier relationships to include sustainability aspects. The minister set the bar higher. He invited thirty-four high-level stakeholders to a round table and made clear that he expected them to do much more to change the status quo—and above all to do it jointly or else he would think about legal ways to ensure supply-chain responsibilities. The outcry among companies was tremendous. Not only did they think he made demands impossible to implement, but they also felt that their current activities to improve the situation had largely been ignored. Emotions ran high, press statements became fierce, and industry associations got nervous as their members expected them to fight back.

It took another large gathering of all stakeholders to get people into a more constructive dialogue that became the starting point for an unexpected process—the co-design of a textile alliance committed to economic, environmental, and social sustainability along the entire textile value chain. Although the task seemed overwhelming, already busy people committed to join the alliance development process, creating a sector-wide approach to sustainable textiles.

Why was this an innovative process? All stakeholders knew they were venturing into the unknown, embarking on a learning journey with unclear outcomes. Although many different sustainability standards already existed, none of those approaches addressed the entire supply chain. Looking at all sustainability issues at the same time and bringing all actors on board was entirely new. Experts from industry, trade, business associations, NGOs, and standards organizations participated in co-design working groups that tackled such issues as a holistic supply-chain analysis, the definition of most critical improvement areas, and the definition of minimum sustainability standards to implement for a membership in the alliance. Six months later the co-design process produced the official launch of a German sustainable textile alliance with an ambitious action plan that was creating an impact on the entire textile sector. What made all the experts and professionals put in the extra time this innovative co-design process required?

- Despite the fact that the minister was criticized for his forceful approach and perceived lack of knowledge about the complexity of the sustainability issues, it was his decisiveness that pushed the process forward. Beyond his pressure, the issue itself tapped into already existing ambitions. Most stakeholders had been working on similar sustainability issues for years with considerable frustration about the absence of a joint approach. Here was a window of opportunity opening up for people to see the larger vision—the possibility of really making a difference in the textile sector (FUTURE POSSIBILITIES—*decisiveness/future orientation*).
- It was clear that each of the stakeholders held part of the knowledge required for a holistic approach. It was the diversity of knowledge and expertise that became important. Bringing together this diversity was more than an additive process (COLLECTIVE INTELLIGENCE—*dialogic quality/diversity*).
- As the working groups looked into the mapping of the entire textile supply chain, the spirit of co-design took root because everybody began to more deeply see the entire picture of challenges and possibilities. It became even more clear that solutions could only be found in a collective effort among all stakeholders (WHOLENESS—*contextuality/ mutual support*).

- While the process of getting all stakeholders in a structured co-design process was seen as chaotic in the beginning, a committed project secretariat streamlined it and built trust among stakeholders through a transparent and reliable sequence of workshops, regular information, and the establishment of a stakeholder-composed steering structure that would oversee the entire process until the launch (ENGAGEMENT—*process quality*).[8]

Driving Social Innovation: The Rock Your Life Movement

Sometimes it's personal connections that determine the way a person develops professional potential. Some people have many such connections, forming a strong network; others don't. Among those who don't are often people from disadvantaged groups in society. When a group of students studied the challenge of equal opportunity in education in 2008 at the Zeppelin University in Friedrichshafen, Germany, they thought something needed to be done in practice to change the situation beyond just study-ing the issue. They wanted to bridge the gap between the privileged, who studied at the university, and the growing number of pupils from the lower secondary school for whom the university was completely out of reach.

The idea was simple: If every student at the university helped one lower secondary pupil to advance his or her career potential at least a little bit, the societal change for equal opportunities in education would be tremen-dous. In 2009 the group started a mentoring program with forty university students who supported one another to advance their mentoring skills. As word of mouth traveled, more university students joined. These students were not the only ones interested; more and more people were enticed by the thought of making a difference. Soon the group made connections to companies because an apprenticeship was the logical next step to advanc-ing the career potential of most of the secondary school pupils. Since 2010, "Rock Your Life" has existed as a nonprofit organization supporting "bridging the gap" mentoring and coaching for many more pupils.[9]

With growing success, funders became interested, partners joined, and the movement grew. In 2014 the organization was present in thirty cities with two thousand people involved. They have established a professional qualification program for university students to ensure that their coaching and mentoring has high impact helping disadvantaged pupils on the path toward higher education. But the potential is even higher. The university students are future decision makers engaged in forming a highly effective action network. This experience will have an impact on their career choices, sense of social responsibility, and larger vision for the well-being of society. Mentoring and coaching, as such, are not new, but the fact that a group of students were committed to the idea of contributing to society led to a social innovation. How did they make it happen?

- The starting point was a concern for equal educational opportunities coupled with a creative idea: One privileged person helping an underprivileged person could make a difference. The idea was easy for everybody to understand (INNOVATION).
- The mobilization of a latent desire to make a difference was kindled in friends and acquaintances by that idea. A sense of *contribution* developed, combined with the understanding that every person was able to make a difference (WHOLENESS).
- Rather than needing to engage people into an abstract idea, the activity—helping disadvantaged pupils—was a one-on-one encounter based on both humanness and coaching skills. Above all, it required and further encouraged *empathy* (HUMANITY).
- Simply starting the mentoring project was a step into *collective action* with practical results that could be shared and evaluated. Successes fueled encouragement and made it easier for other people to join. Gradually the idea required a structured "home" in the form of an organization that could become the center for the *connectivity* of the developing network (ENGAGEMENT).
- The more the movement grew the more professional it became, particularly in setting standards for mentoring and coaching. The initial training and professional exchange, as *iterative learning*, secured the further growth (COLLECTIVE INTELLIGENCE).
- Rock Your Life encourages *future orientation* by helping people see and believe in their individual potential, yet keeping the larger vision present of a society in which "young people are able to literally ROCK their lives." This empowering approach also required *decisiveness*: focused plans, organizational development, and program monitoring to develop a structure that can support the growing impact (FUTURE POSSIBILITIES).

Chapter 18

The Five Principles of Scaling Up Collaborative Impact

Scaling up our global collaboration competency can be a learning journey with a meandering path. As with all journeys, we may take a wrong turn, hit an obstacle, or miss a bus. The goals might get lost at times when we are in the midst of turmoil, have become victims of our own collaborative efforts, or fall back into thinking we know the only right way to do things. Detours are part of the deal, but the following ideas can help remind us of obstacles that we can anticipate and navigate around. They remind us of the most common mistakes made in collaborative efforts and how to avoid them. When we are often in danger of getting lost in the complex cross-currents of collaboration, these pointers help us design collaborative change processes that have the resilience to weather the storms of diverse stakeholder interests and contradictory expectations. What are the five essential principles for scaling up our collaboration competency?

1. **Take collaboration seriously.** Avoid sliding into competition while believing you're collaborating.
2. **Shift the focus from events to collaborative change processes.** Learn how to take care of a system of collaborating actors so that they develop the cohesiveness the aspired change requires.
3. **Combine structural change with dialogic change.** Create an appropriate balance between open dialogic exchange and the safety of structures and procedures.
4. **Design integral approaches.** Attend to wonderland as much as to flatland, and don't get lost in one particular way of doing things.
5. **Take the path with heart.** Discover and revive the passion for collaborative change.

Let's look into each principle.

Taking Collaboration Seriously

Here is a typical sustainability challenge. An agricultural commodity is produced in just a few countries in Africa. As usual, small-scale producing farmers are organized in cooperatives, but these have competency gaps in management. Many traders bring the commodity to each national commodity board. In one country all commodities needed to be auctioned; in another they could be auctioned or traded directly to the buyers. At the level of individual farms, practices might not be transparent—or could be appalling. Child labor is still common on farms. The on-farm practices are at the core of the sustainability challenge.

International buyers, mostly companies from Europe or the United States, have been buying the commodity without concern for working conditions or child labor on farms; they either did not know or did not care. On-farm practices went unnoticed until some of the consumer brands were attacked by NGOs for materials produced with child labor. As the issues became publicly known, buying companies began to get interested in what happened upstream on the farms.

The good news is that many buyers invested in projects to help cooperatives or farms learn management skills and ensure that working conditions were up to international standards. In several cases innovative approaches led to significant improvements in the management skills of the farmers and subsequently their income. Some buyers also joined industry-wide initiatives and round tables to better address the issues and take a more holistic approach to improving the value-chain relationships of this particular commodity. In addition a number of development agencies looked into the issue of value-chain development and eradication of child labor practices.

The bad news is that producing countries have been overrun by projects. Many companies started implementing projects with farms and cooperatives in an attempt to save corporate reputation, as part of an internal sustainability target, or because they needed to secure the commodity source. Meanwhile traders started to horde the commodity so that they could influence the price, creating a good business for them but with no benefit to the farmers. Some of the projects may have been set up as part-nership projects between corporations and development agencies, others as part of industry platforms. What was the problem? Parallel activities with little or no collaboration among the different projects despite working with the same target group led to innovative, far-reaching projects that fell short of a potential impact. People collaborated within their project, yet were competing among projects.

Sometimes parallel activities cannot be avoided, but it helps to check what else is taking place before we even start planning activities. This sounds obvious but in my experience is often ignored. If we really want to contribute to better co-creation, we need to take collaboration seriously and move beyond the interests of territory or ego to look at what truly helps shift a system toward sustainability before we design interventions. The strategies shown in table 18 can be applied.

Remember that platforms of different stakeholder activities only work if people get to know one another and the story behind a project and if all stakeholders can connect with a larger emotionally charged goal. Taking collaboration seriously also means that we learn what it means to gradually get a complex system of actors into collaboration. We need to focus on planning a collaborative change process.

Table 18. Strategies for Shifting a System Toward Sustainability

Dimension (Aspect)	Strategy
WHOLENESS (*contextuality*)	Check the context. Check what is going on in the same field, the same area, or the same country by other companies or organizations. Map the different approaches and see where yours fits. Address gaps rather than doubling or tripling similar approaches.
ENGAGEMENT (*collective action*)	Consider joint projects. Integrate the project into existing activities or join up with other actors to jointly implement a larger project.
COLLECTIVE INTELLIGENCE (*iterative learning*)	Create a learning platform. If there are already many activities going on, at least share lessons, approaches, successes, and failures.
ENGAGEMENT (*connectivity*)	Create a coordinating platform. Increase collective impact by setting up structures that allow actors to create joint agendas, joint monitoring systems, joint progress reviews, and regular communication.

Shifting Focus from Events
to Collaborative Change Processes

Imagine the following scenario: A government minister in a European country decides that he wants to develop a new agricultural support strategy taking into account a shift toward more sustainable agriculture. He wants to do this together with as many national stakeholders as possible. His intention is undoubtedly good, yet he is also pressured by his own aspiration to gain public attention as a politician who is a force for good. He gives a press interview on the new strategy without consulting the respective experts in his ministry; here he announces the stakeholder collaboration process. The planning department gets active immediately, but staff members are reactive, as they had not been informed of the new strategic move. They do not have sufficient time to prepare the participatory process. The minister wants publicly visible action as soon as possible and simply sets a date for the first public event, a stakeholder dialogue. This first event should be followed by five thematic events leading to a draft policy paper to be publicly reviewed and then consolidated into a final draft. He urges his senior staff to identify a steering committee composed of selected knowledgeable stakeholders. The aim is to finalize a consensual policy paper within six months.

Now here's what actually happens. The big public launch event places more emphasis on featuring important speakers for panel discussions than getting stakeholders into dialogue. Despite this, interest is high and people have great hopes for the ambitious move by the minister. The willingness to contribute is tremendous and vocally expressed. Then very little happens after the launch because the supporting secretariat has no time to think about the necessary engagement process and keeps itself busy preparing the follow-on five thematic stakeholder events. In these events there is again little emphasis on actually getting stakeholders into a conversation. Nobody recognizes the importance of responding to the vocal commitment of the many stakeholders and keeping key actors on board by attending to their expertise. Instead, attention is focused on logistical preparations for the upcoming events and the publicity they might receive. Not surprisingly, key stakeholders get disengaged, withdraw their commitment, and publicly accuse the minister of underutilizing their expertise. The follow-on events receive much less interest, the minister's initial credibility is severely damaged, and most stakeholders begin to criticize both the process and the strategy. What went wrong?

Despite the best of intentions, the ministry underestimated the need to build a cohesive system of willing but disparate actors. Being driven toward public recognition, the actual purpose of stakeholder consensus was lost. The step-by-step engagement process that consensus-building collaboration requires was entirely missing. Nobody bothered to grasp the context by asking experts about the current hot spots in the discussion on national sustainable agriculture. In a nutshell—nobody thought about *preparing* a system of actors for consensus-building collaboration.

This might sound astonishing, but it does happen. People tend to focus on events and on publicity and forget that consensus building for a policy strategy is a slow change process requiring attention to people's expertise as well as sensitivity to societal dynamics, power dynamics, and a culture of genuine dialogue. In fact, consensus building requires solid process architecture—the design of the overall preparation, implementation, and review process for a collaboration initiative. This architecture includes the sequence of informal as much as formal communication events, such as one-on-one engagement conversations, small workshops, and larger events that bring stakeholders together into structured conversations designed to lead to a desired outcome. Large events are publicly perceived milestones, but most of the work takes place behind the curtains of the public stage.

What can we do in an environment where people focus on public events and don't understand our talk about process, cohesiveness, dialogue, or relationship building? We can introduce the Collective Leadership Compass as a quality check for good process design. Only well-designed collaboration leads to the envisioned outcomes. Each little step is important. The process architecture can be seen as a guiding structure, almost like a balustrade that keeps the complex set of actors relatively stable and within a frame of action that everybody understands. It helps to prevent chaos, but allows enough freedom for the different forms of communication that collaboration requires. The more difficulties, conflicts, and differences of interest that can be expected among stakeholders, the more structure the process architecture needs to provide. It gives all actors the minimum degree of certainty in a complex and uncertain environment. It helps stakeholders develop a sense of cohesion, it gives orientation, and it safeguards against unhelpful interventions. The underlying intent of good

Table 19. A Sample Road Map

Dimension	Process Design Concept
Future possibilities	Live the future now.
Engagement	Build a strong container and create an engaged network of actors. Make the process design transparent to everybody.
Innovation	Bring in expertise as needed and let expert groups resolve specific content issues.
Humanity	Build resonance both for the goal and for collaboration among all actors that matter.
Collective intelligence	Get the system of collaborating actors into a conversation with itself and create a task-orientated spirit. Allow differences to emerge first, but in a structured way.
Wholeness	Find the common ground.

process architecture is to enhance the ability of differing stakeholders to think together and work toward a future-oriented consensus. Such a structured conversation or stakeholder dialogue takes place among people who matter and those for whom the issue matters.

We can use the Compass as a process quality check by allowing its dimensions and aspects to inspire design concepts pointing to the necessary elements of successful collaboration.

Gandhi's philosophy that "we need to be the change we want to see in the world" carries a deep truth. Every step in a collaboration process needs to reflect the goal we want to achieve. We build the future by living the future now. This means we need to operate right from the start in exactly the same way we want the collaborating actors to operate. Keep the goal

Guiding Questions
Is the purpose of the participatory strategy development clear to everybody? Do we sufficiently empower people to participate in creating a joined strategy? Is the outcome clearly defined, and are the implications transparent?
Have we designed a solid process architecture that makes it clear to everybody how the strategy will emerge? Have we built a cohesive system of actors with the necessary expertise, and do they feel sufficiently acknowledged? Have we created circles of engagement that allow people to work on concrete results—leading up to the final draft strategy?
Have we brought in new and creative ways of seeing or solving the current challenges, or overcoming differences? Have we ensured that best practices and up-to-date scientific and experiences-based knowledge inform the strategy development? Are we prepared to take the risk of not being able to control the outcome?
Do we understand the sensitivities of certain stakeholders? Do we know what people are passionate about and have we taken this into account? Have we planned dialogue settings that allow different stakeholders to understand one another's viewpoints?
Have we planned dialogue settings that allow stakeholders to move toward a culture of thinking together? Are we aware of all differences and conflicts among stakeholders? Have we built a structure of iterative learning into our process design?
Have we taken into account the wider national and international context that influences our strategy? Do all participating stakeholders feel sufficiently supported to contribute? Have we communicated how the strategy will contribute to societal and global development?

high on the agenda. If conflicts arise, it is the emotional connection with the goal that gets people back on track.

A cross-sector core group of actors emotionally engaged with the goal can hold the collaborative process as a kind of container—an image that conveys that people in a well-functioning group of actors jointly carry the process forward, hold one another in mutual respect, and maintain their connection to the goal. The stronger this core group and the better equipped it is with collaboration skills, the better members will be able to weather the storms of complex stakeholder settings. The complex environment of a collaboration process can feel threatening to participants. The most typical human reaction is to criticize process or content (when one is not in charge) or to tighten control (when one is in charge).

A transparent and agreed-upon process design—this can also be called a road map—serves as a GPS device for all stakeholders. When people see what will happen when, who has which role, and who takes over what responsibility, they can relax enough to move forward in a consolidated way. Acknowledging existing expertise within the group is important. Bringing in expertise is helpful when it encourages people to step out of their comfort zone, get inspired by something new, or learn more by receiving information they did not have before. A collaboration process where people have built trust balances appropriate use of group knowledge with delegating difficult content issues to expert working groups. People whom we want to engage need to be taken care of. Building trust, keeping participants informed, and showing appreciation for expertise all contribute to success.

Good conversations change the way people think and act. People who acknowledge each other as people more easily overcome differences. Public events with keynote speeches and panel discussions may serve a purpose, but they do not get people into good conversations. We need to create stakeholder meetings during which people can talk in small groups, can diagnose the current reality together, and can design a desired future. When people work on a task together and achieve a joint result, they align and produce tangible outcomes more readily. Ignoring differences among people does not work in these situations. The opposite is true—it helps to remind us that collaboration is about transforming differences into progress. We are better off getting the hot spots on the table as soon as possible, understanding how the system of actors operates, seeing where the lines of conflict are and where we can find alliances. This is a prerequisite for the next step—consensus building. And there is always a common ground that people can access. It's much easier to enter a common space when people understand the why and the how of their differences and know the story and the logic behind various positions. This acknowledgment opens a pathway to compromise—or sometimes to a better and new solution.

When we start designing road maps for high-quality collaboration processes, we can more consciously plan for both structure and open dialogue to take us farther. For the scenario above, such a plan could resemble table 19.

When we start designing road maps for high-quality collaboration processes, we can more consciously plan for both structure and open dialogue to take us farther.

Combining Structural Interventions
with Dialogic Intervention

The world is made up of structures—physical, mental, virtual. We need them; life is organized in ordered patterns. The human community is part of the living system and capable of self-organizing. If we want to move toward a more sustainable world, we need to observe which structures help us become more effective and which prevent us from delivering an impact. We need to learn how much structure is required to enhance our collaborative effort.

What is a structural intervention in a collaborative change process? It's a deliberate move to create rules, procedures, regulations, plans, or forms of organization that guide or support collaborative efforts, or enhance the delivery of results. Collaboration often starts with a declaration of interest that may be put into writing. It moves on to agreements or even official memorandums of understanding. Some forms of collaboration, such as stakeholder partnerships, require signed contracts. Most often the collaborative effort is accompanied by a plan, a road map, sometimes detailed into milestones and deliverables with clear allocation of responsibilities. In more complex collaboration settings this is complemented by organizational structures—a project secretariat, or even the foundation of a jointly governed institution with a management structure.

Most collaboration efforts include several institutions, often across different stakeholder groups that expect adequate representation in governance structures—such as steering committees, sounding boards, advisory councils, and so on. Regular meetings, general assemblies, and stakeholder events become part of process architectures. Some collaborative initiatives develop complaint mechanisms and rules of participation that regulate who is in or out, the requirements for joining, and the financial implications. They also decide on structured feedback mechanisms such as monitoring and evaluation. Each step of the way, the structural intervention may gradually become more binding.

Structures are important to make collaboration work, yet they can become an impediment when other elements are ignored.

Here is a scenario that may sound familiar. A collaborative stakeholder initiative to improve water resource management has taken great steps to bring together different stakeholders from the corporate world, the public sector, and civil society. Because the initiators are high-level leaders, a press conference and the signing of a memorandum of understanding accompany the public launching event. To ensure adequate representation of different stakeholders in the initiative, an elected steering committee governs the collaboration process with the support of a project secretariat. An organization is planned that will have a proper management structure to drive the initiative's goals.

All this takes time to set up, and some participants become impatient when they can't see results on the ground. Much time is spent in discussions about who needs to be included in which structure, while the initiators complain that they do not want to see too much money spent for administration costs that do not deliver direct impact on better water management. Some threaten to withdraw from the initiative. What has happened?

Structures took precedence over content, over emotional identification with the goal, and over lean, practical delivery mechanisms. When structures take over, they deaden passion for change. People become more concerned with territorial interests, and goals get lost. How can we prevent such a development? The answer is simple, yet not easy. For successful collaboration processes, we need to prepare a system for structures. If we create structures too early that are too rigid, the above scenario plays out. If we do not create sufficient structures, though, the initiative withers. How can we get the balance right?

Let's take a quick look at the purpose of structures. They contribute to identity, to the flow of information among participants, and to networked relationships—all around an issue of common concern.[1] Structures are supposed to support a community for change. *Identity* relates to the emotional connection of collaborators with the envisioned change. *Flow of information* is vital because it not only enhances identity—the feeling of being part of a joined endeavor—but also enables all actors to effectively act, respond, learn quickly, and deliver. The moment information is restricted—often simply in ignorance of its importance or because of time constraints—actors start complaining or, worse, disengage emotionally. *Networked relationships* are the cornerstone for effective self-organization and a prerequisite for fast delivery. If people have easy access to other people, they get things done more quickly.

The first step toward effective use of structures is to evaluate them against their purpose. Do they contribute to the three elements: identity, flow of information, and networked relationships? The second step is to acknowledge that all three elements require dialogic interventions. People need to connect, dialogue, and engage with one another in a meaningful and mutually inspiring way—and not just because the structures force them to. A dialogic intervention is any deliberate move that helps people communicate and connect with one another and with a larger goal. It helps people build relationships, support and get inspired by one another, and see their individual stories woven into the larger story of the change endeavor.

How can we combine structural moves and dialogic moves in collaboration? Pay attention to the stage of development and maturity of a collaboration system and—as we have seen before—take a step-by-step approach to ENGAGEMENT by offering *process quality*, fostering *connectivity*, bringing in HUMANITY, and ensuring *collective action*. One way of doing this is applying the Dialogic Change Model—a guiding structure for planning and implementing stakeholder collaboration and attending to the needs of such a process in four phases (see table 20).[2]

1. **Exploring and Engaging.** This phase is about engaging a system of actors for change, ensuring that a committed group drives the change and understands what factors impact the vision. This phase raises the energy for change and focuses on dialogic structural interventions.
2. **Building and Formalizing.** This phase involves consolidating the willingness to change into a joint future plan of action, consolidating the system of engaged stakeholders, and creating an identity of the initiative—a prerequisite for a commitment to joint action. The typical features of this phase are one or several stakeholder workshops. Planning them such that they take care of all the dimensions of the Collective Leadership Compass helps ensure success.
3. **Implementing and Evaluating.** This phase is about getting things done—agreed-upon or recommended activities, showcases for change. It includes the evaluation of progress or outcomes. Stakeholders implement activities either jointly or at least in a coordinated way. Most collaboration initiatives establish some kind of regular stakeholder meetings for the review of progress and the adjustment of implementation strategies. Attending to the dimensions of the Collective Leadership Compass helps keeping stakeholders engaged and activities on track.

Table 20. Structural and Dialogic Interventions

Dialogic Change Principles	Dimensions (Aspects)
Phase 1: Exploring and Engaging	
Creating resonance	FUTURE POSSIBILITIES (*future orientation*) HUMANITY (*empathy*)
Understanding the context	WHOLENESS (*contextuality*) INNOVATION (*excellence*)
Building a container for change	ENGAGEMENT (*connectivity*) COLLECTIVE INTELLIGENCE (*dialogic quality, iterative learning*)
Phase 2: Building and Formalizing	
Clarifying common goals and resources	FUTURE POSSIBILITIES (*future orientation, empowerment*) COLLECTIVE INTELLIGENCE (*dialogic quality, diversity*)
Planning the future together	FUTURE POSSIBILITIES (*decisiveness*) WHOLENESS (*contribution*) INNOVATION (*creativity, agility*)
Consolidating agreements and establishing structures	ENGAGEMENT (*collective action*) FUTURE POSSIBILITIES (*decisiveness*)
Phase 3: Implementing and Evaluating	
Ensuring transparency and communication	ENGAGEMENT (*connectivity*) FUTURE POSSIBILITIES (*empowerment*)
Creating results and celebrate success	ENGAGEMENT (*collective action*) INNOVATION (*excellence*) WHOLENESS (*mutual support, contribution*)
Establishing learning mechanisms	COLLECTIVE INTELLIGENCE (*iterative learning*) FUTURE POSSIBILITIES (*decisiveness*)

Structural Interventions	Dialogic Interventions
None	Having personal contact/meeting with potential actors; engaging in appreciative, inspiring conversations; establishing common ground for change; opening up possibilities and invitations to join
Getting facts and figures on the table	Exploring the situation; checking what others do in the field; using interviews as part of engagement; analyzing stakeholders; finding out what stakeholders think
Finding an agreement in a core group of change makers on what and how (does not need to be written); taking preliminary plan of action including how to engage more stakeholders	Investing in the quality of relationships and dialogue; addressing all dimensions in meetings
Organizing well-prepared stakeholder meetings and results-oriented meeting agendas	Creating meeting designs that foster person-to-person interaction; ensuring the quality of dialogue during stakeholder events; bringing in different stakeholder perspectives and expertise
Developing future scenarios, creating a joint picture of what the future can look like	Designing a joint diagnosis of an issue or problem; creating a step-by-step consensus-oriented future planning process; focusing on common vision and emotionally charged goals
Signing a memorandum of understanding; creating a joint action plan; finalizing a contract; establishing implementation structures; deciding on monitoring and evaluation systems	Keeping an eye on the quality of relationships and dialogue
Establishing rules of communication and appropriate forms of keeping all stakeholders informed; setting up meeting structures for the core group or a project secretariat	Attending to relationship building and high-quality dialogue during meetings; ensuring a quality check of meetings and information material with the Collective Leadership Compass; inviting feedback to the core group or project secretariat; ensuring the flow of information
Focusing on tangible outcomes and low-hanging fruits	Fostering identification with the initiative; bringing stakeholders together into review conversations; ensuring the dialogic quality of meetings; fostering relationships
Implementing jointly agreed monitoring and evaluation systems; regularly reviewing progress in stakeholder meetings	Keeping an eye on the quality of relationships and dialogic quality of meetings

4. **Replicating and Institutionalizing.** In this phase we take the collaboration initiative to the next level, expanding or replicating its activities
   and creating long-lasting structures for the change envisioned.

The appropriate balance between structural interventions and dialogic
interventions improves the efficiency and effectiveness of the collaboration
initiative. The Collective Leadership Compass can be used as a planning
tool or a quality check for events for the entire process. It can also be used
for idea generation, if the collaboration process or outcomes are endangered, or as an evaluation tool.

When we carefully design a balance between structural and dialogic
interventions, we need to take into account that it is the integration of
flatland and wonderland that makes our joint efforts successful.

Designing Integrated Approaches

As human beings we build our action and collaboration for change
on our personal model or theory of change. We may not be entirely
conscious of how we think change happens and how people can best
be influenced to change. We adopt a theory of change based on the
assumption that we can know the causal processes through which
people both change their thinking and act as a result of an intervention.
Most initiatives, projects, or program strategies follow a single implicit
theory of change, yet people are varied. Assumptions and experiences
are formed by culture, knowledge, theories, and practice. Education,
societal values, trends, and knowledge generation influence our way of
seeing reality and, therefore, our change strategies. Depending on background and education, we may favor particular strategies while ignoring
or disputing others.

In stakeholder collaborations, participants sometimes get into arguments about the most suitable strategy to realize change. At such a point,
awareness is curative, and a glimpse into the aforementioned approach of
Ken Wilber's flatland and wonderland is helpful. We need both objective
analytical knowledge (flatland) and subjective experiential knowledge
(wonderland) for successful collaboration. Incorporating both aspects into
our strategy design helps progress.

When challenges are urgent, collaboration initiatives for sustainability tend to only focus on flatland: the exterior envisioned results, the regulations to be put in place, the actions to be monitored, and the information to be distributed. Wonderland is seen as the realm of the individual. The Collective Leadership Compass takes care to bring both flatland and wonderland aspects into strategizing collaborative change.[3] In my work with collaboration initiatives I have repeatedly experienced that people started quarreling about the one and only right approach to change and got so entangled in advocating for their particular view that they missed out on a much larger opportunity to achieve results. But this is human—unless we make a conscious effort, we all tend to focus on one or two particular approaches to change.

The most ignored aspect of collaborative change is in the realm of wonderland—the transformation of individual consciousness. Many people would agree that nobody can change them unless they decide to change by themselves—through insight, experience, or personal development. Collaboration among different stakeholders has an impact on individual change. Sometimes we only notice years later how we changed a view of the world, a belief system, or an attitude because of exposure to an ambitious collaborative effort. A change may be more obvious when crises occur.

Such a crisis arose in the international sustainable coffee initiative when a document that had been prepared by a cross-institutional stakeholder group had to be checked for legal implications by one of the participating large food companies. The lawyer, a single-minded young man who had not been involved in the stakeholder collaboration so far, took the liberty of rewriting the document without any consultation with the engaged stakeholders. He simply insisted that changes were necessary for his company's legal environment. The document was supposed to be agreed upon by all at the next stakeholder meeting. The lawyer announced that his company would step out of the collaboration process unless all stakeholders accepted his rewritten version of the document. He was not the least aware that he had just endangered two years of trust building among NGOs, companies, and producer organizations.

A night shift of backstage diplomacy by facilitators, project secretariat, and representatives from three other companies resulted in a compromise that rescued the collaboration initiative, yet delayed the process by a few months. The compromise was that the document that had been agreed on by stakeholders would be the starting point for the discussion, and he could bring in his suggestions for changes paragraph by paragraph. We might consider this too large an investment for one person to threaten, but at the end of the meeting the lawyer understood the sensitivity of the consensus-building processes in a multi-stakeholder environment. He was so fascinated by the collaboration initiative that, on the way back to the airport, he told me he would change his job. He wanted to become a force for good and work on such initiatives. Collaboration changes the way we see the world.

The second element of wonderland that people often underestimate in collaboration is conscious attention to the communicative culture and relationships. Some consultative dialogues ignore existing expertise, some collaborative initiatives underestimate the importance of engaging people one-on-one, and some stakeholder workshops allow only question-and-answer sessions rather than deep dialogue after panel discussions. I have sometimes wondered if in the public domain we forget what is self-evident in the private domain—that we can appreciate one another, get into genuine dialogue, find ways of reconciling differences, and accept that not everyone must have our opinion. The human capacity to negotiate about the future is built on mutual respect and trusting relationships. We must build these.

Collaborative initiatives cannot dwell in wonderland alone. While it is more important than most realize that we attend to wonderland, we also need to be conscious of different approaches to flatland change interventions. The most common approach to changing individual behavior patterns is broadly extending information. We know that the introduction of information technologies has an enormous impact on behavioral change. Some believe that this is the only way to change the world toward sustainability—via information, incentives, and technological devices to help us implement or monitor more sustainable behavior, be it in relation to our health, the purchasing of goods, or the tracking of our environmental footprint. The spread of information through mobile phones or Internet access has also made an incredible difference to the empowerment of remote communities, which can now more easily find markets, search for price trends, and understand environmental issues.

There is another, more indirect, yet also powerful approach to change—to transform systems—through the introduction of regulations or laws, or the establishment of institutional structures. These often have a long-term and far-reaching impact as they determine people's behavior. The introduction of labor laws or environmental laws is an example of how the insight into necessity is turned into a regulation to ensure widespread application. As in other human endeavors, we need in stakeholder collaboration organizational structures, plans, and monitoring systems because they are a way of guiding joint human efforts. They are effective in the sense that they provide security, protection, and a certain degree of the predictability required to move a system of actors toward results. Once established, they can reveal their own dynamic and so need to be reviewed for usefulness.

Each of the approaches to change is important for collaboration to reach results. They offer four complementary perspectives that—if all used for the planning of an initiative—increase the likelihood of positive outcomes. When planning and implementing stakeholder collaboration, it is helpful to cross-check whether the process design takes into account all four ways of initiating change in collaboration efforts:

1. **Transforming Individual Consciousness.** Staying aware of the importance of personal encounter in collaboration as a prerequisite for change of attitudes and the willingness to work together. This serves HUMANITY and ENGAGEMENT.
2. **Changing Behavior Patterns.** Identifying the significance of information, contextual understanding, and background knowledge for the success of the collaborative initiative. This serves INNOVATION, WHOLENESS, and FUTURE POSSIBILITIES.
3. **Changing Structure and Systems.** Sticking to programs, announcements, and process plans, which create a reliable structure that helps stakeholders handle complexity. This serves FUTURE POSSIBILITIES and ENGAGEMENT.
4. **Transforming Culture and Relationships.** Ensuring that the more powerless stakeholders are listened to and that they have the opportunity to tell their story, designing elements of exposing participating actors to one another's worldviews and experience. This serves COLLECTIVE INTELLIGENCE and HUMANITY.

Both individuals and collaborative groups can draw on flatland and on wonderland. We may think that telling a story is of no particular use in a stakeholder collaboration that aims at ambitious outcomes. We are hooked on tangible results; it is the changed numbers that we like to point to as success. Yet it is the human heart that holds the thread of change; connections with one another and with the big dream propel us forward. Sometimes the most important route to success is remembering the role of the human heart in collaborative change.

Taking the Path with Heart

For me there is only the traveling on paths that have heart, on any path that may have heart, and the only worthwhile challenge is to traverse its full length—and there I travel looking, looking breathlessly.

CARLOS CASTANEDA
The Teachings of Don Juan: A Yaqui Way of Knowledge
(Deluxe 30th Anniversary Edition)

Have you ever experienced an ambitious collaboration effort for sustainability that lost its intention? Have you come across deadening administrative cooperation procedures, bureaucratic structures, and territorial fights? Have you even become tired of organizing stakeholder meetings that required huge efforts in backstage diplomacy to get to results? Have you thought about giving up collaboration and just getting things done?

There is a strange symptom of the human effort to collaboratively work toward a better world. We tend to get off track, resort to controlling the future by establishing rigid structures, and forget that it is the human connection, the individual story woven into a larger story, that will create a future we all want to live in. Even if we set out to make a difference in the world and join the collaboration journey, our passion can dwindle in our hearts. We become so busy organizing the change we want to see that we feel exhausted, overworked, and uninspired. Yet when passion is missing in our collaborative endeavor, our contribution lacks strength and spirit, and the difference we want to make fades. Our initiative is likely manifesting far below its potential. When this happens we have become disconnected from our heart. We begin to settle for the substitute—being busy for the sake of being busy and administering flatland activities.

If any of the above situations sound familiar to you, it's time to pause. It's time to reflect and to ask difficult questions. Why are we doing this?

Does what we do answer our hearts? These are questions we need to ask ourselves at regular intervals. There will always be times when commitment to a cause of action pushes the heart into the background. We can accept this reality in a pragmatic way. But if our heart's desire diminishes over a longer period of time, if we do not know anymore how to respond to these questions, if most of the collaborative action we are engaged in does not qualify for a positive answer, if the desire to combat others outweighs our ability to answer the questions, then it's time to halt, to withdraw, to create space within and around us, to start a dialogue with ourselves and people close to us. We need to refocus. We need to find the path that has a heart.

There is a journey waiting for us that is asking us to renew our quest for a better world. We need to get passion back in our collaboration initiatives. We need to connect with our story and the stories of others. We need to renew our emotional connection with the goals we set out to achieve or the contributions we wanted to make. We need to remind ourselves of the larger purpose that our collaborative initiative will contribute to. If our passion withers we can assume that the same happens to other people, whether they are aware of it or not. This is the time to invite wonderland back into our collaboration process; it is time to focus on the aspects of the Collective Leadership Compass that connect us with the depth of life and with one another. It is time to uncover our humanity. What can we do to reconnect with our heart and bring the human-to-human connection back into our collaborative initiative?

When passion is lost, we need to use inquiry to take us back to our own deeper journey. It furthers our dialogic quality. Engaging in inquiry means to be willing to look into what we do not know or understand and to search for the coherence of a situation that tires us. A question is an opening to a new form of life; it allows the reorganization of our thought patterns—a prerequisite for something new to develop. Inquiry is not only a technique but also a way of being. It requires courage, allowing empty spaces to exist on our collaboration journey, and above all the willingness to learn and to listen to ourselves and to others. Depending on the depth of the relationship we have developed with our collaboration partners we can embark on a collective inquiry—even if it is simply getting into conversations with people about how they feel, what keeps them going, what energizes or drains them. Real service to the future of humankind needs the engagement of the heart. We need to reconnect with a big dream or a visionary concept that guides the process of our collaborative initiative.

In collaboration initiatives people often reconnect with their heart when they see purpose—how and why this initiative is contributing to a larger goal. Attending to wholeness is an important move to revive passion. People re-engage when they feel that their contribution is part of a larger movement toward sustainability in the world. They shift back to an aspiration to serve. With more emphasis on enhancing one another's potential, the quality of collaboration increases. We don't just administer change; we remember why we embarked on this process of creating a better world. We get back to supporting one another's journeys, and as we do so we gradually notice that our own journey grows stronger and the people we collaborate with reestablish their ability to move beyond obstacles and see future possibilities.

How can we contribute to wholeness more consciously? We need to complement our outward leadership for sustainability with our own internal change. If we remain fragmented and *dis*-integrated as we walk through life, we will create the same outside ourselves. The more balanced and flexible our identity becomes, the less energy we need to spend on self-defense and territorial fights. We become stronger the more we support other people's journeys. We are able to ask in a different way what a situation requires to propel it forward or to move it toward more constructive co-creation. We can integrate feedback and collective learning. We can help other people see a larger story by looking at a situation from different perspectives. We can bring together people who would otherwise not talk with each other. We can reconcile different worldviews, and we can help find solutions to challenges together. We can respect different viewpoints in a way that brings about new insights and inspires people to join in. We can support one another in our efforts to bring about a more sustainable world.

Connectivity and interdependence are then no longer theoretical constructs. They have a direct bearing on the way we perceive the potential of collaboration and take us back to creating relationships, enhancing authenticity in people, listening for what wants to emerge, looking for common ground, and feeling empathy. Reconnecting with our heart and reviving our passion for collaborative change is a journey with no final destination, but a journey that offers us a promise: We will become more consciously part of the larger story and the potential of human evolution.

An Invitation to Join
the Collaboration Journey

The view over the silent early-morning Lake Geneva is breathtaking. Two dark mountains frame a picture that looks like a gateway into another world, snowcapped peaks in the far distance. A world of dreams is slowly awakening on a sunny October day in 2006 in Montreux, Switzerland. The project team that prepared the founding meeting of the Common Code for the Coffee Association worked late into last evening and started again before breakfast. They cannot hide their excitement, which is fueled by both joy and fear. Joy, because none of them would have assumed a few years ago that this group of diverse global stakeholders would become such a committed community for change in the coffee sector. Fear, because the moment has come to create an institutionalized structure and emotions are erupting; previously united stakeholders have started fighting over details of procedures and committee compositions. The international group has gathered for the eighth time. It almost feels like a family gathering when the coffee producers, company representatives, and experts from civil society organizations greet one another while entering the meeting room and looking for their name tags at one of the round tables. The initiative has grown up.

We've been through ups and downs, threats and achievements, agreements and major fights. What started as a dream by a few people has become reality: a basic sustainability standard for green coffee production aiming at enhancing the livelihood of people growing coffee. From here the road is clear—the initiative will grow into a formal structure, the 4C Association, with an executive board, a management team, and a stakeholder-composed council.

In 2006 thirty-seven organizations decided to join and finance a pivotal collaboration approach that shows how working together along the entire value chain is not only possible, but benefits all involved. The 4C Association is a remarkable example of a global community that joined forces to improve social, environmental, and economic conditions through the application of a code of conduct, support mechanisms for farmers, and a verification system. More than one hundred representatives from over twenty-five coffee-producing countries participated in the development process.[1] In 2014 over 350 members come from more than forty countries. These members represent producer organizations in all coffee-producing countries, trade and industry, civil society, research, and support organizations.

Stakeholders from the entire value chain address sustainability issues of green coffee production collaboratively and in a pre-competitive way. Large companies like Nestlé and Kraft Foods have publicly announced their sustainability goal of only sourcing coffee that has been produced in a sustainable way. I had been accompanying the initiative as a strategic adviser through conflicts and successes into collaboration agreements and results.

It was a learning journey for all of us, but there was also a method to the magic. Our continuous attention to the presence of the six dimensions of the Collective Leadership Compass helped us navigate complexity, crises, insurmountable challenges, and human differences. The project secretariat's deliberate focus on high-quality process designs, engagement, and trust building did the job—as did our ability to value the differences in expertise, experiences, and interests as collective intelligence. The dialogic quality we maintained helped us stay in conversations when emotions erupted and stakeholders threatened to leave the initiative. The mindfulness we all learned over time helped us stay in touch with the future possibility of our contribution to a more sustainable future. Our agility allowed us to find the meandering paths toward continuously improving solutions via iterative learning. And our atmosphere of decisiveness prevented us from falling into the trap of false compromises and watered-down commitments.

When the initiative started in the year 2003 it was globally one among a few collaboration initiatives that dared to bring together such a variety of stakeholders into one room and into a joint global action project. As we move into the era of the post-2015 sustainable development goals, this coffee initiative is one multi-stakeholder process among many—globally, regionally, nationally, and locally. A multitude of similar initiatives exist, not only in responsible supply-chain management but also in all other areas of sustainable development, from energy efficiency to resource management, social cohesion, and good governance.

When Thomas Berry in 1999 reminded us of the need for the "Great Work" that would need to be done in the twenty-first century, he framed it this way: "The Great Work now, as we move into a new millennium, is to carry out the transition of a period of human devastation of the Earth to a period when humans would be present to the planet in a mutually beneficial manner."[2] The complexity of social, environmental, and economic challenges humankind is facing calls for the scaling up of collaboration among the public sector, private sector, and civil society at all levels of global development. In 2011 Paul Gilding reminded us in his *Great Disruption* that our current economic model has established a systemic structure that inherently creates our environmental and social problems.[3] But he emphasized that it is also inherently human to change and find new solutions to systems that do not work any longer—if we decide to change.

The post-2015 development agenda is one such attempt at a global scale.[4] It emphasizes the importance of a global approach to working together for a future that is people-centered and planet-sensitive. Multi-stakeholder collaboration has emerged as a promising approach to address these sustainability challenges. This is why the number and forms of collaboration initiatives have risen tremendously in recent years. Cross-sector partnering has moved onto the agenda of most international organizations, the public sector, and a considerable number of large companies. In the emerging global field of collaboration, we are seeing more and more research on stakeholder collaboration, best practice exchange, and capacity building for partnering. This is not surprising, because collaborating will remain a challenge and we need to practice how to do this in the best possible way. Many existing collaborations are not delivering to their full potential. Developing new cross-sector collaboration initiatives is usually slow with high transaction costs, in part because partnering across societal sectors is easy to espouse but difficult to implement. It entails bringing together organizations with different drivers, resources, time scales, values, and cultures. Finding common objectives that fulfill the objectives of all sides is not an easy task. Building trust and equity among the collaborating partners is hard work and often outside the comfort zone of the individuals involved. This work stretches our imaginations, and we need to develop a degree of patience and empathy that may be entirely new for us. Moreover, because knowledge on good collaboration practices is fragmented, many collaboration attempts reinvent the wheel. There is no common set of good practices references.

Still, with collaboration now so high on the global agenda, we are seeing a rich tapestry of approaches, from multi-sector initiatives to individual business–NGO partnerships; from global collaborations to local collective action; from those that aim to achieve transformational, systemic change, to those that deliver project-specific results. Certainly we need to look more deeply into the quantity and quality of our multi-actor collaboration efforts. Where silo mentality and competition still prevail, we need to foster a collaboration consciousness and equip ourselves with skills to implement joint approaches. Where people already partner, we need improve or expand the impact by attending to the quality of collaboration.

The collaboration journey is an adventure with uncertain outcome, but no choice to return. As Paul Gilding puts it: "This is just the beginning of what will be seen by historians as the next step on our long evolutionary journey from apes to our full human potential. It has not been and it will not be a smooth ride, but it will sure be a ride to remember."[5] We need to learn how to develop effective multi-actor governance structures, and how to build consensus step by step rather than overriding skeptical stakeholders by pressure. We need to understand what forms of agreements among diverse actors serve their purpose without becoming worthless paper documents. We must learn to encourage one another with best practices without becoming competitive. We need to know when laws and regulations support progress and when dialogue on the best way forward is the better route to take.

We have only started the collaboration journey. While our sustainability challenges are complex, we have also grown a complexity of responses that will invite us to learn the *art of leading collectively*. But the dream is much bigger than just learning how to collaborate; it is also about remembering that we are human—and that the more human we are, the more we're in tune with the planet to which we belong as humankind. We can build economies of the future rather than replicating industrialization from the past. We can leapfrog traditional infrastructure and take advantage of innovative solutions to connect people. We can increase transparency and empower citizens to have a voice. We can stop pillaging natural resources and reverse environmental degradation. We can make education available everywhere to everyone, men and women. We can change the world—one step at a time. Learning the art of leading collectively is essential to building toward more sustainability, more human thinking, a better distribution of resources, and more equal societies.

When Ban Ki-moon gathered the twenty-seven-member High-Level Panel of Eminent Persons from around the world in 2012 to work on a global development framework for the period beyond 2015, he did something extraordinary: He built a group of global citizens committed to achieving an outcome—the recommendations for a "future worth choosing"—that would inspire future-oriented action in the world by governments, citizens, civil society organizations, and the corporate world.[6] Whether we agree or disagree with the composition of the panel, it was a diverse group of actors with equal representation of men and women, from a variety of countries, and with a broad range of thematic and life expertise. Though they only represented a fraction of humankind and certainly the more privileged side, they became a temporary community of change thinkers—a collaboration system that served a common purpose for the future of humankind.

Like all actors in such collaboration systems they needed to get acquainted with one another, learn to bridge gaps of understanding, and develop the empathy to look at issues from different perspectives. The panel's working process built on COLLECTIVE INTELLIGENCE, which led to an experience of a shared HUMANITY that was then noticeably written into the report. Accepting one another's expertise and shortcomings, interests and passions must have triggered a sense of WHOLENESS that surfaced as the responsibility for the future of our human evolution. The FUTURE POSSIBILITIES that emerged as the five transformative shifts mentioned in the preface of this book are not entirely new. What is new is the emphasis on human values that we all share—community, equality, care, participation, peace, and collaboration. It is time to take up the call to action and move from the conceptual insight that we need to collaborate across nations, institutions, and cultures to mastering the art of leading collectively in a complex world.

The Collective Leadership Compass is the collaboration journey's guide to action and reflection. It is not a substitute for everything we need to learn about partnering for change. It is not a substitute for structures we need to put in place, for rules and procedures we need to agree on, or for a detailed road map. It is a tool that helps us see, discover, and strengthen a pattern of human interaction that enhances life. Learning events that include the six dimensions will have better outcomes. Governance structures that take the Compass into account will function better. Process and action plans that consider the pattern of human competencies will lead to faster results. Organizations that manage around the six dimensions create staff willing to make a difference for a better world. Cross-sector collaboration initiatives that work with the Compass will more likely achieve results.

Conscious collaboration—setting up a temporary or lasting system of multi-stakeholder actors—is a form of creating life. Whether we manage to bring a sufficient degree of life to such a system determines whether it becomes successful or not. Despite our human shortcomings, there is an essential drive to build a good future together. The human mind loves achievements, and the human heart thrives on helping others. Bringing both together is what we need now.

A people-centered and planet-sensitive future requires us to build many nested *Collaboration Ecosystems*—issue-based systems of (institutional) actors aiming to change the status quo (usually a common good) for the better. The envisioned change benefits all actors involved—and our planet earth. In well-functioning Collaboration Ecosystems, the diverse stakeholders bring in concerns, interests, and expertise, and learn from one another about their respective thematic knowledge and geographic context. They identify key challenges and articulate goals together; drawing on their complementary roles, strengths, and agility, they realize their shared vision. Collaboration Ecosystems can exist at many levels of the global society; they can overlap, interact, and collaborate. The better we understand collaboration, the more we know about the art of leading collectively, the more likely our hoped-for outcomes become.

I invite you to join the collaboration journey and become part of a community of collaborative change makers. If you are already a master collaborator, I encourage you to use the wisdom of the six dimensions of the Collective Leadership Compass. It will train your collaboration muscles, ease complex processes, revive the spirit of working together, strengthen your way of mastering your leadership challenges, improve the culture of your organization, and encourage your team to drive the future.

It combines our desire for progress with our longing for meaning. It revives human competencies and brings them into fruitful interaction.

There is nothing more enticing than the opportunity to make a difference for the future of the human civilization. The Compass helps us keep this possibility alive—through ups and downs, hurdles and stories of relief and success. Welcome to a community of change makers; welcome to mastering the art of leading collectively.

You will find more inspiration, a summary of the Compass, exercises, and recommendations and tips for assessments on our website: www.theartof leadingcollectively.net.

Acknowledgments

The journey of writing a book that captures more than two decades of experience in complex multi-stakeholder collaboration starts long before the actual writing. Events happen, insights emerge in conversations, knowledge matures, encounters with people in different cultures develop, and life and work teach unexpected lessons. Constructing a navigating tool like the Collective Leadership Compass is a daring act that gains its credibility only from its tested effect in practice and because it has been inspired by success, encounters with uncounted numbers of professionals, and an immersion into the writings of many thought leaders and scientists. In that way many people contributed to this book consciously or unconsciously, and the author just crafted a compelling storyline, adding experience, further thought, and creativity. I am grateful to all those who knowingly or unknowingly added a further piece to a complex puzzle.

Then there is the actual work of writing the book that lives thanks to many from contributors, supporters, critics, and encouragers. I want to especially thank Glenda Wildschut for her unshakable belief in humanity as an underlying force in the world that needs to be accessed again and again; Dominic Stucker for his continuous support on the journey of completion, and for his contributions; Jade Buddenberg for her conceptualizing idea, her contributions, and a critical review of the first draft; Adele Wildschut and Nizar Thabti for bringing in case studies; Diana Wright for asking inconvenient questions as well as shaping the structure in the first round of editing; and Joni Praded for an encouraging cooperation in the developmental editing.

Notes

Foreword

1. The United Nations. (2014). *The Secretary-General's high-level panel of eminent persons on the post-2015 development agenda.* Retrieved from http://www.un.org/sg/management/hlppost2015.shtml
2. The United Nations. (2014). *A new global partnership: Eradicate poverty and transform economies through sustainable development,* 8. Retrieved from http://www.un.org/sg/management/pdf/HLP_P2015_Report.pdf
3. Weizsäcker, E. et al. (2009). *Factor 5: Transforming the global economy through 80% improvements in resource productivity.* Droemer, Germany.
4. Plato, *Timaeus,* 29-30.

Introduction

1. B'Hahn, C. (2001). Be the change you wish to see: An interview with Arun Gandhi. *Reclaiming Children and Youth, 10*(1), 6–9. Retrieved from http://reclaimingjournal.com/sites/default/files/journal-article-pdfs/10_1_BHahn.pdf
2. KPMG. (2012). *Expect the unexpected: Building business value in a changing world.* Retrieved from http://www.kpmg.de/docs/expect-unexpected.pdf
3. Lutkehaus, N. (2008). *Margaret Mead: The making of an American icon.* Princeton, NJ: Princeton University Press, 261.
4. Accenture. (2013). *The UN Global Compact–Accenture CEO study on sustainability: Architects of a better world,* 12. Retrieved from http://www.accenture.com/Site CollectionDocuments/PDF/Accenture-UN-Global-Compact-Acn-CEO-Study -Sustainability-2013.PDF
5. Lowitt, E. (2013).
6. Confino, J. (2012, April 24). Unilever's Paul Polman: Challenging the corporate status quo. *Guardian.* Retrieved from http://www.guardian.co.uk/sustainable-business/paul -polman-unilever-sustainable-living-plan
7. United Nations Global Compact & Bertelsmann Stiftung. (2012). *A strategy for the commons: Business-driven networks for collective action and policy dialogue: The example of global compact local networks.* Retrieved from http://www.bertelsmann -stiftung.de/bst/en/media/xcms_ bst_dms_36090_36091_2.pdf
8. Carus, F. (2013, February 15). Will Nike deliver on its 2015 performance standards? *Guardian.* Retrieved from http://www.theguardian.com/sustainable-business/blog /nike-deliver-2015-performance-innovation

Part One. Turning Challenges into Opportunities

1. Alexander, C., Ishikawa, S., & Silverstein, M. (1977). *A pattern language: Towns, buildings, construction.* Centre for Environmental Structure Series. California: Oxford University Press.
2. Alexander, C. (2002). *The phenomenon of life: An essay on the art of building and the nature of the universe: Vol 1. Nature of order.* Centre for Environmental Structure Series. California: Oxford University Press, 134.

1. How Collaboration Helps Us Manage Complexity

1. Collective Leadership Institute. (2006). Study on the impact of voluntary sustainability standards, carried out for the German Federal Ministry of Economic Cooperation and Development. Not publicly available.
2. Global Social Compliance Programme. *Welcome to the Global Social Compliance Programme*. Retrieved from http://www.gscpnet.com
3. Confino, J. (2012, November 9). Moments of revelation trigger the biggest transformations. *Guardian*. Retrieved from http://www.theguardian.com/sustainable-business/epiphany-transform-corporate-sustainability
4. Geising, E. Personal conversation. (2002).
5. Unilever. (2010). *Unilever unveils plan to decouple business growth from environmental impact*. Retrieved from http://www.unilever.com/mediacentre/pressreleases/2010/Unileverunveilsplantodecouplebusinessgrowthfrom environmentalimpact.aspx
6. The phrase *triple bottom line* was first coined in 1994 by John Elkington, the founder of a British consultancy called SustainAbility. His argument was that companies should be preparing three different (and quite separate) bottom lines. One is the traditional measure of corporate profit—the bottom line of the profit and loss account. The second is the bottom line of a company's "people account"—a measure in some shape or form of how socially responsible an organization has been throughout its operations. The third is the bottom line of the company's "planet" account—a measure of how environmentally responsible it has been. The triple bottom line (TBL) thus consists of three P's: profit, people, and planet. It aims to measure the financial, social, and environmental performance of the corporation over a period of time. Only a company that produces a TBL is taking account of the full cost involved in doing business. Source: http://www.economist.com/node/14301663
7. Inspired by Otto Scharmer: Scharmer, O. (2007). *Theory U: Leading from the future as it emerges*. San Francisco, CA: Berrett-Koehler Publishers.
8. Personal conversation with several high-level managers in multinational companies.
9. Kauffman, S. (1995). *At home in the universe: The search for laws of self-organization and complexity*. New York, NY: Oxford University Press.
10. Accenture, *The UN Global Compact–Accenture CEO study on sustainability*.
11. KPMG, *Expect the unexpected*.
12. United Nations Global Compact & Bertelsmann Stiftung, *A strategy for the commons*.

2. From the Individual to the Collective: A Paradigm Shift

1. Senge, P. (2010). *The fifth discipline: The art and practice of the learning organization* [Kindle version, Cornerstone Digital], Position 3832. Retrieved from amazon.de.
2. Isaacs, W. (2005). *Leadership for collective intelligence*. Retrieved from http://www.dialogos.com/materials/LCI2005Mkt.pdf
3. Ibid.
4. Koch, G. (2010, November 29). Coca-Cola's water stewardship strategy drive. *Guardian*. Retrieved from http://www.guardian.co.uk/sustainable-business/coca-cola-water-efficiency-drive

5. Griefahn, Monika. Interview. (2012). In preparation for the publication of Petra Kuenkel, and Kristiane Schaefer. (2013). *Shifting the Way We Co-Create*. Collective Leadership Institute. Available at http://stakeholderdialogues.net/media/uploads /Collective_Leadership_Studies_Vol1-Shifting_the_Way_We_Co-create.pdf

3. Why We Need a Compass for Better Co-Creation

1. Rapp, T., Schwägerl, C., & Traufetter, G. (2010, May 3). Klima: Das Kopenhagen-Protokoll. *Spiegel*. Retrieved from http://www.spiegel.de/spiegel/0,1518,692438,00.html
2. Senge, *The fifth discipline*, Position 1679.
3. Sharma, R. (2008). *Face fear fast*. Retrieved from http://youtu.be/_LfW27Q6rWw
4. Hall, E. (1976). *Beyond culture*. New York, NY: Anchor Books.
5. Wilber, K. (1995). *Sex, ecology, spirituality: The spirit of evolution* (2nd ed). Boston, MA: Shambhala Publications.
6. Dolman, E., & Bond, D. (2011). Mindful leadership: Exploring the value of a meditation practice. *360°, The Ashridge Journal*. Retrieved from http://www.ashridge .org.uk/website/content.nsf/w360/2011_S_Mindful_leadership
7. Kuenkel, P. (2008). *Mind and heart: Mapping your personal journey toward sustainability*. Potsdam, Germany: Collective Leadership Institute.
8. Jaworski, J. (2012). *Source: The inner path of knowledge creation*. San Francisco, CA: Berrett-Koehler Publishers.
9. Accenture, *The UN Global Compact–Accenture CEO study on sustainability*, 12.
10. This information is available from Catalyst, a leading nonprofit organization with a mission to expand opportunities for women and business. Retrieved from http:// www.catalyst.org/knowledge/women-ceos-sp-500
11. Sandberg, S. (2013). *Lean in: Women, work, and the will to lead*. New York, NY: Borzoi Books.
12. Smedley, T. (2012, October 11). Women leaders in sustainability: Live discussion highlights. *Guardian*. Retrieved from http://www.guardian.co.uk/sustainable-business /women-leaders-sustainability-discussion-highlights
13. Good summary information on the Chinese philosophical concepts of yin and yang is available online at https://en.wikipedia.org/wiki/Yin_and_yang. Access date: September 14, 2015.
14. The three levels of action, structure, and space go back to a conceptual discussion with William Isaacs and Peter Garrett, with whom I led a five-module leadership development program in 2002 at Dialogos LLC. www.dialogos.com
15. Sharma, R. (2013). *Little black book for stunning success*. Retrieved from http://www .robinsharma.com/pdf/Robin%20Sharma%20-%20The%20Little%20Black%20Book %20for%20Stunning%20Success.pdf
16. Senge, *The fifth discipline*.
17. Horx, M. (2009). *Das Buch des Wandels: Wie Menschen ihre Zukunft gestalten*. Berlin, Germany: Deutsche VerlagsAnstalt.

Part Two. The Collective Leadership Compass

1. de Luca, D. Personal conversation. (2013). Denise de Luca is a leading-edge thinker, educator, and practitioner in biomimicry, biomimetics, and business inspired by nature. More information at http://businessinspiredbynature.com/bci-people/denise-deluca

4. A Glimpse into the Conceptual Background

1. This section is taken from the following article: Kuenkel, P. (2015). Navigating change in complex multi-actor settings: A practice approach to better collaboration. *Journal of Corporate Citizenship*, 58.
2. Senge, P., quoted by Jaworski, J. (1996). *Synchronicity: The inner path of leadership*. San Francisco, CA: Berrett-Koehler Publishers, 3.
3. Kellerman, B. (2012). *The end of leadership*. New York, NY: Harper Business.
4. Senge, P. (1999). *The dance of change: The challenges to sustaining momentum in a learning organization*. New York, NY: Random House, 16.
5. Porter, M., & Kramer, M. (2011). Creating shared value. *Harvard Business Review*. Retrieved from http://hbr.org/2011/01/the-big-idea-creating-shared-value
6. Jaworski, *Synchronicity*.
7. Scharmer, *Theory U*.
8. As one well-known example: IDEO. (2008). Design thinking. *Harvard Business Review*. Retrieved May 4, 2014, from http://www.ideo.com/by-ideo/design-thinking -in-harvard-business-review
9. Krishnamurti, J., & Bohm, D. (1986). *The future of humanity: A conversation*. New York, NY: HarperCollins.
10. Varela, F. (1999). *Ethical know-how: Action, wisdom, and cognition*. Stanford, CA: Stanford University Press; Capra, F. (1996). *The web of life*. New York, NY: Anchor Books.
11. Sahtouris, E., & Lovelock, J. (2000). *Earthdance: Living systems in evolution*. New York, NY: iUniversity Press.
12. Luhmann, N. (1990). *Essays on self-reference*. New York, NY: Columbia University Press; Capra. *The web of life*.
13. Berry, T. (1999). *The great work: Our way into the future*. New York, NY: Bell Tower Press; Elgin, D. (2000). *Promise ahead: A vision of hope and action for humanity's future*. New York, NY: HarperCollins; Capra, F. (2003). *The hidden connection: A science for sustainable living*. London, UK: Flamingo Press.
14. Isaacs, W. (1999). *Dialogue and the art of thinking together: A pioneering approach to communicating in business and in life*. New York, NY: Currency Doubleday; Wheatley, M. (1999). *Leadership and the new science: Discovering order in a chaotic world*. San Francisco, CA: Berrett-Koehler Publishers.
15. Waddell, S. (2011). *Global action networks: Creating our future together*. Hampshire, UK: Palgrave Macmillan.
16. Alexander, *The phenomenon of life*.

5. Rediscovering Human Competencies

1. Kotter, J. (2012). *Leading change*. Cambridge, MA: Harvard Business Review Press; Covey, S. R., et al. (1994). *First things first*. New York, NY: Fireside; Covey, S. R. (2004). *The 7 habits of highly effective people*. New York, NY: Simon & Schuster; Sharma, R. (2011). *The leader who had no title*. New York, NY: Simon & Schuster.
2. Owen, H. (1999). *The spirit of leadership: Liberating the leader in each of us*. San Francisco, CA: Berrett-Koehler Publishers, 66.
3. Kuenkel, P., Gerlach, S., & Frieg, V. (2011). *Working with stakeholder dialogues*. Norderstedt, Germany: Books on Demand.

4. Browne, J., & Nuttal, R. (2013, March). Beyond corporate social responsibility: Integrated external engagement. *McKinsey Quarterly*. Retrieved from http://www.mckinseyquarterly.com/Beyond_corporate_social_responsibility_Integrated_external_engagement_3069

5. Briskin, A. (2009). *The power of collective wisdom: And the trap of collective folly.* San Francisco, CA: Berrett-Koehler Publishers.

6. Scharmer, O. *Theory U.*

7. IDEO, Design thinking; Plattner, H., Meineil, C., & Leifer, L. (2010). *Design thinking: Understand—improve—apply.* Heidelberg, Germany: Springer.

8. von Stamm, B. Personal conversation. (2013). Dr. Bettina von Stamm is an original and visionary thinker in the field of innovation. She is the founder and director of the Innovation Leadership Forum (ILF). http://www.bettinavonstamm.com

9. Confino, Moments of revelation.

10. Wildschut, G. Personal conversation. (2012). Glenda Wildschut is a member of the Truth and Reconciliation Commission in South Africa.

11. Ibid.

12. Isaacs, *Dialogue and the art of thinking together.*

13. Kline, N. (1999).

14. Berkes, H. (2012, February 5). Remembering Roger Boisjoly: He tried to stop shuttle Challenger launch. *NPR: The Two-Way.* Retrieved from http://www.npr.org/blogs/thetwo-way/2012/02/06/146490064/remembering-roger-boisjoly-he-tried-to-stop-shuttle-challenger-launch

15. Wheatley, *Leadership and the new science*, 73.

16. Senge, *The fifth discipline*, Position 5836.

17. Confino, Moments of revelation.

18. Buber, M. (1962). Werke 1. Bd., *Schriften zur Philosophie: Die Krisis des Menschen als eine Krisis des Zwischens.* Koesel, Lambert, Schneider; Munich, Germany, 280.

19. For an insight into the groundbreaking collective leadership for transformation and excellence of Jonathan Jansen, vice chancellor at the University of the Free State in South Africa, check out this video: https://www.youtube.com/watch?v=nfSEMoQr0AI

20. Jansen, J. University of the Free State, Interview Series, Jonathan Jansen, *Transformational Leadership, Interviews by Pumla Gobodo-Madikizela.*

6. Becoming a Collective Leader

1. Covey, *The 7 habits of highly effective people.*

7. Navigating Collaboration

1. Sarasvathy, S. (2008). *Effectuation: Elements of Entrepreneurial expertise.* Cheltenham, UK: Edward Elgar Publishing, 23.

2. Greenleaf, R. (1977). *Servant leadership.* Mahwah, NJ: Paulist Press, 16.

3. For more information on the FeedForward tool, go the the website of Marshall Goldsmith: http://www.marshallgoldsmithfeedforward.com

4. See, for example, Robin Sharma: Check out his YouTube webinar, *How to build willpower and self-discipline.*

5. O'Toole, J. (1995). *Leading change: The argument for values-based leadership.* New York, NY: Ballantine Books, 1.

6. Ibid., 3.
7. Ibid.
8. Lutkehaus, *Margaret Mead.*
9. Jaworski, *Synchronicity,* 57.
10. Sharma, R. (2013). *Leadership wisdom from the monk who sold his Ferrari.* Mumbai, India: Jaico Publishing House.
11. Kuenkel, P. (2013, August 16). Inquiry is a good friend in a crisis. *Living Collective Leadership.* Retrieved from http://petrakuenkel.wordpress.com/2013/08/16/inquiry -is-a-good-friend-in-a-crisis
12. Zafón, R. (2012). *The cemetery of the forgotten books* [Kindle edition, HarperCollins].
13. Krishnamurti & Bohm, *The future of humanity.*
14. Among many other possibilities for more information on meditation, see, for example, a range of comments cited in www.meditationfoundation.org showing the business benefits gleaned by organizations introducing meditation free to their staff, including Google, PricewaterhouseCoopers, Deutsche Bank, Apple Computers, Pacific Bell, NASA, Yahoo, AOL, AstraZeneca.
15. Pór, G. (2008). Collective intelligence and collective leadership: Twin paths to beyond chaos. *Sprouts: Working Papers on Information Systems, 8*(2). Retrieved from http:// sprouts.aisnet.org/8-2
16. Peter Garrett has been a pioneering thinker and practitioner of dialogue; more information is available at www.dialogue-associates.com/our-directors
17. Schein, E. (2003). On dialogue, culture, and organizational learning. *Reflections, 4*(4), 27–38.
18. See, for example, the work of pioneering dialogue expert Peter Garrett at http://www.dialogue -associates.com/publications; Schein, *On dialogue, culture, and organizational learning;* Bohm, D. (1996). *On dialogue* (L. Nichels, Ed.). London, UK/New York, NY: Routledge.
19. Grube, T. (Director). (2008) *Trip to Asia.* This video is a documentary about a journey of the Berlin Philharmonic Orchestra to Asia, available in German with English subtitles.
20. Kania, J., & Kramer, M. (2011). Collective impact. *Stanford Social Innovation Review.* Retrieved from http://www.ssireview.org/articles/entry/collective_impact; Hanleybrown, F., Kania, J., & Kramer, M. (2012). Channeling change: Making collective impact work. *Stanford Social Innovation Review.* Retrieved from http:// www.ssireview.org/blog/entry/channeling_change_making_collective_impact_work
21. Coelho, P. (2009). *The Zahir.* New York, NY: HarperCollins.
22. Jobs, S. (2005, June 12). *You've got to find what you love.* Commencement address delivered at Stanford University.
23. Grube, T. (Director). (2008) *Trip to Asia.*

8. Approaching Change and Strengthening Our Leadership

1. Weisbord, M., & Jannoff, S. (2000). *Future search: An action guide to finding common ground in organizations and communities,* San Francisco, CA: Berrett-Koehler Publishers; Owen, H. (2008). *Open space technology: A user's guide.* San Francisco, CA: Berrett-Koehler Publishers; Cooperrider, D., & Whitney, D. (2005). *Appreciative inquiry: A positive revolution in change.* San Francisco, CA: Berrett-Koehler Publishers.
2. Jones, M. (2000). *Artful leadership: Awakening the commons of the imagination.* Orillia, Canada: Pianoscapes.

3. Ibid., 15.

4. Purt, J. (2012, April 12). What qualities do future leaders need to meet the challenges of the 21st century? *Guardian*. Retrieved from http://www.theguardian.com /sustainable-business/future-leaders-sustainability-21st-century

5. For recommended exercises please go to the www.theartofleadingcollectively.net and view a shortcut to applying the Collective Leadership Compass.

9. Observing Our Pattern

1. The online questionnaire helps you to identify your strength in the six dimensions of the Collective Leadership Compass. You can find it at www.theartofleadingcollectively.net

10. Empowering Action Groups

1. For a more elaborate explanation of building strong containers for collaboration, see also Kuenkel, Gerlach, & Frieg, *Working with stakeholder dialogues*.

2. The online questionnaire helps you to identify your team's or organization's pattern in the six dimensions of the Collective Leadership Compass. You can find more information online on www.theartofleadingcollectively.net

3. *Getting active: The dialogic change model*. Retrieved from www.stakeholderdialogues .net/learning/textbook/getting-active/dcm

11. Building Communities of Change Makers

1. Kuenkel, P., & Schaefer, K. (2013). Shifting the way we co-create: How we can turn the challenges of sustainability into opportunities. *Collective Leadership Studies, 1*. Retrieved from http://www.stakeholderdialogues.net/media/uploads/Collective _Leadership_Studies_Vol1-Shifting_the_Way_We_Co-create.pdf

12. Getting into Collaborative Action

1. Owen. *Open space technology*. For easy access to the methodology, see also http:// www.openspaceworld.org

2. *Getting active: The dialogic change model*.

3. Design thinking is a methodology for practical yet creative resolution of problems by focusing on the future intent. For more information, see also Brown, T. (2009). *Change by design: How design thinking transforms organizations and inspires innovation*. New York, NY: HarperCollins; IDEO, Design thinking.

4. The dialogic practices are usually referred to as voice, listen, respect, and suspend. They originate from the dialogue work of Peter Garrett and William Isaacs. More information can be found in Isaacs, *Dialogue and the art of thinking together*; and in Kuenkel, *Mind and heart*.

5. Ethical Trading Initiative. Retrieved from http://www.ethicaltrade.org

Part Four. Scaling Up Collaboration for a Better Future

1. Leadbeater, C. (2012, January 3). Why cooperation will be more important than ever. *Guardian*. Retrieved from http://www.theguardian.com/sustainable-business /co-operation-more-important-competition-charles-leadbeater

2. Ibid.

3. Sahtouris & Lovelock, *Earthdance*, 109.

4. Ethical Trading Initiative. Retrieved from http://www.ethicaltrade.org; Global Sustainable Seafood Initiative. Retrieved from http://www.ourgssi.org; ACCORD. Retrieved from https://bangladeshaccord.org

13. Improving Stakeholder Dialogue

1. Kuenkel, Gerlach, & Frieg, *Working with stakeholder dialogues.*

2. See, for example, (1) online resources for stakeholder collaboration available at http://www.stakeholderdialogues.net; (2) resources on partnering available at the Partnering Initiative, www.thepartneringinitiative.org; and (3) research on partnering at the Partnership Resource Centre available at http://www.partnershipsresourcecentre.org

3. Tchibo Corporate Responsibility. Retrieved from http://www.tchibo.com/content /893154/-/en/corporate-responsibility.html

4. Common Code for the Coffee Community. Retrieved from www.4c-coffeeassociation .org; Fair Trade. Retrieved from http://www.fairtrade.net; Rainforest Alliance. Retrieved from http://www.rainforest-alliance.org

5. Ethical Trading Initiative. Retrieved from http://www.ethicaltrade.org; Round Table Codes of Conduct. Retrieved from http://www.coc-runder-tisch.de

6. Worldwide Enhancement of Social Quality. *WE: Added value for development cooperation.* Retrieved from http://we-socialquality.com/WE-and-You /Development-cooperation.aspx?l=2

7. Bergstein, Nanda. Personal interview. Bergstein is the Head of Vendor Relations and Sustainability at Tchibo.

8. Kuenkel, P. (2013, April 10). Stakeholder engagement: A practical guide. *Guardian.* Retrieved from http://www.theguardian.com/sustainable-business/stakeholder -engagement-practical-guide

9. Ibid.

10. Coca-Cola. *Water stewardship.* Retrieved from http://www.coca-colacompany.com /sustainabilityreport/world/water-stewardship.html; Nestlé Cocoa Plan. *Our commitments.* Retrieved from http://www.nestlecocoaplan.com/ourcommitments; Cocoa Life. Retrieved from http://www.cocoalife.org

11. The term *base of the pyramid* refers in economics terms to the largest but poorest socioeconomic group in the global society. For more information, see Prahalad, C. K. (2006). *Fortune at the bottom of the pyramid: Eradicating poverty through profits.* Upper Saddle River, NJ: Pearson Education.

12. For more information on high-quality stakeholder engagement, see also Stakeholder Dialogues. Retrieved from http://www.stakeholderdialogues.net

13. Government of Rwanda. (2013). Rwanda Vision 2020: Economic Development and Poverty Reduction Strategy. Retrieved from http://edprs.rw/content/vision-2020

14. World Bank. (2013). *Doing business 2014: Understanding regulations for small and medium-size enterprises.* Washington, DC: World Bank Group.

15. Wildschut, A. & Rugamba, D. Personal conversation. (2014). Adele Wildschut is the director of integrated capacity development at the Collective Leadership Institute, www.collectiveleadership.com\. And David Rugamba is the head of the Strategy and Competiveness Division at the Rwanda Development Board.

16. Ibid.
17. Ibid.

14. Cultivating Effective Cross-Sector Partnering

1. Porter, M., & Kramer, M. (2011). Creating shared value. *Harvard Business Review*. Retrieved from http://hbr.org/2011/01/the-big-idea-creating-shared-value
2. KPMG, *Expect the unexpected*.
3. The SADC Public–Private Partnership Network. Retrieved from http://www .sadcpppnetwork.org. Supported by Deutsche Gesellschaft für Internationale Zusammenarbeit (GIZ); Nepad Business Foundation. Retrieved from http:// nepadbusinessfoundation.org
4. Documentation of introductory speeches of the Public Private Dialogue Forum on Infrastructure, 23rd and 24th October, 2013 in Johannesburg, South Africa. More information is available on http://www.sadcpppnetwork.org/events/2nd-global-free -trade-special-economic-zones-exhibition-summit/
5. Ibid.
6. Deutsche Gesellschaft für Internationale Zusammenarbeit (GIZ). Retrieved from http://www.giz.de; African Cashew Alliance. Retrieved from http://www.africancashew alliance.com; FairMatch Support. Retrieved from http://www.fairmatchsupport.nl; TechnoServe. Retrieved from http://www.technoserve.org
7. Interview recording done by the Collective Leadership Institute, February 2015.
8. National Forest Products Statistics, Lao PDR. Retrieved from http://www.fao.org /docrep/005/ac778e/AC778E12.htm

15. Invigorating Sustainability Leadership

1. Young Leaders for Sustainability. Retrieved from www.youngleadersforsustainability.de
2. The Intercultural Innovation Award. Retrieved from http://interculturalinnovation .org/case-studies/diversecity-onboard
3. Collective Leadership Institute, Documentation of keynote speech held by Cornelia Richter at the annual gathering of the Young Leaders for Sustainability program in 2012.
4. WWF. *One planet MBA—University of Exeter, UK: Developing a new generation of business leaders; One planet leaders: Business transformation for a living planet*. Retrieved from https://www.imd.org/programs/oep/execution/opl/upload/IMD _WWF_OPL_Brochure.pdf
5. WWF. *One planet leaders philosophy*. Retrieved from https://www.imd.org/programs /oep/execution/opl/upload/IMD_WWF_OPL_Brochure.pdf
6. Ibid.
7. Möller, C. Personal conversation. (2013).

16. Building Networks for Change

1. Hawken, P. (2007). *Blessed unrest: How the largest social movement in history is restoring grace, justice, and beauty to the world*. New York, NY: Penguin Books.
2. Waddell, *Global action network*.
3. Avaaz. Retrieved from http://avaaz.org/en
4. 350. Retrieved from http://350.org

5. Not For Sale. Retrieved from http://www.notforsalecampaign.org
6. Department for International Development, United Kingdom Government. (2002). *Better livelihoods for poor people: The role of land policy.* London, UK: Department for International Development.
7. Information obtained from an interview with Steve Waddell. (2014, June).

17. Turning Innovation into Collective Design

1. Schumpeter, J. (1939). *Business cycles: A theoretical, historical, and statistical analysis of the capitalist process.* New York, NY: McGraw-Hill Book Company.
2. Innovation Leadership Forum. Retrieved from http://www.innovationleadership forum.org/About.aspx
3. von Stamm, B. (2008). *Managing innovation design and creativity* (2nd ed.). Chichester, UK: John Wiley & Sons.
4. von Stamm, B., & Trifilova, A. (2009). *The future of innovation.* Surrey, UK: Cower Publishing.
5. See, for example, IDEO, Design thinking.
6. von Stamm, *Managing innovation design and creativity.*
7. Collective Leadership Institute, interview documentation with Uew Luebbermann. (2013).
8. Deutsche Gesellschaft für Internationale Zusammenarbeit (GIZ). Retrieved from http://www.giz.de
9. Rock Your Life. Retrieved from http://www.rockyourlife.de

18. The Five Principles of Scaling Up Collaborative Impact

1. Wheatley, *Leadership and the new science.*
2. *Getting active: The dialogic change model.*
3. or more information on the concepts of flatland and wonderland, see Wilber, K. (2000). *A theory of everything: An integral vision for business, politics, science and spirituality.* Boston, MA: Shambhala Publications.

Epilogue: An Invitation to Join the Collaboration Journey

1. 4C Official Press Conference. (2007, 23 April).
2. Berry, *The great work*, 3.
3. Gilding, P. (2011). *The great disruption: Why the climate crisis will bring on the end of shopping and the birth of a new world.* New York, NY: Bloomsbury Press.
4. United Nations. (2014). *The secretary-general's high-level panel of eminent persons on the post-2015 development agenda.* Retrieved from http://www.un.org/sg/management /hlppost2015.shtml
5. Gilding, *The great disruption*, 256.
6. United Nations. (2014). *A new global partnership: Eradicate poverty and transform economies through sustainable development.* Retrieved from http://www.un.org/sg /management/pdf/HLP_P2015_Report.pdf

Index

········ About the Author ········

Petra Kuenkel is a full member of the Club of Rome and leading strategic adviser to pioneering international multi-stakeholder initiatives that
tackle sustainability issues, and the founder and executive director of
the Collective Leadership Institute (CLI), a German not-for-profit social
enterprise building competency for collaborative change and advocating
for high-quality dialogue and cooperation. As a lead faculty member, she
designed and conducted high-potential international leadership programs
in the United States and the United Kingdom. Based on successful change
processes, she developed dialogic change methodology and the Collective
Leadership Compass, a guiding tool for navigating change in complex
multi-actor settings. Kuenkel's writing has appeared in the *Guardian*
Sustainable Leadership hub, numerous professional journals, and on her
blog, *The Future of Leadership Is Collective*.

For more information, please visit www.theartofleadingcollectively.net
and www.petrakuenkel.com.

About the Foreword Author

Ernst Ulrich von Weizsäcker is co-president of the Club of Rome and
co-chair of the International Panel for Sustainable Resource Management
at the World Resources Council. Previously, he was dean of the Bren School
of Environmental Science and Management at the University of California,
Santa Barbara; president of the University of Kassel; director of the UN
Centre for Science and Technology in New York; director of the Institute
for European Environment Policy in Bonn, Paris, and London; and president of the Wuppertal Institute for Climate, Environment and Energy
in Germany. He has also been a member of the German Parliament. The
author of *Factor Five* and numerous other publications, von Weizsäcker
was honored with the Takeda Award in 2001.

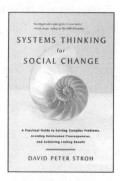
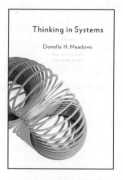
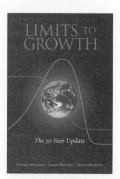